Servicing International Markets

To our colleagues at the Management Centre

Servicing International Markets

Competitive Strategies of Firms

Peter J. Buckley, C. L. Pass and Kate Prescott

BLACKWELL
Business

Copyright © Peter J. Buckley, C. L. Pass and Kate Prescott 1992

The right of Peter J. Buckley, C. L. Pass and Kate Prescott to be identified as authors of this work has been asserted in accordance with the Copyright, Designs and Patents Act 1988.

First published 1992

Blackwell Publishers
108 Cowley Road
Oxford OX4 1JF
UK

Three Cambridge Center
Cambridge, Massachusetts 02142
USA

British Library Cataloguing in Publication Data

A CIP catalogue record for this book is available from the British Library.

Library of Congress Cataloging-in-Publication Data

Servicing international markets: competitive strategies of firms /
  edited by Peter J. Buckley, C. L. Pass and Kate Prescott.
    p. cm.
  Includes bibliographical references and index.
  ISBN 0-631-18189-X
    1. International business enterprises—Management. 2. Marketing—
Management—Case studies. 3. Competition, International—Case
studies. I. Buckley, Peter J., 1949–   . II. Pass, C. L.
III. Prescott, Kate.
HD62.4.S47 1992
658'.049—dc20   92-8133
                                                                 CIP

Typeset in 10 on 11.5 pt Times New Roman
by Graphicraft Typesetters Ltd, Hong Kong
Printed in Great Britain by Biddles Ltd., Guildford, Surrey

This book is printed on acid-free paper

Contents

Figures

Tables

Acknowledgements

Our primary debt is to the Economic and Social Research Council (ESRC) for the majority of the funding for this study under its Competitiveness and Regeneration of British Industry Initiative (Grant No. F20250027). We are also grateful to Beddows and Company for funding the retail banking studies. The coordinator of the Competitiveness Initiative, Dr Arthur Francis, provided continued support throughout the project and we would also like to thank Professor Neil Hood for his assistance. Other members of the competitiveness initiative project teams provided constructive criticism as the work progressed, notably Mark Casson, Steven Young, John Cantwell, Bob Pearce, and Jim Hamill.

An atmosphere of constructive cooperation was engendered in the meetings of the 'internationalization phase' of the competitiveness initiative. Other useful comments have been made by David Storey and our colleague Hafiz Mirza.

We owe a great deal to the help of our industry consultant Mr John Martin who provided introductions and help with arranging and carrying out interviews.

The time given to us by the top executives who we interviewed was of crucial importance in completing the study. Many of the insights presented here originate from them. We hope that this book represents some return to them for their time and assistance.

The hard work of processing and reprocessing the many drafts of this book fell to Mrs Chris Barkby and we are indebted to her for her skills, good humour and willingness to undertake tasks beyond the call of duty. We would also like to thank Mrs Brenda Atter and Mrs Sylvia Ashdown (as always).

We are grateful to the following publications for allowing us to use material previously published elsewhere. An earlier version of chapter

2 appeared as 'Measures of International Competitiveness: A Critical Survey' *Journal of Marketing Management*, Vol.4, No.2, Winter 1988, pp.175–200. A part of chapter 3 appeared as 'Measures of International Competitiveness – Empirical Findings from British Manufacturing Industry', in *Journal of Marketing Management*, Vol.6, No.1, Summer 1990, pp.1–14. An earlier version of parts of chapter 5 appeared as 'The Implementation of an International Market Servicing Strategy in UK Manufacturing Firms', *British Journal of Management*, Vol.1, No.3, September 1990, pp.127–36 and 'Foreign Market Servicing by Multinationals: An Integrated Treatment', *International Marketing Review*, Vol.7, No.4, 1990, pp.25–40.

1

Introduction

The growing 'openness' of the world economy fostered by trade liberalization programmes and the formation of various free-trade blocs and
common markets, together with the expansion of multinational companies (MNCs), has served to sharpen the competitive pressures facing
UK companies in international markets. In this book we report the
results of a study of the foreign market servicing strategies of a sample
of UK manufacturing and retail financial services firms, in their attempts to advance and protect their international competitiveness.

We begin by looking at a number of general aspects of competitiveness
and foreign market servicing strategies.

1.1 Basic Concepts

1.1.1 Competitiveness

'Competitiveness' may be defined as the ability of a firm to meet and
beat its rivals in supplying a product on a sustainable (long-term) and
viable (profitable) basis. In the international context, this rules out, for
example, short-term 'dumping' where market share is 'bought' by selling the product at unprofitable prices.

Immediately, this suggests that competitiveness is a dynamic concept
where planning must incorporate both long-term and short-term objectives in order that it be sustainable. Porter (1985) believes that competitive
success is underpinned by the possession of firm-specific advantages
over rival suppliers. These can be assessed at a point-in-time, and conclusions, drawn about the competitive stance of a firm *vis-à-vis* its rivals,

can be made on a static basis. However, firm-specific advantages can be eroded, and without management of resources to maintain advantages in the face of changing market conditions, the firm will lose its competitive edge. This highlights the importance of regarding the issue of competitiveness as *a process*, wherein firms pursue a goal of long-term profitability through exploitation of firm-specific advantages, and the reallocation of profits to enhance continually firm-specific advantages.

In the international arena, the level of international coverage attained by a firm is, in itself, becoming a source of advantage permitting firms to exploit rapidly changing technologies in a wide market, and to draw new inspiration from a broad customer base, whose changing needs stimulate new directions for business activity. Clearly the process of competitiveness must be managed to incorporate all parts of the internationalized network, which requires careful integration into an overall coherent strategy of the firm's various constituent divisions. Possibly, then, the key to competitive success rests with management, whose task it is to organize its operation to produce and exploit advantages in an integrated way.

1.1.2   Foreign market servicing strategy

There are three generic strategies which may be deployed by firms in supplying their products to overseas markets: exporting, licensing and foreign direct investment (Buckley and Casson, 1976). The first two forms of market servicing can be used by firms operating out of a single 'home' country base, while the latter is the hallmark of a multinational company (i.e., a firm which owns income generating assets – mines, manufacturing plants, offices, sales subsidiaries – in two or more countries).

Exporting (X) involves production in one country, with products being sold in overseas markets. This can take the form of indirect exports with the firm using various market intermediaries (agents, distributors, trading companies, etc.) to handle overseas sales, or direct exports handled by the firm's own export departments. Licensing (L) involves the assignment of production and selling rights by a firm to producers in target markets in return for a lump sum and/or on-going royalty payments. Foreign direct investment (FDI) involves the firm establishing its own production and selling facilities in overseas markets. This can take the form of a new greenfield investment, a merger with, or takeover of, an established supplier, or a joint-venture arrangement (Root, 1989).

At its most simple, X can be distinguished from the other two methods of market servicing by the *location effect*, as with exports the bulk of value adding activity takes place in the home country, whilst the other two methods transfer all, or a high proportion of value adding activity to host country markets. Similarly, L can be distinguished from X and FDI by the *externalization effect*. In licensing, the firm sells rights and the use of assets (know-how, production methods, brand names, etc.) to an 'outside' firm, the licencee. In X and FDI such activities are *internalized* and remain within the initiating firm. Broadly then, the location and internalization effects separate the three generic forms of market servicing:

$$\text{Market servicing} = \overset{\text{\Large \textit{Internalization effect}}}{\underset{\text{\Large Location effect}}{X + L + FDI}}$$

1.1.3 Foreign market servicing strategy and its impact on competitiveness

We are now in a position to look at the *interrelationship* between foreign market servicing strategy and the maintenance and enhancement of a firm's competitiveness. The decision to export, invest or license to the foreign market can impact on the ability of the firm to manage successfully the competitive process. Different management systems associated with the alternative forms of market servicing pose different problems for managing for competitive success. Exporting from an established 'home' production plant is a relatively inexpensive and low-risk way of servicing a foreign market (i.e., it obviates the need to invest in overseas plants) and maximum advantage can be taken of centralized production to secure economies of scale and thus lower unit costs. On the other hand, the firm could be put at a competitive disadvantage either because of local producer's lower cost structures (deriving, for example, from lower labour costs) and control of distribution channels, or because of governmental tariffs, quotas and other restrictions on imports, as well as adverse currency movements. Moreover, in the case of indirect exporting, export performance may be retarded by a 'poor' selection of agents and distributors (lacking commitment, motivation and resources to provide satisfactory sales cover and marketing). Licensing may be attractive because it enables a firm, particularly one constrained by a shortage of management and capital resources, to gain rapid market penetration, and because it does not involve direct entry into the market it thus avoids head-on competition with local suppliers. On the other hand, the royalties obtained may represent a poor return on an innovative process or product, with the ultimate danger that the technology or product may be 'captured' and developed further by competitors leading to the elimination of the firm's initial competitive advantage. Foreign direct investment can be expensive and risky, although host country governments often offer subsidies etc., to attract inward investment, and investment costs can be lowered by establishing a joint-venture with a local partner. In many cases, however, the 'prescence' effects of operating locally (familiarity with local market conditions, the cultivation of contacts with local suppliers, distributors and government agencies, and the provision of back-up services such as maintenance and repair) may be important factors in building profitable market share over the long term. Moreover, direct investment by internalizing various aspects of a firm's market servicing operation may enable the MNC both to avoid the transaction costs of using the market (specifically, the costs of concluding and policing contracts with agents, distributions, etc.) and to increase its marketing effectiveness through a greater control of key distribution and marketing functions.

In sum, the selection of an appropriate foreign market servicing strategy designed to enhance and protect the competitiveness of the firm is dependent on an amalgam of *firm-specific factors* (e.g., the nature and 'uniqueness' of the firm's competitive advantage, and resource availability), *industry-specific factors* in target markets (e.g., the level of market concentration and the extent of barriers to entry), and *location/ country-specific factors* (e.g., the extent to which products need to be adapted to meet local requirements, host government policies on tariffs, subsidies, etc.).

1.2 Empirical Study of Policies on Market Servicing: The Research Framework

The main proposition addressed in the study is that the international competitiveness of a firm is dependent on the selection of an appropriate set of foreign market servicing strategies and the effective *management* of the chosen market servicing modes. The study is based on the following analytical schema.

1.2.1 Competitiveness and its operationalization

Competitiveness is defined by three interrelated factors (1) competitive *performance*, (2) competitive *potential* and (3) management *process*. These 'three Ps' describe different stages in the competitive process.

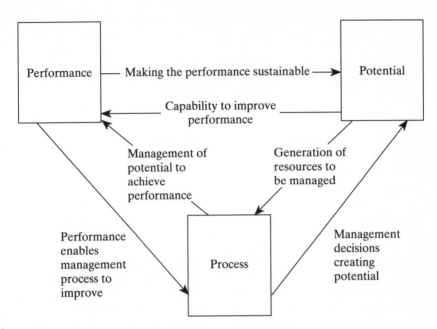

Figure 1.1 The interrelationship between measures of competitiveness

Potential measures describe the inputs into the firm's operation; performance measures the outcome of the firm's operations; process measures the management of the firm's operation. From this perspective, competitiveness cannot be considered as a static concept, but rather as a multi-faceted ongoing process. Figure 1.1 depicts the interrelationships between the three aspects of competitiveness.

Clearly, no single measure of competitiveness alone can fully explain the nuances of competitiveness as a dynamic process. If only performance measures are considered, the question of the *sustainability* of such performance remains unanswered. Too many uncertainties remain concerning the management of success, and the regeneration and maintenance of competitive potential, which is part of the process of planning for future competitiveness. Conversely, where only competitive potential is measured, no indication is given of whether or not this potential is turned into performance. Assumptions based on the idea that advantages necessarily result in success ignore the possibility of unrealized potential and may consequently lead to distorted results. Management processes by their very nature are difficult to quantify and thus 'qualitative' observation has to be relied on in the main. As the concept of competitiveness fundamentally depends on comparison, qualitative assessment of management process alone may prove unsatisfactory, as it makes no reference to the fruits of management activity in the form of performance measures. It is, however, a critical aspect of research into the process of competitiveness, as it describes how managers turn potential into performance. Therefore, a composite, interactive measure covering performance, potential and process is essential. This is done both by theoretical review (see chapter 2) and empirical investigation (see chapter 3).

1.2.2   Choice of foreign market servicing mode

Market servicing policies concern the choices between exporting, foreign licensing and foreign direct investment. Studies of macro data on exporting, licensing and foreign direct investment reveal wide variations across industries and foreign markets. Consequently, an element of the primary research concentrates on industry and market dependent variables shaping foreign market servicing decisions. Other factors, however, are critical to the foreign market servicing decision, notably issues of channel management. The orthodox theory of international business has paid far less attention to the non-production functions of stockholding, distribution, promotion, generating customers and transport than to production. The marketing and transport functions are either ignored or are implicitly assumed to be governed by the same factors that determine production in the international business literature. The literature on international marketing, by contrast, concentrates on operational details of distribution and control of agents and tends to provide an arbitrary cut-off, ignoring forms of doing business abroad other than exporting.

Figure 1.2 is an attempt to encompass the key elements of the market servicing decision. The key functions are shown: production, which may be a multi-stage process, stockholding, distribution control, promotion, generating customers, transport and retailing. These various functions are interdependent and are linked together both by a flow of physical product and by a flow of information. The physical flow runs through the production stages, distribution and retailing to the customer. These functions may be internalized or undertaken by external intermediaries, depending upon a number of considerations such as the extent of cost savings arising from combining together sequentially-linked production processes, stockholding costs and the incidence of various market 'transaction costs' (the costs associated with finding suitable input suppliers and distributors and in negotiating, concluding and monitoring contracts with other firms). Information flows between the functions, in particular those relating to the promotion of the firm's products and the generation of a customer base are equally crucial. Again, the importance of information flows may dictate whether functions are internalized or externalized.

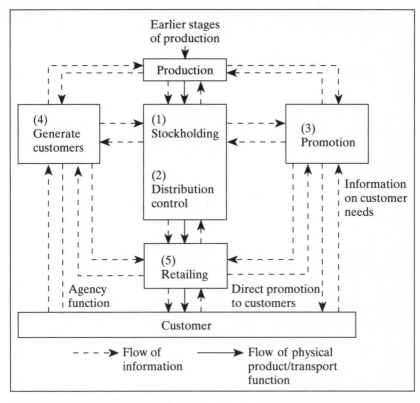

Figure 1.2 A schematic diagram of the key constituent elements of the firm's activities (developed from Buckley and Casson, 1976, p.51)

The local knowledge, specialist skills and customer contacts of independent intermediaries may favour externalization. In other cases, the need for secrecy and the avoidance of misinformation may encourage internalization. Additionally, information flows are an integral element in sustaining competitive advantages, in particular in establishing 'first-mover' advantages through obtaining prompt and accurate data on, for example, changing customer tastes and preferences, new materials and packaging techniques, etc. Therefore, any analysis of the foreign market servicing decision must consider all the activities listed and the key elements determining their location and internal versus external performance. The activities cannot and should not be considered in isolation. It is the interrelationships and interdependencies between the activities which make the market servicing decision so complex. Because of the many factors affecting the configuration of activities, policies should be constantly under review.

1.2.3 Impact of foreign market servicing on competitiveness

Building on the two theoretical strands above, the impact of foreign market servicing on competitiveness can be analysed.

As indicated earlier, market servicing policies concern the choices between exporting, foreign licensing and foreign direct investment. They vary widely at the macro level across industries and across foreign markets. At this level the forms can be differentiated by the location effect, which splits exporting (production in the home country) from foreign licensing and investment, where production takes place abroad, and by the internalization effect which splits foreign licensing (a market relationship) from exporting and direct investment, where control is internal. However, when we consider multi-function and multi-product firms, examining both entry into foreign markets and switches of market servicing mode, the picture becomes much more complicated. Production is not the only function whose location and control can be varied. Similar decisions must be made throughout the marketing channel. Thus research and development, stockholding, distribution, retailing, the agency function and promotion can be located at home or abroad and be internalized or externalized. Thus, a potentially rich pattern of activities can be delineated.

In view of the complexity of competitiveness and market servicing strategies it is clear that (1) the strategic move to be analysed must be carefully described in several dimensions and (2) the impact on competitiveness must be traced through all its (interacting) mechanisms.

The model we envisage is shown as figure 1.3. The change in market servicing strategy may impact upon (1) competitive performance (2) competitive potential and (3) management process. There is also a potential dynamic interaction or feedback between each of these inter-related measures of competitiveness.

The decisions made by firms are constrained by the nature of the product, the firm's previous involvement with the market, the actions of competitors, demand conditions in the market, financial and cost considerations. However, despite these constraints, a range of choice is available to firms, not only between the three generic modes of market servicing, but also within mode. This latter point emphasizes the importance of channel decisions within the firm's strategy, as adaptations to channel structure can have an important impact on elements within the competitive process. The impact of between-mode and inter-mode changes on the three aspects of the competitive process are not always

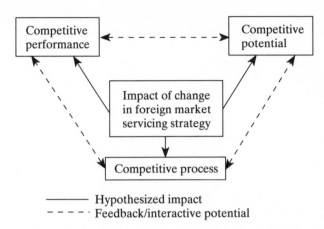

Figure 1.3   Hypothesized impact of foreign-market servicing changes on competitiveness

positive, and in some instances foreign market servicing decisions involve a trade-off between the various competitive elements and require possible adverse effects to one element in the short-term to be considered in a broader, long-term perspective.

1.2.4   The empirical study

To reiterate, the basic hypothesis of the study can be presented as:

Competitiveness of British Firms	is a function of	appropriate market servicing strategies and other variables

From this, using the definition of competitiveness elaborated above this becomes:

Competitive Performance	Competitive Potential	Competitive Process	$= f$ (market servicing strategies and other variables)

A priori, it can be postulated that both host country and industry variables will affect the outcome of a strategic move. Further, the type of strategic move, for example, from no foreign involvement to exporting through an agent or from exporting through a distributor to a foreign direct investment, is likely to have an impact on the components of competitiveness. The hypothesis now becomes:

Competitive Performance	Competitive Potential	Competitive Process	$= f$ (type of market servicing change, industry factors, host country factors and other variables)

So as to minimize the impact of variables other than the change in market servicing strategy, the study was limited to a small number of target markets (in particular, Germany,[1] France, USA and Japan) and a small number of industries (glass, industrial gases, consumer paint, scientific instruments, pharmaceuticals and retail financial services). However, the changes in other variables which might have affected the outcome are specified where appropriate. Competitor firms from USA, Japan, France and Germany are included in the study as comparators.

In-depth interviews were conducted with 15 manufacturing firms and 24 retail financial services firms. All were British owned and their head offices were in the UK. The manufacturing sector sample comprised five pharmaceutical firms, five scientific instruments firms, three paint firms and one firm each from the glass and industrial gases industries (grouped together as 'national champions'). The manufacturing firms varied greatly in size and degree of internationalization. Four distinct groups may be identified: (1) Small firms with a primarily national orientation, targeting maybe one or two international markets as a first step to reaching a wider international market. The turnover of firms within this group rises to approximately £25 million. (2) Medium sized firms in a comparatively early stage of internationalization, seeking a more consolidated approach to their overseas investment, often involving capital investment for the first time. The turnover range for this group is £25m to £100m. (3) International firms who are players in most, if not all, of the significant national and regional markets in their industry. There may be significant gaps in the global coverage of these firms who may be dominant in one or two regions and weak in others. The turnover range of this group is £100–£1000 million. (4) Global firms, who are major players in oligopolistic world markets and whose turnover exceeds £1000 million.

The retail financial services firms covered by the study comprised six banks, eight building societies and ten insurance companies. In order to achieve comparability of activities across these three sectors it was necessary to restrict the analysis to European activities, given that UK building societies are not permitted to service markets outside Europe.

Again, the firms varied greatly in size and the degree of international involvement.

Four groups of firms were identified:

1 Firms planning a defensive stance in the light of possible threat to the UK market from European financial liberalization after 1992. Included here are also those firms showing some vague (unformulated) interest in potential niche markets.
2 Firms scanning Europe for opportunities.
3 Firms who have identified target markets and are in the process of establishing operations.
4 Firms with established operations in one or more European market.

Experience of many firms in the financial service sector is skewed more towards first-time expansion than strategies for consolidation of international activities.

In addition to the interviews conducted with UK firms, a series of interviews were carried out with foreign firms who had been identified as direct competitors by British managers. These interviews provide a 'yardstick' for our observations and establish whether our findings are peculiar to UK firms – or to firms, in general, across each identified industry sector. Although the sample size in each sector is relatively small, the analysis provides some interesting differences which raise a series of questions and issues regarding the competitiveness of UK firms.

The sample of comparator firms totals 14: five in France, six in Germany, two Japanese and one American. They cover four of the identified sectors: pharmaceuticals (four) scientific instruments (four) national champions (one) retail financial services (five – incorporating two banks, two housing finance and one insurance firm).

Notes

1 Although West Germany and East Germany were unified in October 1990, most of the statistical data and primary research pre-dates this and consequently relates to W. Germany.

2

The Meaning of Competitiveness

2.1 Introduction

A review of recent literature on competitiveness yields an array of measures which purport to be surrogates of competitiveness. A cursory examination of the measures shows that they vary enormously in scope and in terms of the level of analysis (that is, at country, industry, firm and product levels). Usually single measure proxies of competitiveness have been used to illustrate single issues, for example, declining export market share as an indicator of loss of 'export competitiveness'. In this chapter the limitations of current concepts and measures of competitiveness are examined and an attempt is made to propose an approach which will have wider use than in a single project.

2.1.1 Definitions

Competitiveness at the level of the firm Few definitions of competitiveness exist in the literature, but of those that do, the Report from the Select Committee of the House of Lords on Overseas Trade (1985) (The Aldington Report) best summarizes those which are tailored to the competitiveness of firms. 'A firm is competitive if it can produce products and services of superior quality and lower costs than its domestic and international competitors. Competitiveness is synonymous with a firm's long-run profit performance and its ability to compensate its employees and provide superior returns to its owners'.

This suggests that measurement of a company's 'competitiveness' should incorporate quantitative measures of costs, prices and profitability, and qualitative indicators of non-price factors, specifically quality, if the definition is to be satisfied. These are not, however, the only measures

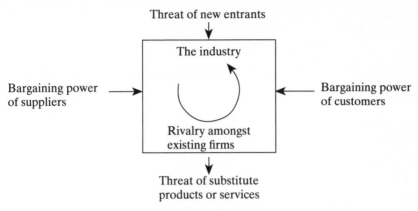

Figure 2.1 Competitive strategy: forces driving competition in a market

cited in the literature. A parallel approach is taken by the European Management Forum, which defines competitiveness as 'the immediate and future ability of, and opportunities for, entrepreneurs to design, produce and market goods worldwide, whose price and non-price qualities form a more attractive package than those of foreign and domestic competitors' (European Management Forum, 1984).

The above definitions suggest what attributes a competitive firm should possess, but provide little information about *how* a firm becomes competitive. The 'strategic' aspects of competitiveness – that is, the formulation by the firm's *management* of an appropriate 'competitive strategy', is critical to long-term success. According to Michael Porter (1980) a main concern of competitive strategy is to identify (1) the firm's own and rivals' competitive strengths and weaknesses and (2) the nature and strength of the various 'forces' driving competition in a market (see figure 2.1). The key to a successful competitive strategy is then (3) to understand fully what product attributes are demanded by buyers (whether it be low prices or product sophistication) with a view to (4) establishing, operationally, a position of competitive advantage which makes the firm less vulnerable to attack from established competitors and potential new entrants, and less vulnerable to erosion from the direction of buyers, suppliers and substitute products.

There are three generic strategies for competitive success (see figure 2.2): cost leadership, product differentiation and 'focus'. Low costs, particularly in commodity-type markets, help the firm not only to survive price competition should it break out, but also, importantly, enable it to assume the role of market 'leader' in establishing price levels which ensure high and stable levels of market profitability.

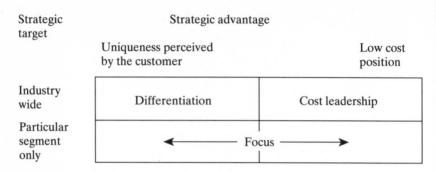

Strategic   Strategic advantage
target
           Uniqueness perceived   Low cost
           by the customer   position

Industry
wide   Differentiation   Cost leadership

Particular
segment   ◄———————— Focus ————————►
only

Figure 2.2   Competitive strategy: three generic strategies

Cost advantages over competitors are of two major types: (1) absolute cost advantages, that is, lower costs than competitors at all levels
of output deriving from, for example, the use of superior production
technology or from vertical integration of input supply and assembly
operations (2) relative cost advantages, that is, cost advantages related
to the scale of output accruing through the exploitation of economies of
large scale production and marketing and through cumulative experience
curve effects. Over time, investment in plant renewal, modernization
and process innovation (either through in-house research and development, or the early adoption of new technology developed elsewhere)
is essential to maintain cost advantages.

By adopting a product differentiation strategy a firm seeks to be
unique in its market along a dimension that is valued by its potential
customers. Product differentiation advantages derive from (1) a variety
of physical product properties and attributes (notably the ability to offer
products which are regarded by customers as functionally 'better than'
or having 'unique' qualities, compared to competitors' products) and
(2) the particular nuances and subliminal images built into the firm's
product by associated advertising and sales promotion. Again, given the
dynamic nature of markets, particularly product life-cycle considerations,
competitive advantage in this area needs to be sustained by an active
programme of new product innovation and upgrading of existing lines.

General cost leadership and differentiation strategies seek to establish a competitive advantage over rival suppliers across the whole market.
By contrast, 'focus' strategies aim to build competitive advantage in
narrow segments of a market, but again either in terms of cost or, more
usually, differentiation characteristics, with 'niche' suppliers primarily
catering for speciality product demands.

Competitiveness at the national level   Competitiveness can also be examined more generally in the context of the competitiveness of nations.

At this level of analysis, the absence of definitions is more marked, but one obvious example was gleaned from the literature. 'The definition of competitiveness for a nation must similarly be tied to its ability to generate the resources required to meet its national needs' (Aldington Report, 1985). This definition is equivalent to that adopted by Scott and Lodge (1985): 'National competitiveness refers to a country's ability to create, produce, distribute and/or service products in international trade while earning rising returns on its resources' (p.3).

Measuring competitiveness in terms of 'national needs' is clearly a difficult task as it requires a careful clarification of the national needs of each country separately analysed. A great deal of attention has recently been paid to the 'loss of competitiveness' of the US economy. See *inter alia* US Department of Commerce (1987), Baumol et al. (1989) Feenstra (1989) and Dertouzos et al. (1989). Most recent research avoids this issue and concentrates on relative performance measures, cost advantages or qualitative assessments of countries' international business ratings.

The work of Scott and Lodge (1985) explicitly concentrates largely on the perceived trade off between national competitiveness and social goals. Countries are placed, in the chapter written by Scott, in a matrix which has 'development oriented strategies' on the vertical axis (work, saving, investment) and 'distribution oriented strategies' (economic security/entitlements, income redistribution, short-term consumer benefits) on the horizontal axis. These competing national strategies, growth/productivity and external competitiveness versus domestic economic security and redistribution of income are deemed to account for differences in the dynamics of changes in rankings of international competitiveness.

A further study which emphasizes the importance of national characteristics in competitiveness is Michael Porter's The *Competitive Advantage of Nations* (1990). Porter's basic proposition is that 'Companies benefit from having strong domestic rivals, aggressive home-based suppliers and demanding local customers'. This is encapsulated in Porter's 'diamond', shown in figure 2.3. A basic starting point is a country's factor endowments, such as plentiful (i.e., cheap) labour or skilled labour, raw materials and capital stock, together with its underlying scientific and technological infrastructure. With regard to demand conditions it is not so much the size of the home market (although it is accepted that a large home base may be necessary to underpin economies of scale in lowering supply costs and prices) as its nature that matters. Porter emphasizes the importance of the presence of sophisticated and demanding buyers in stimulating the innovation and introduction of new products capable of being 'transferred' into global markets. The category of 'related and supporting industries' provides an important bedrock

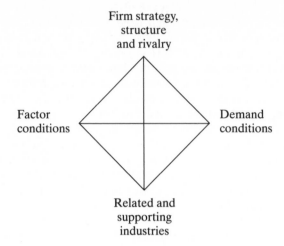

Firm strategy,
structure
and rivalry

Factor
conditions

Demand
conditions

Related and
supporting
industries

Figure 2.3 The Porter 'Diamond'

to competitive success through a network of suppliers and commercial infrastructure. The final quadrant 'firm strategy, structure and rivalry' Porter suggests may be the most important of all, especially the element of fierce local competition. While international rivalries tend to be 'analytical and distant' local rivalries become intensively personal, but nonetheless beneficial in providing a 'springboard' for international success. All these factors, it is suggested, are interrelated, creating a 'virtuous circle' of resource generation and application and sensitivity in meeting customer demands. Of course, in the last analysis 'competitiveness' applies as a general rule to *companies* or *industries* not nations (while, for example, a country which is deemed to be price uncompetitive in world markets, because of inflation, may attempt to 'correct' this by devaluing its currency, whether this is sustainable or not will ultimately depend on the cost-effectiveness of a range of individual companies and industries). This said, nation-specific factors provide an important 'backdrop' to the creation and enhancement of company competitive advantage on a global basis (see also Porter, 1986). For example, companies may base themselves in a more technologically advanced country in order to draw on that country's embodied scientific and technological infrastructure and skills to develop and innovate new processes and products (for instance, Japanese pharmaceutical companies which have established R&D facilities in the US and the UK). Alternatively, companies may establish manufacturing plants in less developed countries in order to access raw materials and cheap labour.

2.1.2   Categories of measures of competitiveness

An immediate problem thus arises: at what level should the analyses of competitiveness take place? Should it be measured at the firm, industry or national level? Any analysis must specify clearly the level at which measurement is taking place and must specify the unavoidable constraints. Our major concern is with competitiveness at the level of the firm but it is essential also to review macro measures of competitiveness. The time horizon of the analysis needs to be spelled out because binding constraints in the short run become flexible in the longer time period. Further, the issue of the inclusion of social goals in the definition of competitiveness is open to question. Many of the 'measures' of competitiveness implicitly or explicitly include issues of employment generation, quality of employment, distribution of income or other, wide objectives.

The diversity of the measures of competitiveness used by researchers, suggests that ideas about this complex concept vary greatly. For some, competitiveness is seen as the ability to perform well, for others, it is the generation and maintenance of competitive advantages, and for the rest it is the process of managing decisions and processes in the 'right' way. Consequently measures can be categorised into three groups:

COMPETITIVE *PERFORMANCE*
COMPETITIVE *POTENTIAL*
MANAGEMENT *PROCESS*

By categorizing the measures in this way it becomes apparent that the 'three Ps' describe different stages in the competitive process. Potential measures describe the inputs into the operation, performance measures the outcome of the operation, and process measures the management of the operation. From this perspective, competitiveness cannot be considered as a static concept, but rather, as discussed in chapter 1 (section 1.2.1), as an ongoing *interactive* process. When statistical measures have been used to show, for example, that one firm performs better in the market place than its competitors, and has generated and sustained more competitive potential, the qualitative information derived from researching management processes helps to explain the reasons for success.

It is essential also to classify the measures according to whether they are at national level, or applicable to the firm, the industry or the product. Tables 2.1 to 2.3 categorize the most frequently used measures at each level.

From this viewpoint it would seem, therefore, that single measures

The Meaning of Competitiveness

Table 2.1 Performance measures by level of analysis

Country
 Export Market Share
 % Manufacturing in Total Output
 Balance of Trade
 Export Growth
 Profitability

Industry
 Export Market Share
 Balance of Trade
 Export Growth
 Profitability

Firm
 Export Market Share
 Export Dependency
 Export Growth
 Profitability

Product
 Export Market Share
 Export Growth
 Profitability

alone fail to capture the nuances of competitiveness. This, however, is not the only point of contention. Increased internationalisation of trade has meant that the boundaries of business can no longer be limited to single countries, which complicates measurement and analysis. Measures of competitiveness should, therefore, consider the impact of not only exports but also sales arising from foreign direct investment and licensing. Figure 2.4 summarises the important issues to be addressed at each stage in the international competitive process.

Thus, measures of competitiveness must be extended beyond parent company boundaries, as well as beyond single measures. Section 2.2 of this chapter highlights the limitations of performance measures of competitiveness and section 2.3 the limitations of measures of potential. Section 2.4 reviews some of the advantages offered by incorporating qualitative research into management processes in an assessment of competitiveness. Section 2.5 presents some of the important issues raised by the literature in an attempt to outline a clearer understanding of the concept of competitiveness, which has important implications for measurement and analysis. The conclusion, section 2.6, suggests the key elements which should fill in the 'empty boxes' of our approach.

Table 2.2 Measures of potential by level of analysis

Country
    Comparative Advantage
    Cost Competitiveness
    Productivity
    Price Competitiveness
    Technology Indicators
    Access to Resources (May vary by industry)

Industry
    Cost Competitiveness
    Productivity
    Price Competitiveness
    Technology Indicators

Firm
    Cost Competitiveness
    Productivity
    Price Competitiveness
    Technology Indicators

Product
    Cost Competitiveness
    Productivity
    Price Competitiveness
    Quality Competitiveness
    Technology Indicators

Table 2.3 Management process measures by level of analysis

Country
    Commitment to International Business
    Government Policies
    Education/Training

Industry
    Commitment to International Business (Trade Associations etc)

Firm
    Ownership Advantage
    Commitment to International Business
    Marketing Aptitude
    Management Relations
    Closeness to Customer
    Economies of Scale and Scope

Product
    Product Champion

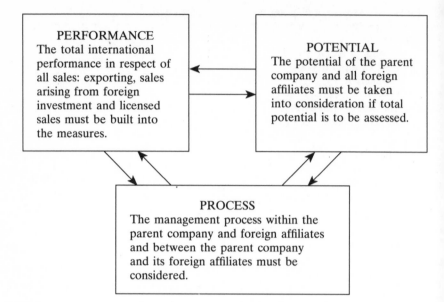

Figure 2.4   The competitiveness of an international company

2.2   Measures of Performance

2.2.1   Export market share

The percentage share of exports relative to a matched comparator is frequently cited as a measure of competitiveness (Krugman and Hatsopoulos (1987), Lipsey and Kravis (1987), Kirpalani and Balcome (1987)). At a macro-economic level, countries' export market shares are measured across all industry groups on the assumption that global export volume is indicative of competitive performance. Such a measure, however, fails to give insights into countries' balance of trade and economic strength through its failure to consider imports (Krugman and Hatsopoulos (1987), Francis (1987). In addition, only exports are considered as elements in competitiveness, thus ignoring sales arising from foreign affiliates and foreign licensed sales. Exports account for only 55 per cent of the total foreign sales of British companies (1983 figure from Buckley and Prescott (1989)). Therefore, a shift in the market servicing policy of firms can radically affect any such measure of competitiveness.

A more sophisticated measure of competitiveness is obtained by examining the export market share by industry. The view here is that a declining market share in high technology industries and an increased share in less sophisticated products is thought to be a reflection of a decline in competitiveness. This view derives from a stance which injects social goals (quality of life, nature of employment) into competitiveness measures, for it is by no means obvious that the technology content of trade is a good proxy for competitiveness.

The measure can be further improved by examining the destination of exports. The argument here is that export market shares maintained through exporting to less developed countries are less indicative of high degrees of competitiveness than are those won in the more advanced countries. This may be regarded as a proxy for the time frame of competitiveness – based on the lower growth rates of less developed countries – building into an argument of sustainability, but again there is no intrinsic relationship between market share in particular foreign markets (designated 'more dynamic' or 'highly competitive') and competitiveness.

Export market share is also frequently used at the level of the firm. However, it fails to account for instances where market share is maintained through drastic price cutting, which would consequently have an adverse effect on profitability and possibly on long-term performance. The measure also cannot cope with multiproduct firms whose performance varies according to product (Kirpalani and Balcome (1987)) and firms operating in market niches.

All market share measures suffer from the defect that they ignore margins. A crucial problem is that market share can (at least in the short run) be bought by underpricing – 'dumping' in the international context. Consequently, the sustainability of market-share measures is constantly open to question.

2.2.2 Percentage share of world manufacturing output

An alternative to market share measured through exports, is market share measured through the national share of world manufacturing. The basic assumption underlying this measure is that a fall in the percentage share of world manufacturing is an indication of declining competitiveness. It is assumed that a fall in share denotes an erosion of a country's manufacturing base by more competitive countries. However, factors other than competitiveness may affect both the numerator and denominator of the fraction. The numerator, that is, the value of a country's manufacturing, is tied in with demand, and is consequently affected by the economic environment of the domestic market, and overseas markets in which a country's companies operate. A fall in demand in the domestic market obviously has the greatest impact. In terms of international trade, however, the effect may still be marked where demand falls in a particular overseas market on which a country is heavily dependent. As the international trade of many countries is biased towards a small number of world markets, a fall in demand in any one country may have a significant impact on their percentage share of world manufacturing. It does not, however, hold that if a country maintains its share of world manufacturing in the face of declining demand, it is maintaining its competitive position.

Compensatory price cutting and market dumping may be employed to sustain sales at the expense of generating and maintaining competitiveness. The single measure fails to highlight how far this is so, or whether the position is truly related to competitiveness.

The denominator, that is, the value of world manufacturing, is tied to the manufacturing base of each country. Increased manufacturing resulting from new businesses does not necessarily indicate an increase in 'competitiveness', but may simply be part of the development of previously non-industrialised countries. Added volume of manufacturing in one country will cause a fall in share in other countries purely as a result of the mathematical relationship. If such an increase in volume acts to generate world demand without reducing the volume of manufacturing in other countries, then the fall in share experienced by some countries cannot be explained by declining competitiveness. Consequently, the single measure may be misleading.

In addition, a fall in share of world manufacturing may be caused by a change in the numerator or denominator, the implications for each being very different. As a result, the simple assumption that a fall in share of world manufacturing indicates a decline in competitiveness, cannot be substantiated. Competitiveness is only one factor which may impinge on the movement in share of world manufacturing, and thus, before such an assumption can be made, many other factors need to be tested for.

2.2.3   Percentage share of domestic manufacturing in total output

This measurement is based on the assumption that to be competitive a country's strength should be in manufacturing as opposed to services. (Krugman and Hatsopoulos (1987)).

A fall of manufacturing in total output is considered to be a measure of uncompetitiveness. The basic arguments underlying this assumption are twofold. First, services are considered to be less tradeable, and secondly many services are thought to ride on the back of manufacturing industries, and thus a decline in one will effect a decline in the other. The first point fails to account for the continuing increase in trade in services which, despite the fact that there is less tradeable volume, does not consider the long-term potential of tradeable value. Second, it is argued by Francis (1987) that declining manufacturing is partly due to this sector buying in more services from outside concerns, as opposed to producing them internally.

A further issue which must be considered is the basis of measurement. An apparent decline in manufacturing can result from an increase in services. Consequently, an absolute decline in manufacturing should be ensured before assumptions of declining competitiveness can be made. In the case of the UK, Francis (1987) argues, even where an absolute decline in manufacturing as a percentage of gross domestic product is apparent, the decline in manufacturing is due to an increase in 'other' activities, namely North Sea Oil. As a result, the measure may be misleading in terms of traditional manufacturing sectors which may continue to be competitive.

2.2.4 Balance of trade

Some studies suggest that competitiveness can be measured according to the balance of trade between countries. The measure is not, however, without its limitations: 'The most obvious indicator of US competitiveness in manufacturing is the raw trade balance. This indicator by itself, however, can be misleading. A decline in demand for manufactures abroad can lead to a trade deficit by reducing US exports, even if US firms remain competitive' (Krugman and Hatsopoulos (1987)).

2.2.5 Export measures at firm level

Two measures of competitive performance are export sales growth and export dependency (the ratio of exports to domestic sales). In the former case, these may be simply compensatory for a decline at home; in the latter, the use of domestic sales as the denominator biases the measure.

2.2.6 Profitability

Profitability, or relative profitability, is rarely referred to in the literature as a proxy for competitiveness. Partly, this is because of the extreme difficulty of measuring profitability across industries and particularly across countries. However, profitability is arguably the single most important measure of competitive success. Profit objectives may be firm specific and complications arise when companies of different size are compared. Some firms (and some nationalities of firms) may forego short-term profits for long-term growth and on a short time horizon they may appear to be uncompetitive, despite the fact that they are developing competitive advantages in the markets in which they operate. In many countries, stock exchange valuations and the takeover threat are constraints on this behaviour, leading to accusations of 'short-termism' in company planning. At the product level, company profitability may obfuscate the relative performance of different products in the portfolio. Highly competitive products earning high margins may compensate for uncompetitive products in other sectors.

Despite these comments, long run profitability is essential for survival and profitability must be an important element in any assessment of competitiveness. The point of time nature of measurements of profitability mean that it is most useful as an adjunct measure, even a constraint, in more complete encapsulations of the competitiveness concept.

2.2.7   Competitive performance measures reviewed

The quantitative measures reviewed thus far can be categorized together in that they all measure relative competitive 'performance'. What is being measured is the *outcome* of the competitive process and past performance. They provide a historical perspective, and are all characterized by their inability to provide insights into the sustainability of such performance. Using only these measures leaves too many questions unanswered.

All of the measures reviewed, except profitability, ignore margins. All the other measures examine shares of world markets or segments of that market or changes in export performance. This must be tied to measures of the profitability of achieving such shares. The point of time, non-dynamic nature of profitability measures also makes such measures suspect as proxies for competitiveness. In terms of *outcome* measures, relative market share with a profit performance criterion represents the best approach, but even such a composite outcome measure leaves open the question of sustainability.

2.3   Measures of Competitive Potential

The above section showed the importance of the dimension of potential in studies of competitiveness. This section reviews such measures.

2.3.1 Comparative advantage

The fundamental assumptions of the standard Hecksher–Ohlin model
of international trade are that factors of production are immobile between countries and that these factors are used in different combinations
to produce different goods. A country then possesses a comparative
advantage in good X if the country is relatively well endowed with
factors which are used intensively in the production of X.

The concept of 'revealed' comparative advantage (RCA) was put
forward by Balassa (1965 and 1977) because of the view that cost
comparisons were an inadequate surrogate for comparative advantage.
Balassa used export performance to measure RCA but even the most
detailed trade statistics relate to product groups rather than individual
products, and consequently countries often appear as importers and
exporters of the same product categories. The growth of intra industry
trade is well documented (see Greenaway and Milner (1986)). As a
result, therefore, the generally preferred method of analysing comparative advantage is through net exports (exports minus imports) as
opposed to absolute. (See Bowen (1983)). Criticisms and extension have
been made by Scott (1985), Cable (1983), UNIDO (1986) Cantwell
(1987) and Webster (1988).

The work of Leamer (1984) shows that empirical content can be
given to concepts of comparative advantage (however at a very high
level of aggregation – only ten aggregates were used in the main analysis
(p.xv)). Leamer feels that the main currents of international trade can
be well understood in terms of the abundance of a remarkably limited
list of resources. The key factors are natural resources, work forces and
savings rates. Physical capital emerges as an important determinant of
comparative advantage in manufactured products.

However, there are three important limitations of research into
comparative advantage. Firstly, agglomeration across industries, and
across firms, suggests inadequate results, as different factors contribute
to the advantages of different products and firms trading those products.
Secondly, the macro-economic country perspective ignores overseas trade
other than exports. Finally, the choice of factors which are thought to
contribute to the advantage is an arbitrary one, and it is possible that
apparent key factors will supplant the real elements which make
countries/industries competitive.

2.3.2 Cost competitiveness

'Cost competitiveness' is often used as a measure of competitiveness at
industry and firm levels. The general principle behind this thinking is

that the lower the costs a firm/industry incurs, the more competitive they will be.

Costs enable a comparison to be made between the position of firms using different methods of foreign market servicing. Using labour costs, some idea of relative positions of industries across nations may also be made. Cost analysis, however, fails to take account of the performance of industries and firms. It is possible for a firm/industry to be cost competitive but fail to earn satisfactory returns as a result of poor market positioning or product image. In this sense, then, are they truly competitive? 'If the performance of the country's industry is good irrespective of, e.g., poor cost competitiveness, it means that the industry has chosen the markets, the strategy and other competitive means which have led to successful results.' (Artto (1987) p.48).

2.3.3 Productivity

The productivity of a firm is sometimes tied in with competitiveness and adds another variation to the theme of cost competitiveness. The cost of labour, and raw materials can provide a company with productivity advantages over its competitors, but how it uses these advantages in the market place is more critical to understanding competitiveness than merely being aware of their existence.

Labour productivity – macro level   Fagerberg (1988) puts the proposition that 'Few would probably disagree with the view that [international competitiveness] refers to the ability of a country to realize central economic policy goals, especially growth in income and employment, without running into balance of payments difficulties,' (p.355). He suggests that a theory of international competitiveness must establish a link between the growth and balance of payments position of an open economy and factors influencing this process. The primary quantitative measure of international competitiveness has been 'growth in relative unit labour costs'.

However, this is at odds with the evidence that the countries with the fastest growth of exports and GDP have at the same time experienced much faster growth in unit labour costs than other countries and vice versa: 'the Kaldor paradox' (Kaldor (1978), see also Thirlwall (1979)).

The problem of these interpretations is that they depend exclusively on price competitiveness and that prices depend exclusively on labour costs. Fagerberg (1988) produces a model which includes not only price competitiveness but also the ability to compete in technology and the ability to compete in delivery (ability to deliver proxied by capacity). The model suggests that the main factors influencing international competitiveness (identified as growth in GDP at constant prices with the alternatives of growth in market share for exports and imports) are technological competitiveness and ability to compete on delivery. There are, of course, many problems in measuring technological competitiveness. In addition, ability to compete on delivery is proxied by gross fixed investment as a percentage of GDP, which is capable of many other interpretations. Perhaps the best summary of Fagerberg's results is that investment plays the crucial role both in creating production capacity and in evolving new technology. This, rather than cost competitiveness, is supported as a key factor in international competitiveness.

Labour productivity – industry level   An examination of labour productivity at the industry level has been conducted for the UK relative to the US and Germany (Smith et al. (1983)). This enables an identification to be made of those sectors where British performance has been comparatively good or bad. In justifying labour productivity as the key measure, Smith et al. say, 'At the national level, output per man, and by extension, output per head of the population, is the basic determinant of living standards. At the sectoral level, since labour costs bulk large in many economic activities, differences in labour productivity levels are a major determinant of inter-industry costs and international competitiveness,' (p.13). After allowing for environmental and structural differences, the authors point to differential sector performance where Britain performs worst in industries where the British activity is under capitalized relative to the foreign counterpart and where its scale of activity is below that of its competitors (i.e., opportunities for specialization were not being taken). British productivity tends to be especially poor in industries where plant size is typically large. In addition, the more vertically integrated is British industry compared to its competitors the better is its labour productivity performance.

Labour productivity – firm level   A study by Pratten (1976b) of labour productivity differentials within international companies found that 'economic causes' accounted for over half the observed productivity differential. These were: differences in rates of output of products and length of production runs (the key difference UK versus USA), differences in plant and machinery plus other economic causes (differences in product mix, substitution of labour for material or better quality materials, capacity utilization and availability of labour). Behavioural causes were incidence of strikes and major restrictive practices and differences in manning and efficiency (estimated to be the key difference in the case of Germany). Management attitudes were felt to underlie much of the observed discrepancies in UK productivity.

Pratten's comparative study of Swedish and UK companies also concentrates on labour productivity (1976a): one key element in the relative success of Swedish companies was that foreign investment was more deliberately used as a weapon in controlling overseas markets and securing exports. A higher capital intensity and economies of scale in specialized product areas were also part of a nexus of factors contributing to Sweden's relative success.

Support for the importance of achieving competitive cost positions through economies of scale is provided by Owen (1983). Owen found that, in general, relative plant size was more important than relative firm size; economies of scale resided in manufacturing rather than in the overhead functions performed by the company. Company size is important in so far as it enables managements to rationalize manufacturing operations to achieve common specification and plant specialization. There are also significant industry differences: in the case of motor car production the company seemed to be the important dimension, in white goods the product line was most important. Owen's work also supports the view that management attitudes to exporting are crucial for competitiveness. Regarding domestic sales as the basic business and exports as a bonus is a disastrous mistake: exporting is necessary to survive in home markets.

2.3.4 Price competitiveness

Price competitiveness, is clearly related to cost competitiveness, and, therefore, this measurement also plays an important part in determining the location of production. Several measures of price competitiveness may be employed. For example:

Relative export prices: the ratio of export prices of UK goods to a weighted average of export prices of the UK's main competitors.

Import price competitiveness: the ratio of UK wholesale prices of goods to the price of imported goods.

Relative wholesale prices: the comparison of prices in the UK domestic market with the prices against which UK exports will be competing in other domestic markets.

Such measures give an indication of an industry/product's potential for competitiveness but give no insight into how they turn such potential into performance. A company may be price competitive, but through poor product quality/brand image/market servicing/product positioning may be unable to turn such potential into sales and profits.

2.3.5 Quality competitiveness

Measurements of quality at greater than the product level are difficult. Surrogates such as value:weight, value:labour input and value added:output do not capture the nuances of quality competition (Slater (1988)). Measurements of quality could encompass: concern with the technology of ensuring close tolerances in manufacture, consistency and conformity of output; product achievement standards (reliability, longevity, etc.); concern with design or image.

Competing on price is not necessarily the optimum form of competition. Where quality is thought to be a key competitive element, producing down to price may be an inappropriate strategy to follow. Price may also act as an indicator of quality and consequently lower prices may suggest poorer quality, and thus deter sales. Quality achievements are not an end in themselves but are a means to match consumer wants. We therefore consider quality competitiveness to be subsumed in profitable market share.

The idea that cost based competition is becoming a failed strategy to achieve international competitiveness is taken further by Piore and Sable (1984) and other champions of flexible specialization. The basic idea is that seeking the mass market and maximum economies of scale can be contracted with the flexible utilization of multi-use equipment, skilled workers and the creation of a community that restricts the forms of competition to those favouring innovation. The spread of flexible specialization therefore amounts to a revival of craft forms of production. Although somewhat idealistic across a broad range of industries, in certain sectors this alternative must merit consideration, particularly in niche markets and production areas dominated by fashion.

2.3.6 Technology as an indicator of competitiveness

Much of the recent research into competitiveness focuses on technological activity and development as the key to competition. Many indicators of technical intensity are postulated as indicators of competitiveness.

These include R&D expenditure (Pavitt (1984), Cantwell (1987)), employment of qualified scientists and engineers, number of patents (Patel and Pavitt (1987)), royalty income and licensing and value to weight indicators. However, these measures must be supplemented by some notion of the outcome of the technology process. Comparative studies of the innovation process can shed light on straightforward indicators (see for example Whittaker (1990)).

Added to this, different distributions within R&D may impinge on performance: 'A heavily R oriented industry may not have an impact for some time. A heavily D oriented industry may 'appear' less advanced but may have a more immediate impact,' (Sciberras (1986) p.6).

It is the *outcome* of R&D which is important to the firm and industry, not the level of spending. Firms may spend extensively on research and development, but may fail to produce products which match the needs/ wants of the market place.

2.3.7 Access to resources

Access to key inputs may be a wellspring of competitiveness. Resources which may give rise to a competitive advantage could include access to capital, skilled labour including management and natural resources. These resources are often regarded as location specific (i.e., immobile) and in a geographical sense this is, of course, true. However, it is not true where firms are mobile. Multinational firms may go international precisely to gain access to such resources (Dunning (1981), Buckley and Casson (1976)). Therefore, access to resources may be a consequence of internationalization, not a constraint on it. However there may well be competitive advantages which arise because of the domicile of firms, or because of constraints on internationalization and an access from firms of other nationalities.

Access to capital It has been argued that British firms suffer from a lack of 'patient money'. The stock exchange is adduced to require rapid returns and the valuation of companies is suggested to be over sensitive to short-term performance. This accusation of 'short-termism' in the British stock market (similar charges have also been laid in the US) is regarded as a competitive disadvantage as it prevents long-term planning and constrains coherent long-term plans, for example, for internationalization and for research and development.

Access to skilled labour Shortages of skilled labour are again often seen as a constraint on competitiveness. At the firm level, as with many of the other issues we consider, this is a constraint in the short run. In the long run, the firm can train labour, buy in key workers from elsewhere (including other countries) and influence public policy to rectify shortages. In periods of rapid expansion, shortages of key workers may constrain response to opportunities.

Access to raw materials Competitive advantages may arise because a firm has cheaper access to raw materials through its location. Transport costs and trading rigidities will often raise the costs of key inputs to foreign firms. This provides a key motive for foreign direct investment, to take advantage of cheaper inputs.

2.3.8 Competitive potential measures reviewed

This second set of measurements refers only to the inputs which generate competitive potential, but fails to consider if, and how this potential is turned into performance. It cannot explain why a company which appears cost competitive, price competitive, spends a high proportion of its profits on R&D, has a high percentage of technical personnel, lodges many patent applications and shows high relative income from licenced sales, can still fail to perform well in the market place. In other words the commercialization process, transforming potential into outcome, is ignored.

It is clear, however, that two elements of potential are crucial to the sustainability of competitive performance. These are technological development and price/cost effectiveness. Technological development, and technological awareness are vital if a company is not to be overtaken by superior products. In the long run, too, price and cost competitiveness are essential even in high margin markets.

In most of the literature, assessment of competitiveness generally appears to focus *either* on the outcome of the performance *or* the inputs which generate competitive potential. Research studies which measure both input and performance are much fewer in number. One example is Oral and Reisman (1988) which envisages competitiveness as a function of industrial mastery (defined as success compared to its competitors in terms of generating and managing capital and other operational resources), cost superiority and political/economic environment. Thus, notions of comparative, potential and current competitiveness are encompassed.

Even where potential and performance measures are incorporated, there still remains the issue of *how* the most apparently successful and competitive firms translate their potential into performance. What is pertinent here is an assessment of the competitive process which relates to the effectiveness of corporate and divisional decision making. In terms of analysis, this demands a qualitative study of management processes at the level of the firm, and government management of the economy at the national level. As firms operate in different markets, and governments in different countries, they are consequently faced with different opportunities and constraints, a situation-specific analysis is necessary. The following section highlights some of the important competitive process issues.

2.4 Management Process

The task of transforming competitive potential into performance is the task of management. It is the performance of management on which the competitive process rests. Approval of the performance of management is essentially qualitative and particular elements of the management process have been singled out by various writers. Our review attempts to pick out the key elements in this complex picture. In addition, fundamental issues concerning governments' management of the economy are also addressed.

2.4.1   Ownership advantage

The concept of ownership advantage has been used to explain the ability of firms to secure and retain profitable market share. Ownership advantages form one of the major planks of Dunning's 'eclectic theory' of multinational enterprise, the others being internalization advantages and locational advantages (Dunning (1981 and 1985)). Porter's work places a great deal of stress on the generation and retention of competitive advantage (Porter (1985)).

A basic problem with ownership advantage as a source of competitiveness is that it ignores the means by which the advantage was built up in the first place. It is a static concept which is of very limited use when analysing a dynamic situation. There is a great danger of regarding ownership advantages as fixed and immutable (Buckley (1983 and 1988)). It is undeniable that a major driving force of international competition (and foreign market servicing policies) is the generation and protection (prevention of dissipation) of ownership advantages but ownership advantages may well be a consequence and not a cause of foreign expansion – a crucial element may be feedback of knowledge from overseas (Casson (1988)). Internalization theory can explain why this feedback must be internalized within the firm and why foreign direct investment is often preferred to other market routes, for example, licensing (Buckley and Casson (1976 and 1985)).

In the present context, ownership (or competitive) advantages are exogenous to our explanation, not a separate determining factor of competitiveness.

2.4.2   Commitment to international business

Much of the literature refers to Western countries' (governments'), industries' and firms' lack of commitment to international trade. A lack of international orientation in the education system, resulting in low levels of proficiency in foreign languages and cultures, and government policies which frequently focus more on domestic issues (Hannay and Steele (1986)) and firms lack of global distribution networks as a method of exploiting technology (Rugman (1987) pp.94–95) are thought to contribute to uncompetitiveness.

2.4.3 Marketing aptitude

Several elements contribute to the marketing aptitude of firms. In much of the literature, this is generally referred to as 'non-price' competition. This extends the notion of competitiveness to the level of consumers in whose hands the ultimate success, and consequent 'competitiveness' of a product – and hence a company lies. 'The marketing concept holds that the key to achieving organizational goals consists in determining the needs and wants of target markets and delivering the desired satisfactions more effectively and efficiently than competitors,' (Kotler (1984) p.22).

As has been noted earlier a company can be both cost, and price 'competitive', but may fail to be truly competitive in the market place through poor product design, product performance, positioning, servicing and a poor understanding of the market. Arising from this, it must be noted that non-price competition does not depend upon offering better specification, higher quality, more effective marketing and/or more service, but rather that it depends upon offering the *right mix* of these factors to cater for the needs and wants of consumers in different segments of the market. It is not a matter of customers putting 'a price' on the different elements of this mix: what is important is that the mix matches consumer perceptions.

2.4.4 Management relations

Two elements of management relations can be contributors to improving competitiveness: internal relations and external relations, particularly with foreign intermediaries.

Internal relations   A major part of the task of management in transforming potential into performance is that of motivating and organizing the workforce. Industrial relations therefore play a part in the management process. Improving productivity and overall cost performance clearly contribute to competitiveness as do the elimination of labour frictions, disputes and strikes. The development of a harmonious and well motivated workforce is often stated to be the basis of Japan's competitive success. This has led to a spate of suggestions that management relations should be developed along Japanese lines. This, together with the adaptation of quality circles and just-in-time (Kanban) production philosophies are deemed to provide a key to emulating Japanese success (for example, Pascale and Athos (1982)).

This raises a major question for assessments of competitiveness: how far can successful techniques be transferred across countries in order to improve competitive performance? (Buckley and Mirza (1985)). Certainly, management learning and the adoption of new techniques of management can be a key factor in improving performance. Thus, 'proximity to market' has been adduced as an independent factor in competitiveness (Shepherd, Silberston and Strange (1987)).

External management relations   Where business operations are extern-alized – in the case of exporting through agents and licensing, or where firms are involved in joint ventures – relations with intermediaries or partners is important to the performance and competitiveness of firms.

All parties must agree on a common direction, and be motivated to plan for, market, and distribute a firm's products. Such relationships are not easy to manage, and conflicts will undoubtedly affect performance and competitiveness. Success depends on shared commitment, coopera-tion and trust, which require mutual willingness to solve problems, reciprocity and interdependence to sustain the commitment. This all demands time and management resources, careful monitoring and nurturing. How these elements of success are achieved and managed is important to the competitive process.

2.4.5   Economies of scale and scope

Often, competitiveness is associated with reducing costs and, other things being equal, this cannot be denied. From this, commentators often deduce that scale economies are essential to cost reduction and therefore that increased competitiveness is a concomitant of increased scale. How-ever, it must be noted that success is also a function of strategy and that scale economies differ between industries and products and are subject to revision in the light of rapidly changing technology.

Economies of scope arise in multi-product firms where economies of scope in production allow joint costs of two or more products to be less than the sum of stand-alone production costs (Teece (1978)). The key to lateral integration of products within a firm is the free internal transfer of resources, which enables costs to be reduced in areas other than those for which a resource was specifically developed (Buckley (1983)). Similarly, learning-curve effects can be regarded as a dynamic repres-entation of economies of scale (Abernathy and Wayne (1974)).

This brief discussion shows that economies of scale and scope are the outcome of judicious investment strategies on the part of management, rather than as separate elements of competitiveness. Such an investment strategy should be included in overall management processes.

2.4.6   Product champions

At the product level, product managers are responsible for the strategy and performance of goods. Success at this level is often thought to be related to entrepreneurship of such managers whose innovative product management is thought to play an important role in developing a sustainable competitive advantage. Successful managers of this ilk are frequently referred to as 'product champions'.

2.4.7 Management process at the macro level – government management of the economy

The quality, effectiveness and management of government policies are analagous at the macro level to the strategy of the firm at the micro level. Efficacious government policies can help to realize the potential competitive ability of a nation deriving from its natural endowments of resources (its comparative advantage). To do this, macro policies and industrial policies must allocate resources in an efficient manner, or at least help to reduce inefficiency. The methods by which this can be done are, of course, matters of extreme controversy centering on the appropriate degree of interference with the market. Scott and Lodge (1985), for instance, put growth and productivity on an orthoganal axis to redistribution of income in an implied, but unproven, absolute trade-off.

Particular importance is attached to improvements in the natural resource endowment by upgrading the labour force by education and training. Particular attention has been paid to management education in this regard.

2.4.8 Management process indicators assessed

The summary of management process indicators shows that when one looks beyond the broad-brush measures of competitiveness, there exists a complex array of factors which explain some of the finer details of the ability of firms to compete. These include: the experience which a firm has gained over time and which may enable it to make 'better' strategic decisions and consequently win a stronger competitive position; a clear market focus which may enable a firm to adapt quickly to changes in the needs of their customers, or market products in a way which serves the same needs in a better way; a definite commitment to international business which is built into the firm's long-run strategic plan; efforts to overcome the problems of 'foreigners' when doing business abroad; and close liaison with host and foreign governments, may all indicate greater competitive ability, and in some instances may be the key to competitive success.

The problem which arises however is that of comparison and quantification. In multi-faceted, dynamic business situations, it is difficult to assess and compare management processes. Hence the emphasis in the literature on easy-to-measure proxies, largely outcome related. Figures one to three summarise the relationship between potential, process, and performance. In order to understand the competitiveness of firms all three 'Ps' should be considered.

The three different elements are not independent – changes in potential should lead to changes in the management process and consequent performance. In turn, performance feeds back into the firm's future potential. Therefore, the relationship between the three 'Ps' is important in understanding the dynamics of the competitive process.

2.5 Issues Raised by the Literature

Several key points are raised by this critical review of the literature on competitiveness.

Firstly, is there a concept of competitiveness over and above that of efficiency? Efficiency can be described as the optimal allocation of resources to achieve desired ends. Consequently, on this reading competitiveness research involves the search for inefficiency and the policy recommendations are directed to the eradication of such inefficiency. In fact, there is an element in competitiveness which is not present in efficiency and that element is the choice of the most appropriate objectives. In other words, competitiveness includes both efficiency (reaching goals at the least possible cost) *and* effectiveness (having the right goals). It is this choice of industrial goals which is crucial. Competitiveness includes both the ends and the means towards those ends.

Secondly, competitiveness is a relative concept. It must be defined relative to some other state of the world. The possibilities are (1) relative to the situation of a different historical point of time (thus raising issues of *loss* of competitiveness) (2) relative to an existing comparator (at the firm level, perhaps paired groups of firms, either of different nationalities or pursuing different policies or two divisions of the same firm having made different choices) or (3) relative to a well-defined counter-factual position (the alternative position). Each of these possibilities has methodological implications for the empirical measurement of competitiveness. The key point is that as many factors as possible must be held constant in order to ensure that it is competitiveness which is being measured and not the constraints of the environment. To achieve an endogenous performance measure, all the elements of the constraints of the environment must be controlled.

Thirdly, what is the role of trade performance in competitiveness measurement and conceptualization? It is clear that the use of trade performance has an element of mercantilist philosophy as its underpinning. However, it is possible to argue that trade performance is an inefficient proxy for industrial effectiveness. Crude trade balance measures can account only for certain elements of competitiveness. Specifically, they are point of time measures at a given exchange rate and are the outcome of a complex set of factors, many of which have little to do with competitiveness. Capital movements, which are often the *cause* of shifts in relative national industrial effectiveness are treated as balancing flows by this analysis. Rather more sophisticated are measures which take into account the (changing) composition of exports and imports, more specifically the concern that market share in 'sophisticated' products is declining and unsophisticated ones is increasing. The argument then is that sophisticated products are technologically-intensive and that the loss of technology-intensive market share has detrimental social implications including declining employment and increasingly unskilled job provision.

Fourthly, the efficiency and effectiveness of resource use has to be defined with regard to the particular resource. Is it use of labour (or types of labour), capital or management which is inefficient? Perhaps the best response to this issue is to concentrate on inefficiencies in management for it is management which is the key change factor. This raises the issue that, under the perspective of industrial effectiveness, it may be necessary to specify incorrect objectives as a crucial problem of a loss of competitiveness. Consequently, issues such as the time discount rate of managers leading to excessive 'short-termism', a lack of an accurate cultural perception of the international environment, the excessive depletion of non-renewable resources, etc., may inhibit effectiveness. This leads to the issue of how far industrial effectiveness is actually under management control. In the short run, management is heavily constrained, in the long run it is much less so. For instance in the short run the poor quality of technical and/or managerial education is unalterable. In the long run training programmes can be instituted to relieve this constraint. However, it is also the role of government to play a part in providing the institutional and environmental conditions for the exercise of effective management.

This raises the fifth issue which is that of the level of the analysis. Should competitiveness be measured at the firm, industry or national level? What is essential here is to specify clearly which level is implied and to set out the unavoidable constraints. The time horizon of the analysis also needs to be carefully specified because the unavoidable constraints in the short run become flexible in a longer time period.

This perspective of industrial effectiveness, considered at the management level, enables us to link the concept of competitiveness to a

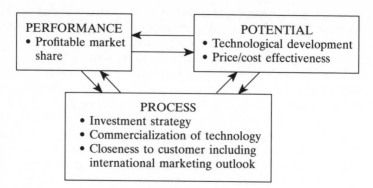

Figure 2.5   Key measures of competitiveness at the firm level

model of market servicing with a view to empirical investigation of the key issues.

2.6   Conclusion

This review of the extant literature on competitiveness has led to the view that single measures of competitiveness do not capture all the elements of the research issue. It is necessary to examine performance, potential and management process in order to evaluate critically changes in competitiveness. This must be done relative to a comparator, which must be chosen in order to hold constant as many extraneous factors as possible. Comparators may be parallel bodies, relative to a historical situation or relative to a well defined 'alternative position'.

The level chosen for our study of the impact of foreign market servicing strategy on competitiveness is that of the firm. This does not mean that other levels are unimportant. Indeed, a study of patterns of perform-ance by industry may well shed a great deal of light on an individual firm's performance.

In terms of specifying measures of competitiveness, it is clear that measurement of *performance* must be wider than a single measure. It is proposed that *profitable market share* should be the key quantitative outcome measure. This means market share whilst sustaining at least the industry norm of profitability. Together with this outcome measure should go some notion of maintaining or improving *potential*. Although measurement is difficult, attention should be paid to the generation of new products and processes through investment in technology and to long-run price and cost control. Finally the management *process* in commercializing this technology should be part of an investigation into management attitudes to internationalization, closeness to the customer and development of the business through an appropriate investment strategy. Our focus is thus upon effective management. Figure 2.5 provides a classification of the key elements of competitiveness.

Finally, the task of measurement and estimation of outcome is simplified by the need only to specify the *direction of change* of our indicators when specific market servicing decisions were taken. An estimate of the extent of change would be a bonus.

It might be argued that this choice of key measures by outside observers does not accord with the stated objectives of managers. The following chapter goes on to test this framework against managers' own perceptions of competitiveness in our sample group of industries.

3

Measures of International Competitiveness in Practice

3.1 Introduction

This chapter, building on the theoretical framework discussed in chapter 2, attempts to 'fill the empty boxes'. Findings from the 16 interviews conducted amongst manufacturing firms, and 24 interviews in the financial services sector, are integrated into the model in an attempt to distinguish the key elements within the competitive process on an industry-by-industry level. Despite the fact that the number of in-depth interviews is relatively small, we believe that the results are widely applicable.

3.2 Pharmaceuticals (five firms)

The pharmaceutical industry is characterized by two very distinct industry groups, branded pharmaceuticals (patent protected products) and generic pharmaceuticals (products for which the patent has expired). Due to the high costs associated with research and development in the creation of patented drugs, and the need to develop scale economies, the activities of small firms are generally skewed towards the generic pharmaceutical divisions. The strategic differences in approach to these industry groups is marked. In addition, pharmaceutical products can be divided according to the 'type' of healthcare they offer. Drugs which are used for clinical treatment of, for example, heart, respiratory, and nervous system disorders (which are more frequently prescription medicines) can be distinguished from those used to treat more minor ailments such as headaches, coughs and colds (which tend to be sold over the counter (OTC)). The former category is generally referred to as 'ethical' pharmaceuticals.

Again, the strategic implications differ between the two product types, importantly in downstream activities, that is, the channels of distribution through which they are sold.

Performance Pharmaceutical firms are acutely aware of market share and market share rankings at product level. This level of analysis is deemed essential due to the diverse nature of products within the industry, making a comparison between, for example, aspirin and antiasthma compounds, nebulous. Each of the five firms mentioned market share as a primary measure of competitiveness. Generally, these were quantified by reference to international comparative statistics (by which the industry is well served) although in the case of the one entirely domestically oriented (small) firm in the sample, it was domestic market share which was examined. Only in one case was market share the sole criterion of performance. Added to this, one firm mentioned market ranking by share of sales volume and growth, and another return on investment. A further firm added distributor performance, as their small market share in various international markets was generally perceived as offering little indication of improved performance. Consequently comparison of their leading competitors' market share is considered as less important than improved turnover by their distributors. A final firm listed 'turnover, profit and market share' as key measures of performance.

Potential In the case of branded pharmaceuticals, the general consensus is that successful performance in the short run depends upon unique products or range of products, which in the long term relies on investment in research and development. Research and development was frequently mentioned as the key to competitiveness in this sector. In the case of generic pharmaceuticals, where non-branded, drugs compete, with off-patent branded pharmaceuticals, development rather than basic research is crucial.

There was virtual unanimity that two of the major factors contributing to success are (1) the quality of the product range and (2) manufacturing and marketing facilities. In the former category, unique patented products are vital to branded drug producers, and these are maintained by R&D expenditure and the recruitment of good researchers. As one manager noted 'good researchers attract good researchers' thus successful R&D departments self perpetuate. Attention was also drawn to economies of scale in R&D. Interestingly, British pharmaceutical companies feel that the lack of good indigenous graduates is a major constraint on future R&D (and thus competitive potential) in the UK. In generics, the key factor is applied development. On the latter point, both patent and generic pharmaceutical manufacturers spoke particularly about the quality of the distribution and marketing operation, specifically the quality of the sales force.

Constraints on competitive potential were identified as a lack of suitably qualified graduates, lack of economies of scale for smaller firms and lack of synergy between individual products (and intra-group companies). Alternatively, in the branded pharmaceutical sector, the British government has set favourable pricing levels recognizing the need for producers to earn continual profits for reinvestment in R&D. Other governments have not been so understanding.

Process   Several aspects of management were identified as contributing to international competitiveness. The degree of focus of management was seen as important by several firms. One manager described the direction of his business as being like roulette. There is a certain degree of risk in choosing particular areas in which to invest in research and development. In the early stages, the area of focus is often perceived as potentially a winner or equally a loser. Thus, of key importance is the interface between technology and marketing. This reduces the risk of backing losers as the direction of research is determined by the needs of the market. Here the sales force is again important in its understanding of the product and its markets. A further management element voiced as important was concentration on objectives. These were often expressed in very general terms, but normally related to quality of products within a continual cost-cutting programme. One manager emphasized 'selling quality to professionals' as their management objective. Corporate relationships were identified as important and personal contacts, both inside and with outsiders, were mentioned.

One firm gave a clear picture of the international research management process and thus is worth paraphrasing.

'The key management elements are (1) international training: opening people's eyes to global opportunities. (2) Breaking down traditional interfaces by moving personnel across different departments. The 'hands on' experience generates commitment. (3) Problem-solving teams are set up with personnel drawn from various departments. (4) It is essential to maintain control of overseas manufacturing subsidiaries; technical reviewers are sent out who are also problem solvers. (5) No expatriate staff are used in foreign plants – we always hire indigenous people and (6) we have our own apprentice training school which cuts reliance on outside trainees.'

In general, benefits were perceived as being derived from developing an international perspective across all staff within the organization within the confines of an internalized global structure.

Overall, considerable emphasis was given to management aspects in international competitiveness.

3.3 National Champions – Industrial Gases and Glass (2 firms)

This section groups together Britain's national champions in two industries, industrial gases and glass, partly to disguise individual response, partly to draw together aspects of competition based on international oligopolies.

The industrial gases industry comprises a range of gases derived from the atmosphere and from chemical processes. The main atmospheric or 'air separation' gases are oxygen, nitrogen and argon which are produced by liquefaction and distillation of air. Gases derived as by-products from chemical processes include carbon dioxide and hydrogen, and various 'speciality' gases such as sulphur dioxide and gaseous chloride. The industry developed rapidly in the earlier part of this century as a supplier of oxygen to the steel and chemical industries. Today, with the innovation of new gases and user applications, the industry supplies a diverse spread of customers in the food and beverages, metallurgy, electronics, oil and other industries.

The global industrial gases industry is highly concentrated with seven international companies accounting for around 78 per cent of industry sales. In recent years, international competition has increased as the leading companies have moved into each other's traditional spheres of influence. The exploitation of new applications for gas products has been one important competitive stimulus. Another has been the introduction of new manufacturing techniques for atmospheric gases. Industrial gases are difficult and expensive to transport and this has tended to produce local monopolies. Foreign direct investment by the main international companies, together with more 'portable' technologies has increased competition in the industry, but the logistics of gas distribution and established contractual practices mitigate against widespread competitive encroachment.

Flat glass is of two main types, 'raw' or generic flat glass is produced in strips to a variety of specifications (length, sizes and thicknesses, clear and translucent) depending on end usage. Safety glass consists of glass which is 'toughened' (specially heat treated) or 'laminated' (interlayered with a plastic film) to provide greater strength and shatter resistance. Formerly, glass was produced by the 'sheet' and 'plate' processes, but these are now largely superseded by the 'float' glass process. The particular advantages of the float-glass method over the other two processes is that not only is it less costly to produce glass because of savings in the 'forming' stage of manufacture but also the glass produced is of a superior quality (more uniform surfaces and thicknesses, and blemish-free finishes).

Originally, exporting was the principal method of serving international markets, as the massive economies of scale demanded for competitiveness in glass manufacture meant that producers concentrated on developing efficient domestic manufacturing plants. In their search for more effective ways to penetrate international markets, leading global manufacturers looked to take-over opportunities and licensing to extend their operations. As a consequence, the industry developed a global character, with technology developed by multinationals being invested in less economically developed countries. To some extent, however, the traditional market structure of dominant indigenous manufacturers still prevails in developed economies. With the invention of the float-glass manufacturing process in the 1960s, overseas investment in cost-effective manufacturing plants became a more viable option.

Performance   One firm commented that 'basically market share' is their key performance measure. For them, market share is easy to measure as it can be assumed that a constant relationship between market share and installed capacity exists in their industry. The other uses 'ultimately' rate of return on investment, taking into account the environment and potential returns to be made. This measure is used in conjunction with market share. Quality and technical parameters are also considered.

Clearly, both firms, as members of global oligopolies, are acutely aware of their international competition. In one case, one of the firms has chosen to compete on price, consequently profits for all in the industry have been disappointing. The competitive interdependencies of the firms could not be more clearly illustrated.

Potential   Both firms emphasized the role of R&D and continued technical excellence. Quality parameters are estimated and reassessed. One firm felt that its fundamental research was as good as anyone in the world but that in terms of development in the market place it was not as good as its competitors: 'At the end of the day, the game is about selling, not making'. Scale economies were emphasized by both firms and one firm emphasized cost competition and the UK location was favourable to this. Research and development in both new processes and new materials remained the key to competitive potential.

Process   The management process as explained by one firm depends on (1) their aiming for a global balance across major consuming countries (2) their having a policy of hiring local people and leaving them to get on with it ('if they don't perform get rid of them') (3) the importance of good communications, in particular having a flow-back of information to the centre and (4) removing what had in the past been a blinkered view of the market.

3.4 Scientific Instruments (five firms)

'Scientific Instruments' cover a broad spectrum of product categories ranging from sophisticated thermo-analysis equipment down to pipettes and glass beakers. They are principally those products which are designed to provide industrial laboratories, private and national health care-laboratories, and universities and schools with the instruments they require for research and development.

Performance Market share and profitability were again to the fore in the industry, with perhaps more emphasis on profitability than in the foregoing two groups of firms. Market share and profit were mentioned by all firms. One firm's aim was 'to maximize profit'. Measuring market share is not a problem on 'big ticket' orders because market intelligence is highly specific and detailed: all firms in the industry know who got the order if they didn't! However, in other sub-sectors measurement of performance is much more difficult because in the case of Own Equipment Manufacturers, products are incorporated into the manufacturer's portfolio and thus into larger systems, which cannot be split out as individual sales items. Personally tailored customized products therefore tend to use profitability rather than (unavailable) market share.

One privately-owned firm was concerned with return on investment above all else. In the case of a recent foreign investment, its key objective was to recoup the investment in a short period of time and to establish profitable operation. Once foreign operations are established on a profitable basis, market share becomes an important objective.

Potential Product quality and the technology leading to it are crucial in internationally competitive scientific instrument companies. Product quality, design, technical standards, 'finish', 'ease of use' and energy efficiency all are important in giving a product real international potential. Product specialization and flexibility are important and so a balance has to be struck between specialization and versatility. Some firms are much more development orientated rather than research based. Testing and improving standards are crucial.

Generally, companies mentioned distribution and marketing as problems in realising potential. One firm felt that its foreign market servicing stance – relying on agents and distributors rather than sales subsidiaries – was incorrect. Another described British marketeers as 'a bunch of willing amateurs'. Whilst R&D was seen as contributing to improving competitive potential, poor marketing was seen as the key competitive disadvantage. British products were improving technically (for example, machines with a wider temperature range than foreign products) and more 'user friendly; but they were not well marketed.

Process   Product specialization, versatility and performance were seen as key targets for management in this industry but transmission of market information back to head office was emphasized as a key weakness by one firm. One company has a philosophy of small units which gives the firm a focus, which it feels its bigger competitors lack. This firm feels it is not good at 'selling itself' to staff and thus poor at keeping and motivating its staff. Marketing weaknesses were again emphasized.

One firm's manager was highly critical of the private ownership of the company, which he felt was short term and opportunistic in its decision making rather than concerned with long-term strategy. Managers were constrained by the owners and decisions were not delegated. Thus, decisions seemed arbitrary and the long-term strategy was difficult to fathom ('non existent' in his words).

3.5   Paint (four firms)

Until relatively recently, the low-value 'commodity' nature of paint, and its volume bulk, meant that it was not economically viable to export it abroad. This meant that there was little 'global' competition *per se*, the general structure of the market being based on national competition. The product, however, has moved away from being a commodity and has emerged today as a more sophisticated quality product backed by large advertising budgets. As this change took place, successful firms were those which were able to invest in research and development and advertising, which resulted in a concentration of the industry. For example, in the UK there were 250 manufacturers twenty years ago, whereas today there are only four major players. With this increase in added value, it has become possible to export paint profitably, and therefore the industry is becoming more globalized. However, the long-term effects of strong indigenous manufacturing in foreign markets means that they are difficult to penetrate successfully when operating at arms length. Consequently, even when selling through independent wholesalers/distributors, manufacturers see the need to have their own agents 'on the ground' in foreign locations.

Performance   Two firms use market share and profitability as their measure of performance although one of these is financial-performance led. One firm looks at cost and prices and keeps below those of its competitors because there is overcapacity in the industry. It benefits from economies of scale in production and distribution. The final firm uses international brand leadership as its performance measure.

Potential   One firm is a major innovator. Its potential comes from its continual investment in R&D and marketing. This lead arises from the fact that the UK is the most sophisticated market in the world. Because of this reservoir of knowledge, it can serve consumers at different levels of development. There is enormous investment in research, development, innovation and merchandising (i.e., the way its brand is presented). Finally, potential competitive ability is drawn from the fact that they have a European-wide integrated production system. The firm has made several major innovations and it draws on its global experience. These advantages are maintained by a carefully focused strategy.

One firm is focused on cost leadership. It believes that price is the key to success, allied to quality. Scale economies in its UK manufacturing is vital. On the marketing side, the local registration of brand names and relationships with buyers are keys to success.

A third firm is focused on building and maintaining product uniqueness through an R&D programme. The fourth firm builds potential by research but also by a policy of consumer monitoring and attempting to be close to its customers.

Process One firm believes that it is strong strategically but that it occasionally has tactical problems in certain markets. Production restructuring has enabled profits to be earned in a short period of time. A movement of personnel between departments and locations has aided the transfer of knowledge around the organisation. A second firm lays emphasis on a loyal and dedicated staff, which is kept motivated by money incentives and who work as team for the company. Marketing and promotion is identified as the key management task in the third firm. Finally, the fourth firm seeks to maintain a distinct identity with the customer and to pay attention to improving information systems and distribution networks internationally.

3.6 Banks (six organizations)

De-regulation of financial markets in the UK has resulted in a blurring of the traditional boundaries between banks, building societies and insurance companies. Banks, which were once the bastions of current accounts, deposit accounts, unsecured loans and more recently, credit cards, have, in recent years, ventured into the mortgage and insurance markets. The result is that many are now more akin to 'financial supermarkets' than specialist providers of a restricted array of financial services. This trend has resulted in increasing competition in many financial markets and a reassessment by many banks of their overall objectives and future business horizons. A recent Economist survey on international banking (1990) suggests that the new highly competitive market place faced by many banks has made them more aware of the need to be efficient, streamlined profitable organisations with a broader view of potential expansionary paths encompassing international markets. These assertions can be tested by assessing the measures currently being used to assess competitiveness at an international level.

Performance   Return on capital and return on equity were the most commonly cited performance indicators mentioned by all six banks in the sample. The banks are aware that in order to justify investment in foreign operations they have to be confident that capital could not have earned greater returns elsewhere. As their whole business revolves around money management and investment for gain, the culture of banking organizations can potentially act as a barrier to international expansion in that short-term gains may be hard to achieve and investment consequently difficult to justify. This culture is particularly evident in two institutions who have made a conscious decision not to expand internationally in retail financial services at the present time (although they are developing their international corporate banking division). Two banks went on to justify this measure in terms of maximizing returns to shareholders. Three banks indicated that profitability was an important measure, one firm highlighting that the time to profitability is a key consideration in their market servicing decisions, another asserting that profitability is becoming increasingly important as competition intensifies. The latter firm indicated that cost cutting is an important element in maximizing profits, as is 'developing interfaces between products'. This theme was iterated by the third firm that mentioned profitability which is concerned with 'profitability of customer relationships', that is, the maximization of the potential available within their customer base – achieved through cross-selling. Thus, there is clearly some belief that the 'financial supermarket' can provide an important source of profits.

There was some evidence that these measures are not used indiscriminately. One firm indicated that measures depend on the form of market servicing, it being impossible to assess joint ventures in the same way as wholly-owned operations. This stems from the different objectives set for such operations. Another organization stressed the fact that some operations are simply judged on the perceived future potential, which helps to support a progressive, long-term commitment to internationalization.

Unlike the manufacturing sector, market share was not adduced to be an important measure of competitive performance. It was mentioned by only one firm in the sample, which indicated that market share and profitability are more to do with marketing projections than performance measures.

Potential   A wide array of competitive advantages were identified. Two banks highlighted continual innovation as a source of competitive advantage. Whilst accepting that new innovations can be copied rapidly and relatively cheaply, by continually introducing new products they believe that they can always keep one step ahead of their competition. To some extent, it is believed that this is easier to achieve in certain European markets than it is in the UK, due to the fact that markets such as Spain, Italy and Portugal are less developed than the sophistic-ated UK market, and thus the scope for introducing new, and relatively innovative products is greater. Another firm also highlighted the relat-ive sophistication of the UK market as a source of competitive advantage. As the UK market is more developed than many other European markets, they have already dealt with a lot of the new expansions now taking place across Europe and are thus better prepared to manage them. However, they recognize that by trying to deal with the issues in the same way as in the UK they could overlook important issues. Con-sequently, they are prepared to adapt their approach to local market conditions.

One bank stressed customer service as their major advantage, and in this respect they have dedicated themselves to a total quality management approach. They believe that because it is so pragmatic it allows the firm to improve its bottom line. They concern themself with the price of quality and the price of non-conformance. As 'quality' is difficult to measure, they spend time identifying consumer needs and wants and then develop products and systems to satisfy these needs. They also believe that they have a good central delivery system for their card services enhanced by their total quality management initiative.

Another firm mentioned their clearly focused strategy as a source of advantage, identifying areas in which they can excel and make money and thus generate returns to their shareholders. One smaller institution views its size as allowing better lines of communication than many of its larger competitors and a more personalized service to their customers. Other potential indicators, each mentioned by one firm, include size and stature, flexibility, good indigenous management, low-cost pro-duction, a good image and a good network throughout Europe. It is interesting that only one firm felt their European network was an ad-vantage considering that all managers highlighted distribution networks and a well-established customer base as being the key competitive advantages in Europe.

One bank felt that there is very little to differentiate between the clearing banks. Although branding might provide some advantage, and the way they sell and deliver differs to some extent, neither have resulted in growth above and beyond the other clearers.

Process Process indicators fall into four clear groups. Firstly, three firms view good indigenous management, and autonomy of operation of their foreign subsidiaries as giving their organization strength. Within this group, one firm stressed that their reluctance to impose a blueprint for management on their foreign subsidiaries has given the foreign operation the freedom to manage within the constraints of their own local environment. A second firm believes that major benefits accrue from a collective desire to achieve, which will succeed if British and foreign managers work together, all personnel making a contribution to the overall business. The final firm sees employing 'key personnel' with good contacts in the local market as providing the most advantages.

Secondly, there are two firms who regard training as the key potential indicator, and are currently investing large amounts in training staff – particularly retraining 'back-room staff for front-room duties'. As technology supersedes personnel in administrative roles, many institutions are refocusing training on how to sell and how to deal with customers. This approach enhances the drive for cross-selling as more contact time between staff and customers in the bank branches provides the opportunity to sell a range of products to existing customers.

Thirdly, one firm believes its focused approach is the best way to proceed. As firms cannot be all things to all people, by focusing on activities where they display strengths, they can concentrate resources and management time on areas of business where they are confident that they can make returns and achieve performance targets. Finally, one firm believes that developing good technological systems to move money, and process applications quickly is an important part of facilitating the business. However, in this respect, they believe that many banks are on an equal footing, and although it does not provide much of an advantage, it is a prerequisite of competitive performance.

3.7 Building Societies (eight organizations)

Like the banks, the building societies have recently extended outside their traditional spheres of business – mortgage finance – into areas more traditionally associated with banking and insurance companies. Many have also integrated backwards into the estate-agency sector in order to capture business at an early stage in the house-purchase chain. Associated services, such as removals, transit insurance and property insurance have also been explored and developed by some institutions keen to cross-sell services to 'captive' housebuyers.

Unlike the banks, however, building societies have only recently been given permission to extend their selling activities into European markets. Many are therefore at an early stage of development and much of what follows is therefore speculative, based on research of European markets, rather than experience in particular countries.

Performance Among the building societies, more emphasis is placed on profitability than was the case in the banking sector. Six out of the eight sampled firms mentioned profitability as a key indicator. There was also some evidence to suggest that the societies take a longer-term view of expansion. One firm indicated that they accept that initially they have to accept losses, but look to a return to profits in three years, or in some instances, five years. They also recognize that there are loss-leader benefits to be earned. A second firm emphasized that they measure 'long-term profitability' rather than immediate return on their assets. A further firm stressed that at the end of the day what they are trying to assess is how hard their assets are working for the company.

Only two organizations mentioned return on capital. One enumerated their target for new projects as 25 per cent ROCE within the first couple of years. The other suggested that once a new business venture begins to generate profits, then they measure ROC performance.

Other indicators which were mentioned include the extent to which the new venture enhances corporate image and the amount to which it consumes management effort and the opportunities for generating scale and scope economies by linking activities.

Market share was mentioned by two organizations as being of critical importance in the UK market, although in their European developments they expect that it will be a less meaningful indicator in the short-term when activities are small-scale. One manager suggested that, in isolation, market share measures would not provide much information on performance. A move from 0.3 to 0.4 per cent, would only be considered good if return on assets continued to be favourable.

Potential   Again, a wide variety of competitive advantage indicators were provided by interviewees. Three firms mentioned the efficiency of their money management as offering potential advantages and enhancing profitability. Efficient wholesale funding operations provide a solid financial base which is expected to support future expansion and development. One firm, however, noted that their good capital ratios makes them more attractive to predators, particularly foreign firms seeking to enter the UK market. A second source of potential emanates from the relative sophistication of UK building society products over European equivalents. The sophistication of endowment mortgages – which allows customers to borrow up to 100 per cent and the wide choice of products were mentioned by four societies. This was particularly stressed in relation to Southern Europe, whose markets are not perceived to be well advanced. Linked with this, two societies suggested that UK building societies have a good pan-European reputation, being regarded as experts in the field of mortgage finance. For these firms, playing on their corporate name is proposed as a way of promoting quality.

Other indicators include size and security (yielding a good credit rating), customer service and product knowledge.

Four of the eight building societies clearly feel that they have potential advantages which can readily and successfully be exploited in European markets. Two of these stressed that, although they do not consider themselves advantaged over UK competitors, they are confident that they have superior products than many European companies, are leaner and more efficient. The remaining four societies see greater potential, in the short-term, in developing their national activities by extending their regional coverage, rather than planning European expansion.

Process   There is general consensus among the building societies that their lack of international experience serves as a major disadvantage in extending their operations into Europe. Recruitment of personnel with experience in overseas markets is consequently a critical objective for all firms wishing to set up activities overseas. One manager indicated that they can (1) buy in staff with experience (2) train staff to deal with such operations or (3) hire indigenous managers with relevant expertise. Two firms, however, fear that overcoming the problem of lack of experience will not be so easily achieved. As the culture of the organization is domestically oriented, it will take a lot of time to open up the minds and outlook of managers to accept and actively pursue European expansion.

One firm highlighted the disciplinary mix among its top executives as providing a well-balanced management team able to develop the business in all key areas of activity.

3.8   Insurance Companies (ten organizations)

The insurance industry across Europe has witnessed a great increase in competitive pressure over the last few years, partly as a result of the deregulation of financial markets and partly as a result of increasing affluence of European consumers, which has enticed many firms to expand into neighbouring markets. This has put pressure on many of the smaller institutions and resulted in a certain degree of concentration within the industry as firms have sought merger opportunities in order to protect their interests. Another trend is the development of close ties between many insurance companies and banking institutions across Europe, in an effort to expand customer networks through the established branch systems of the leading banking institutions. This latter trend is continuing apace in the UK insurance market, and in the strategies being followed by UK players to extend their activities into Europe.

Performance   Profitability was mentioned by nine out of the ten insurance companies in the survey, but never as a sole indicator of performance. In most instances, the measure is used in conjunction with investment income and fund performance. There were three instances where firms recognize that short-term profits have to be traded for long-term gains. Here the focus was sustained sales growth over the short-term which is expected to yield satisfactory profits in the longer-term. In an effort to achieve profit targets, only two firms highlighted a cost-minimizing strategy. In all other instances increased sales performance was the main thrust of improved performance – achieved through increased productivity of salesmen, regional expansion and geographic diversification. The only firm which did not mention profitability and fund performance, a small specialist motor insurer, was merely concerned with sustained growth of their overseas operation.

Return on capital was only mentioned by two firms, and market share by one organization.

Potential   Product innovation/creativity was mentioned by five of the ten organizations. Three of these, however, recognize that their products are not unique and can be easily replicated by competitors. One firm went on to stress, therefore, that it is not so much the development of new products which is the key to competitive success, but rather the rapid introduction of these products into the market and managing their portfolio to generate maximum gains from innovative products. Their success in this area is enhanced by a wide geographical network. This latter point was mentioned by three firms, who believe that experience in several international markets gives them scope to offer European packages. This, however, is more beneficial to their corporate business than at a retail level. Along with the innovativeness of products, one firm believes the quality of its products enables it to take advantage of earning a high proportion of sales through independent agents, who readily promote their products on their merit. This is, however, difficult to replicate in many European markets where independent agent networks are less developed. The firm is, therefore, actively encouraging independent agents to set up in Spain in order that they can by-pass the tied system between banks and insurance companies. Another firm believes that their strength lies in the differential focus of their products which means that they do not become involved in potentially damaging price cutting strategies. In order to maximize the benefits they have spent a lot on retraining staff towards a customer orientation. Working through agents, however, prevents them from taking this stance abroad.

Efficient money management was adduced to be a major source of competitive advantage by four out of the ten insurance companies. Other advantages mentioned include the strength of indigenous managers in underwriting, the quality of the salesforce (being of graduate calibre which is rare in many European markets), small size which allows for flexibility and greater receptivity to customer needs, and in-depth knowledge of a specific market segment.

Process   There is an apparent divergence of opinion regarding the benefits and pitfalls of autonomous management of overseas operations. Four firms believe that it is a positive approach, allowing the personnel invested with knowledge of the market – competitors and customers – a free hand to plan and develop the business in close proximity to the market. Two organizations, conversely, fear that too much autonomy is given to subsidiary companies and foreign operating units, greater benefits being earned from closer integration of foreign operations and domestic business. One manager stressed this point by asserting that strength comes from interdependence, and scale economies can be achieved by centralizing certain functions rather than the present system of duplicating activities in various locations. However, he recognizes that the present system of autonomous management offers the benefit of greater results accountability, as the operating companies have no one to hide behind. In conclusion, he suggests that a balance needs to be struck between those operations which can be most efficiently managed centrally, and those that need to remain autonomous.

One firm highlighted the importance of constantly reviewing methods of distribution, seeking new ways of delivering products and by-passing the often highly competitive structures in existence in many foreign markets. Two further firms pointed to their focus on core strengths as generating a strong business culture and clear direction for future growth. Other factors include minimizing costs, remaining independent, being small and thus having fewer layers of bureaucracy, and staff training and development.

All firms reiterated the importance of money management and investment decisions, critical to the financial security of the organization and future growth potential.

3.9   Key Findings: The Empty Boxes Filled

The review of the 16 manufacturing companies above, drawn from five industries and 24 financial service firms across three sectors, allow us to make a tentative estimate of the elements of competitiveness which managements deem to be important. In almost every case, the managers seized on elements which are a combination of the three Ps (Process, Performance and Potential). There are also regularities in the environmental pressures which lead to an emphasis on particular components of competitiveness.

3.9.1   Performance

Profitable market share is the best characterization of the most usual performance surrogate chosen by firms in the manufacturing sector. In an industry like pharmaceuticals, this measure is employed at the product level. Knowledge is widely (though not costlessly) available to all firms in the industry and so product ranking in particular markets can be known and targeted. Performance can and is often measured at distributor level and the performance of the sales force down to the individual salesperson can be monitored. In other industries, market share, can be measured by assuming a relationship between installed capacity and market share, although this is dangerous if differentials in marketing skills exist (and it is likely that they do). In several industries and subsectors price competition is 'forced on' UK firms, and in the paint industry where there has been considerable overcapacity, lower prices mean highly effective cost performance and the necessity to reap economies of scale, hence pressures towards production rationalization. In some areas of scientific instruments, it is difficult to measure market share as products are incorporated into a manufacturer's portfolio and individual units are built into a system which is sold. Many firms across industry groups mentioned quality competition as important and growing in importance but it was measured on an ex-post-guesswork basis. Financial targets for return on investment tended to underpin performance measures on a wide basis. Growth was often seen as an end in itself and where mentioned it was sales and profit growth which were deemed important. The goal of operating globally was frequently mentioned by medium-sized firms, which had expanded into a small number of specific foreign markets.

Profitability is also a key indicator in the financial services sectors. Here, however, this is coupled with investment income and fund performance as opposed to market share. This reflects the underlying ethos of financial service firms – investment for gain. To some extent, and particularly in the banking sector, this compounds a short-term strategic focus as investment (particularly in foreign operations) can be hard to justify where capital could have been used more profitably elsewhere.

3.9.2 Potential

The key measure of potential was investment in research and development. This is usually proxied by R&D spending. In the pharmaceuticals industry, R&D spending was paramount. However, the range and quality of product offerings and the maintenance of an active and professional sales-force were equally seen as giving potential to sustain the competitiveness of the firm. Costs were mentioned in relation to potential more in the producers of generics, and here applied research was emphasized more than basic, patent-driven expenditure. In several areas it was felt that the British firm was as good as any competitor in the world on basic research but that commercialization (development in the market place) was less good than foreign competition. Selling skills were emphasized as needing attention in improving potential in a number of areas. Quality and technology were emphasized, as were, less frequently, low cost ('unbeatably low cost' in one manufacturer with economies of scale and experience advantages). The need to match good quality with effective (foreign) distribution networks was emphasized in the scientific instruments sector. Brand names and relationship with buyers were emphasized in our one consumer-goods industry (paint).

In the financial service sector, whilst product innovation (akin to R&D in manufacturing industry) was highlighted by many firms, innovations are easy to replicate and consequently do not necessarily provide a sustainable competitive advantage. Other factors must, therefore, be included. Thus, money management and distribution networks are highlighted as key factors to sustain a strong market position. Given the fact that generating a substantial distribution network overseas is very costly, and gaining access to indigenous distribution through joint ventures not always feasible, there emerges for many organizations, a barrier to achieving international competitiveness. In the short term, many firms are concentrating on their product 'sophistication', (an off-shoot of the intensely competitive UK market, wherein firms have had to differentiate continually their products in order to compete), in the less developed financial service markets of Europe. In the longer-term they hope that the systems they have developed to introduce continually new products will provide a basis for sustained competitiveness.

Some of the smaller firms within the financial service sample, whilst recognizing that their size can be a disadvantage in terms of financial muscle, credit ratings and the size of their customer base, compensate for these disadvantages by stressing their flexibility, lack of bureaucracy and good internal communication flows and receptivity to customer needs.

3.9.3 Process

If there is a surprise in these management assessments of competitiveness, it is the emphasis given to management process factors in competitiveness. Inevitably these are more idiosyncratic than the other two elements but several regularities emerge.

Firstly, there is an emphasis on management focus. Many firms (in both the manufacturing and service sectors) attribute success to clear goals and targets followed through in a relatively narrow area, be it product/market specific, technology specific or related to well defined company goals. Secondly, there is an emphasis on internal and, less frequently, external, relationships. Thirdly, there is a strong presumption that success hinges on tying the production, marketing and research processes closely together and ensuring harmony of goals and planning across these functions. This is linked to good communications within the company and in particular the necessity to have information flowing back to the centre. Several companies identified the lack of good information being transmitted to head office as a major process constraint on competitiveness.

Finally, recruitment, staff training and development were deemed important by a variety of firms, particularly in the financial service sector. Here, the lack of international experience of managers, particularly in firms going international for the first time, was viewed as impeding international competitiveness.

Research in the financial services sector also revealed a conflict between focus strategies, and product diversification, (moving towards a 'supermarket' approach to financial service retailing), across the three sectors. Another area where there are conflicting opinions relates to the benefits and pitfalls of giving autonomous control to foreign operations, which raises the issue of foreign market knowledge. The banks and insurance companies who view autonomy as offering clear advantages do so in the belief that foreign managers are better able to plan and control operations as a result of their first-hand knowledge of the market. Attempting to manage foreign operations along English lines is consciously avoided in recognition of the fact that all markets are different and require adaptation, not only of products, but also business practices and approach. Those insurance companies believing that foreign activities should be more closely integrated with domestic operations stress the economic benefits of avoiding duplication of activities in various locations.

Other management process elements were confined to one or two firms in the manufacturing sector but are worthy of further consideration. One firm described itself as 'not greedy for short term profits'. Several of the larger multinationals felt that breaking down traditional interfaces was crucial to success. Indeed two firms had strategies of moving people around through different departments in order to break down barriers and create a commitment to the firm (rather than to individual functions or units). The creation of teamwork was also mentioned as a key element by several firms. The international dimension of competitiveness was also picked up at the top end of the size range: control of foreign units was frequently devolved entirely to locals but review and feedback procedures were implemented to maximize international synergy. By contrast, flexibility was emphasized by one smaller firm, and one scientific instrument maker had a philosophy of small units to give a focus which larger companies (it felt) lacked. More than one firm felt that it was weak on 'selling itself' to its own staff, and although management, staff and workforces were frequently felt to be process advantages, some unease was often expressed that the maximum competitive advantage was not being made by human resources.

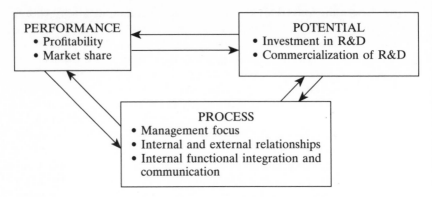

Figure 3.1   Aspects of competitiveness: results for manufacturing sector

3.10   Summary

If we return to the empty boxes of figure 2.2 there is a strong consensus in our sample of manufacturing firms that allows a tentative suggestion for the contents of these boxes. Figure 3.1 summarises this concensus.

Competitive Performance   is best measured by Profitability and Market
                          Share
Competitive Potential   is best measured by Investment in R&D and
                          commercialization of these activities
Management Process   is best proxied by Management Focus,
                          Internal and External Relationships,
                          and Internal Functional Integration
                          and Communication.

Overall, performance measures cited show a high degree of standardization across all manufacturing industry sectors. Thus, profitable market share may be viewed as applicable at national level. Potential measures, whereas not showing a great deal of general applicability, were met with general consensus within different industry sectors/industry groups. These, then, characterize competitiveness at the industry level. Management process indicators, on the other hand, tend to be firm specific, dependent on the historical development and character of the organization.

The picture for financial service firms is as follows:

Competitive performance: Profitability and investment performance
Competitive potential: Product innovation/sophistication
                           Money management
                           European network

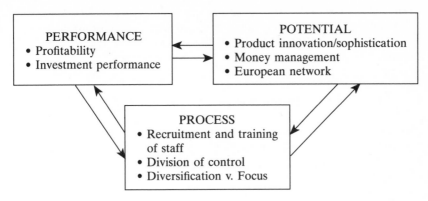

Figure 3.2   Aspects of competitiveness: results for retail financial services

Management process: Recruitment and training of staff
                             Division of control
                             Diversification v. Focus

Overall, whereas in the manufacturing sector performance measures appeared to be universally applicable, and potential measures specific to particular sectors and process indicators firm specific, this kind of distinction is not apparent in the financial service sector. This may be partly due to the blurring of traditional boundaries between the three sectors which has occurred in response to the deregulation of financial markets. As firms are now offering a wide range of products across the traditional business sectors, the diversity of measures identified in each sector may result from the diversity of products being offered. Figure 3.2 summarizes the results.

Some of these differences may be explained in terms of the intertwining of production and retailing in financial services. In the traditional approach to selling financial service products, retailing (through branch networks) is as much a critical part of the business as production. Consequently, overseas location of activities is determined by a separate set of factors. This raises the importance of distribution channels, as considerations extend beyond wholesalers (who build and break bulk in many manufacturing sectors), to the establishment of, or access to, retail outlets. Although such outlets may be replaced by sales representatives (particularly in the insurance sector) or other sales agents (for example, solicitors and estate agents in the case of mortgage sales) the shift of emphasis from up-stream to down-stream activities can be seen to have a pervasive influence. Notably, emphasis was placed on overseas networks as a key area of potential. Recruitment and training of staff reflects the importance of adapting not only products, but also retail functions to suit local market buyer behaviour. Attention to diversification versus focus could, arguably, be equated with the difference in strategy between specialist stores and supermarkets.

3.11   Implications for British Industry

This survey of attitudes to competitiveness in British industry allows us to do two things (1) to characterize the 'competitive organization' and (2) to point to key problems and bottlenecks in achieving competitiveness.

3.11.1   The competitive organization

The stereotypical competitive manufacturing organization has a clear management focus, pays attention to the communication links within and between its constituent parts and to internal and external relationships. Its performance is monitored and managed not on a single measure of output but on the returns from maintaining a strong strategic position (proxied by market share) taking care not to define this too narrowly or in a static fashion. This performance is sustained by attention to investment in research and development and the commercialization of innovations. The competitive financial service organization mirrors its manufacturing counterparts in many respects. Here, however, more emphasis is placed on the management of distribution – establishing foreign networks or gaining access to channels through synergistic collaboration – than is the case in the manufacturing sector. Inclusion of the retailing function in the managerial remit skews the competitive challenge away from a production/distribution focus towards distribution/delivery.

3.11.2   Obstacles to improved competitiveness

The key obstacles to improved competitiveness are lack of skills, notably in people capable of transmitting information across (largely artificial) boundaries in the firm. In smaller manufacturing firms the lack of international orientation and an inadequate foreign distribution/selling organization in particular pose further problems. Access to distribution networks attains even greater significance in the financial service sector in which failure to capitalize on advantages in Europe may stem solely from the inability to secure competitive distribution and delivery systems.

A blinkered attitude to the market and difficulties in commercializing knowledge remain bottlenecks. Particular shortages seem to exist for manufacturing firms in marketing skills and in managing the marketing/ technology interface, and for financial service firms in staff with relevant European knowledge and experience. Finally, many firms alluded to the shortage of 'patient money' in the British economy i.e., funding which allowed the firm to seek its long term objectives un-constrained by the need for short-term payoff. This may be more of a constraint for the smaller firms in the sample.

3.11.3 The need for balance

It is important to take a holistic view of competitiveness and the competitive process. Balance between and within the 'three Ps' is essential. For instance, a large market share without profitability is unsustainable and too much investment in future potential at the expense of performance related results will leave the firm vulnerable to a take-over bid. The three legs of the competitiveness tripod, performance, potential and process, must be maintained in balance.

4

The Design of a Foreign Market Servicing Strategy

4.1 Introduction

This chapter is an attempt to codify and integrate different approaches to the foreign market servicing strategies of international firms. It does so by widening the typical range of functions explicitly considered by the international business literature and by applying a uniform and unifying set of concepts to this enhanced range of functions carried out by the firm. Section 4.2 provides a brief review of the basic concepts and framework of analysis. Sections 4.3 to 4.13 examine the analysis at the level of the individual operations, taking account of both service and manufacturing firms. It will be seen that the orthodox theory of international business has paid far less attention to the non-production functions (stockholding, distribution, promotion, generating customers and transport) than to production itself. The marketing and transport functions are either ignored or are implicitly assumed to be governed by the same factors that determine production in the international business literature. The literature on international marketing, by contrast, concentrates on operational details of distribution and control of agents, and tends to provide an arbitrary cut off point, ignoring forms of doing business abroad other than exporting. An integration is long overdue. The work is exploratory and avoids detail on industry structure and company differences in an attempt to find regularities. The analysis relies on the two key choices for the firm for each function it performs: whether the function should be undertaken by the firm itself or subcontracted and where the function should be performed. These choices – the internalization and the location decision – are expanded below. The following section presents the key issues of our approach, a synthesis is provided in section 4.14 and it is followed by a short conclusion.

4.2 Foreign Market Servicing Strategy: An Overview

The foreign market servicing strategy of a firm is the set of decision on which production plants should be linked to which specific foreign market and the methods or channels through which this should be achieved. The three main generic types of foreign market servicing strategy are (1) exporting (2) licensed sales abroad and (3) foreign direct investment. The foreign market servicing decision is a complex one both theoretically (Buckley and Casson (1985)) and in practice (Buckley and Pearce (1979, 1981 and 1984)).

4.2.1 Elements of a foreign market servicing strategy

The three main generic elements of a foreign market servicing strategy are (1) exporting (X) (2) licensing and other contractual relationships (L) plus (3) foreign direct investment (I). All three cover a spectrum of types of arrangement in which the channels of distribution and relationship with the buyer vary within the type.

Exporting covers the indirect export of goods; through agents, distributors, merchant houses, trading companies and a variety of other intermediaries, and the direct export of goods and services. Its essential feature is that production activities are carried out in the home country, although marketing may well be carried out in the host country, separated by a transport cost barrier.

Exporting is often regarded as merely the first step into a foreign market, but its persistence as a viable strategy mode even in the largest multinationals suggests that it still has a role to play. The sequentialist school has made much of the observed pattern of servicing a foreign market over time which goes X → L → I or X → I. Indeed exporting itself has been analysed as a sequential process (for a review of this literature see Buckley and Ghauri (1991)). Its role in internationalization is well documented but exporting's role in the market servicing pattern of established multinationals is less well understood. To be adequately modelled, the relationship between exporting and other forms of market servicing, must be carefully specified, as must the factors influencing multi-plant operation (Scherer et al. (1975)). New thinking and modelling on strategic trade policy and the new international economics should re-integrate exporting into realistic models of the multinational firm (see Krugman (1986), Dunning and Buckley (1972)).

Licensing is a generic term which covers a variety of non direct investment production operations involving arms length cooperation with an external agency (or agencies). Some element of market transfer is included in this packaged sale of assets and services. A spectrum of relationships is possible ranging from (the rare) simple sale of embodied knowledge or assets (brand name, patent) through franchising, turnkey operations, contract manufacturing, management contracts, etc.

A typology of these forms of international operation is provided in Buckley (1985) where they are classified in five dimensions (1) equity or non equity ventures (2) time limited or unlimited (3) space limited or unlimited (4) extent of transfer of resources and rights and (5) internal or external mode of transfer. (See also Young (1987) for a survey and Luostarinen (1980) for an alternative approach.)

Licensing as a mode of market servicing is often regarded as a transitory mode, perhaps utilized for learning or market testing purposes before a move is made to a foreign direct investment. A minority of firms are regarded as specialist licensors and licensing is often seen as a peripheral activity contingent upon (peculiar) extraneous eventualities, such as government restrictions, as a second best choice.

It is conceivable that changing world competitive structures make this view outmoded. The 'new forms' of international operation may be uniquely well suited to the competitive conditions which prevail in many world markets, including political uncertainty, government restrictions, idiosyncratic markets and residual technologies. Moreover, licensing allows international companies to avoid head-to-head competition by cross licensing, joint marketing and production agreements and knowledge pooling. These cooperative devices may be genuine or may be methods of reducing competition by collusive behaviour (Buckley and Casson (1987)).

Foreign direct investment, too, covers a range of operations. The normal image of a foreign direct investment is a production facility involving a huge capital outlay. This is not necessarily so. A foreign direct investment can be the creation of a sales subsidiary – one person with stock working from his basement with a car! The key feature of foreign direct investment is not scale but control from the parent. This control, exercised most usually through equity ownership enables direct management of a foreign facility rather than control through a contract. These issues are widely debated in the internalization literature (Buckley and Casson (1976 and 1985), Dunning (1981), Hennart (1986), among many others).

Direct investment thus covers marketing operations and production operations, both sales subsidiaries and production subsidiaries ranging from assembly to full production. Moreover, there are other important distinctions: in mode of entry between a greenfield venture and a take-over; in organization form between a joint venture and wholly owned subsidiary.

Direct investment is regarded as the most risky form of entry in terms of capital committed, but is regarded as the most effective in securing market share and strategic competitive advantage. This is confirmed, for instance, in two recent articles on entry into the Japanese market (Buckley, Mirza and Sparkes (1987a and 1987b)). It also confers prestige as an internationalized company and is seen as the key weapon in a global strategy as for instance in the 'triad' concept (Ohmae (1985), Buckley, Mirza and Sparkes (1984)).

It is, however, far too easy and incorrect to assume that direct investment is always the correct form of market servicing. External conditions and internal capabilities often suggest otherwise.

Although, theoretically, the same generic options are open to service firms, certain features of services impact on foreign market servicing choice and deserve comment. Boddewyn, Halbrich and Perry (1986) classify types of international services according to their tradeability, based on the extent to which services are embodied in physical goods and the degree of inseparability (that is the extent to which the provider of the service and the customer need to be present at the point of delivery) in provision of the service:

1 Service commodities, which are distinct from their production process are tradeable across national boundaries and thus exportable
2 Where production cannot be separated from consumption as in the case of legal advice, a foreign presence is necessary
3 Where services comprise a mix of distinct commodities and location bound service elements, some location substitution is possible.

Consequently, a different pattern of foreign market servicing options may be expected in this sector. Hirsch (1986), addressing the implications of the inseparability of production and consumption, notes how the 'simultaneity factor' (that is, the fact that certain services are produced and consumed at the same time) serves to retard export trade. The costs associated with satisfying the need for interaction between producer and buyer are compounded by the high price of international travel and communications, and thus the exporting firm is at a cost disadvantage *vis à vis* its foreign competitors. When the cost of cultural distance, language, nationalistic and legal barriers are added, the cost disadvantages are further heightened. Edvinsson (1981) notes that foreign service providers, lacking any legitimacy and identity in the foreign market, require some kind of 'platform' and local support environment to operate successfully. Although this is also true for goods manufacturers operating abroad, the intangibility of many services(that is, the fact that there is no physical good which can be judged by the consumer) means that uncertainty about performance is higher and thus greater demands are placed on service firms to win the confidence of the consumer through strong referent promotion and a good local image.

Alternatively, the loss of control over operations, which is characteristic of licensing, poses problems of quality control. Again, this is true in goods manufacturing, but as many services are people produced, 'heterogeneity' (variation in the way the service is produced and quality of the service provided) compounds the difficulty of controlling the quality of the delivered service when handled externally.

Both arguments therefore suggest that foreign involvement by service firms will show a higher degree of foreign investment options than is the case in the manufacturing sector.

4.2.2 Cross section analysis of foreign market servicing

The total foreign sales (TFS) of British firms are made up of (1) exports from UK (X) (2) sales abroad licensed by UK firms (L) and (3) sales arising from British foreign direct investment.

$$\text{i.e. TFS} = X + L + I$$

The amounts of each of these can be measured at a point of time, over time and in particular markets, as we will see below.

At its most simple, X can be differentiated from the other two methods by the location effect, as with exports the bulk of value adding activity takes place in the home country, whilst the other two methods transfer much of value adding activity to the host country. Similarly, L can be differentiated from X and I by the externalization effect. L represents a market sale of intermediate goods or corporate assets by the firm. In licensing, the firm sells rights and the use of assets to a licensee. In X and I such activities are internalized (Buckley and Casson (1976 and 1985)). This has important implications. Broadly then, the internalisation and location effects separate the three generic forms of market servicing.

Internalization
Effect

$$\text{TFS} = X + L + I$$

Location
Effect

These simple differentiations are, in practice, highly complex. First, comparative costs are not easily calculable or obvious. In multi-product, process and functional firms, the internal division of labour and the costs associated with each activity are difficult to assess accurately. Further, there are many complex interactions between the activities involved. Location abroad of some activities will have knock-on effects on home costs and those of third countries within the firm's international network. Second, the costs and benefits of internalization are nebulous and difficult to measure. Both sets of complications are entirely contingent on circumstances. The difficulties of these calculations is that the situation is dynamic and the determinants of choice of optimal market servicing strategies are continually shifting.

Cross-section analyses of market servicing are snapshot pictures at a moment in time of a continually changing process. The make-up of total foreign sales into X, L, I, at the macro level can give us a crude picture (Buckley and Davies (1980)) but this pattern is continually changing as the nature of international competition alters. Further, it is difficult to get meaningful comparative measures of the three modes, although this is usually done by estimating final foreign sales in aggregate (Buckley and Davies (1980), Luostarinen (1978)).

A major complicating factor in the analysis of foreign market servicing policies is that the forms are often complements, not substitutes. This fact means that a careful analysis of the relationship between modes is essential. For instance, Hood and Young (1979) point to the existence of 'anticipatory exports' (goods exported from the source country in anticipation of building the foreign plant), 'associated exports' (complementary products exported by the parent after establishment of the subsidiary) and 'balancing exports', which result when the first plant build abroad is operating at capacity.

Also, foreign direct investment has a dynamic effect in maintaining the worldwide competitive position of the investing firm (Hood and Young (1979), pp.313–5).

This suggests that a dynamic analysis is essential. Assumptions in modelling which do not allow for changes in demand conditions – for instance, the existence of a 'presence effect' which results in an increased demand after the establishment of an investment presence (Buckley, Newbould and Thurwell (1987)) – are clearly inappropriate. Similarly models which ignore the competitive process, in particular the role of 'defensive investment', established to protect a market share, are unlikely to capture the nuances of strategy. Models must be organic rather than static and capable of specifying the relationship between exports, licensing and foreign direct investment.

4.2.3 Time series analyses of foreign market servicing strategies

A number of theoretical models of the foreign market servicing strategy of firms are extant. They are almost entirely concerned with the switch

from exporting to a foreign market to investing in it. Licensing is a largely neglected phenomenon in modelling (though see Davies (1977) and Buckley and Davies (1980)).
Comparative Static Analyses   The model used in the Product Cycle approach (Vernon (1966)) is a cost based formulation:

invest abroad when $MPC_X + TC > APC_A$
where MPC_X is marginal cost of production for export
    TC is transport cost to target market
    APC_A is average cost of production abroad

The argument here is that marginal costings are appropriate for exports because domestic production would be undertaken anyway, whilst the foreign unit must bear the full average costs of production.

This move (in the 'maturing' phase of the cycle) can be triggered, or reinforced, by the desire to defend a market established through exports, and most analysts agree that this is best done by a direct investment.

Several other approaches have been suggested to the switch from exporting (or less usually, licensing) to investment. Two comparative static approaches are given by Horst (1971 and 1972) and Hirsh (1976). Hirsh's analysis is based on cost minimization and he derives the following inequalities to give firms in country A simple decision rules on the best way to service the foreign market B, either from source country A by export, or by direct investment in B. (Subscripts a and b indicate location). Therefore, for firms in A:

$$\text{Export to B if} \quad P_a + M < P_b + K \tag{1}$$
$$\text{and} \quad P_a + M < P_b + C \tag{2}$$
$$\text{Invest in B if} \quad P_b + C < P_b + K \tag{3}$$
$$P_b + C < P_a + M \tag{4}$$

Where P_a and P_b are production costs in the two countries, M is the difference between export and domestic marketing costs, C represents the extra costs of controlling a foreign rather than a domestic operation, and K represents firm specific know-how and other intangible income producing assets. All quantities are present values of costs over the life span of a specific investment project. The meaning of inequalities (1) and (2) is that exports should be undertaken if costs of domestic production and export marketing costs are below costs of doing business abroad. Inequalities (3) and (4) suggest that investment should be undertaken when total costs of production abroad (including control costs) are below costs of utilizing the firm-specific advantages (K) in production abroad and below the costs of exporting from the parent country, A.

It should be noted that Hirsh's analysis assumes that demand is insensitive to the location of supply and can therefore be ignored. The analysis is also concerned with an initial investment abroad assuming no excess capacity in the parent country, A, otherwise this would mean exporting until marginal costs of further exporting exceeded revenues. It is thus applicable to the siting of a new additional production facility. No analysis is given of the generation of K (firm specific know-how) and thus no idea of relative costs of investing in R&D (to attempt to generate K) versus other types of investment. K is given as a return from a past sunk cost. No light is shed on the timing of the investment and demand factors are removed by assumption.

Horst's (1971) analysis concentrates on the influence of tariff and tax rates in the 'invest versus export' decision. Rather than being able to throw up simple rules, Horst shows that the analysis breaks down into special cases according to the conditions under which the firm is operating and the level of taxes and tariffs in home and foreign countries. Horst notes the interesting finding that high tariffs are a mixed blessing for MNEs: on one hand they make exporting more costly, on the other they enhance the firm's prospects for increasing profits by allowing increased price discrimination between markets. If the price elasticity of demand is lower in the protected market than elsewhere, then an increase in the tariff will allow the firm to raise its price locally, thereby reducing demand and discouraging investment. Investment policy is further influenced by the conditions of production of the firm and market size: the sensitivity of foreign investment to tariff policy is greatest when the marginal cost of production is decreasing with respect to output. If the protected market is a relatively large one, then there is a certain tariff level beyond which it is optimal for the firm to concentrate *all* production in that market, even if resource costs are higher in the protected market, because saving of tariff costs outweighs additional resource costs. The complexity of decision rules even in this simple model is illuminating. Horst adds industry specific influences on foreign investment (firm size, R&D intensity, concentration of the industry and desire for resource control) to the firm-specific factors above, in a further paper (1974).

The analyses of Hirsh and Horst highlight different aspects of the foreign investment decision. Hirsh's emphasis on marketing and technological costs is complementary to Horst's inclusion of tariff and tax rates. Both include relative production costs at home and abroad, although Horst emphasizes returns to scale. However, neither approach is particularly concerned with the timing of the switch to FDI.

The timing of the switch to FDI Analyses which are concerned with the dynamics of foreign expansion of the firm should be able to specify those factors which govern the timing of the initial FDI. Aliber (1970) attempts to do this by reference to the capitalization of returns from the firm's alternatives: exporting, licensing and foreign investment. Aliber assumes that the firm possesses a 'patent' or monopolistic advantage. He argues that the costs of doing business abroad prevent investment from being the preferred strategy until a certain market size. Only at a particular size of market will the higher capitalization ratio, which applies to source country firms, overcome the cost advantage of a local producer (which can be exploited via licensing the 'patent' to a local firm). In Aliber's system, the source-country firm will always be a higher cost producer than the host-country firm, provided the latter has access to the patent at competitive rates. This limits the analysis by ruling out those situations where the source-country firm (through familiarity with the technology, firm-wide economies of scale, etc.) has compensating advantages *vis-à-vis* host country competitors.

The dynamics of the 'switch' from exporting to licensing and then to FDI are thus dependent, according to Aliber, on the host country market size and the differentials in capitalization ratios between assets denominated in different currencies. The latter is determined by the currency premium in the capital market – the compensation investors require so that they will bear uncertainty concerning fluctuations in exchange rates. Tariffs are easily incorporated into this framework: an increase in the host country tariff will bias the foreign patent owner towards use of the patent in the host-country; the choice between its use in licensing or internally via FDI remains unchanged, the choice depending on whether host-market size allows the capitalization factor to outweigh the cost of doing business abroad.

In a theoretical paper, Buckley and Casson (1985) provide a model which specifies the optimal timing of a 'switch' to direct investment by reference to the costs of servicing the foreign market, demand conditions in that market and host market growth. The market servicing decision is more complex than it appears at first sight, particularly when the initial costs of setting up a foreign investment are time-dependent.

A simple model of a firm facing a growing market is illustrated in figure 4.1. This model specifies two kinds of costs, fixed and variable, and two forms of foreign market servicing: exporting which has low fixed but high variable cost, and foreign direct investment which has high fixed but low variable cost; licensing is an intermediate state, which in this example is never the preferred option. Should foreign market size become greater than Q, then the firm will switch its mode of market servicing to investment in the market. Removal of tariffs may therefore lead to a switch, not to exports (or to exports only as an intermediate stage), but directly to foreign investment by the multinational firm.

This model enables specification of the optimal timing of a switch in modes by reference to the key variables (1) mode related costs (2)

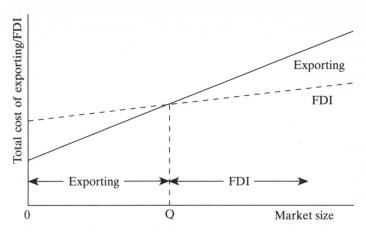

Figure 4.1   The switch from exporting to FDI
Source: Buckley and Casson, 1985.

demand conditions in the host market and (3) target market growth. The introduction of time dependent set up costs, in particular, makes the decisions very complex. A similar model has been developed by Giddy and Rugman (1979).

Enderwick (1989) suggests that incremental internationalization is not possible in many service sectors as a result of the inseparability factor. This restricts the scope of firms to learn about the market by following low-investment exporting strategies and utilizing foreign market intermediaries. Although he introduces this issue to demonstrate the greater risks involved for internationalizing service firms over those in the manufacturing sector, it has important implications for the dynamics of foreign-market servicing in the service sector.

For services embodied in tradeable goods, internationalization may follow a similar pattern to the manufacturing industry, unless firm specific advantages are best exploited through internal hierarchies, or where there are government restrictions on trade. Where production cannot be separated from consumption, however, and foreign direct investment and licensing are the only available options, the increased resource commitment involved in adopting these modes may slow down the process of internationalization. As greater returns are required from domestic operations before resource commitment overseas can be considered, and the market from which returns can be made is restricted (exporting is not a viable proposition), the natural progression to foreign direct investment is not so clear cut. Also, retarding the process of internationalization is the fact that many services are highly localized and industries fragmented, and thus nationalization of innovative services is the focus of strategic growth, not internationalization. A further restricting factor is the lack of learning opportunities, highlighted in the behavioural models of internationalization, offered by indirect exporting modes of foreign market servicing. As knowledge cannot be acquired cost effectively and at little risk through exporting, the uncertainties involved in licensing or investing resources abroad may deter the consideration of international expansion.

This is not to suggest, however, that all manufacturing firms religiously follow such a process of incremental expansion. In chapter 5, it is noted that an unexpectedly high proportion of British manufacturing firms in the survey moved from little-to-no market involvement directly to foreign direct investment. Although this may be partly explained by their experience of other foreign markets, the nature of the product (being bulky and too expensive to transport) and the need to gain a local identity, demonstrate that commitment to the market precluded consideration of export strategies. These factors are not dissimilar to those determining foreign direct investment options in the service sector, that is, the nature of the service dictates production in close proximity to customers, and the need to generate a strong image and goodwill determines foreign investment. Thus, whilst it is useful to identify features of many service industries which dictate particular modes of market servicing, the differences between manufacturing and service sectors should not be over-stated. It is rather the greater number of instances where factors specific to the nature of services dictate foreign direct investment, or some form of market presence which characterizes the service sector, rather than the fact that services, *per se*, are implicitly 'different'.

Returning to the issue of acquiring knowledge through incremental international expansion, although exporting is ruled out where the inseparability factor applies, firms may follow a course of learning through contractual arrangements and joint venture options. Thus, Buckley and Casson's (1981) assertion that licensing should have a place in the internationalization model appears particularly pertinent. However, whereas their model is based on volume-related fixed and variable costs, for service firms it may be more appropriate to consider the different costings of internal and external markets. The cost of lost sales arising from leakage of competitive advantage in the case of licensing may make equity investment through a joint venture a more risk-averse method of gaining market knowledge. Due to increased control which a joint venture affords, the risk of leaked advantages is lessened. When the added advantages of pooled resources and the long-term possibility of increasing the equity stake to achieve majority ownership are considered, joint ventures may appear a more favourable option. The international behaviour of location-bound service firms may, therefore, follow a path from low-risk contractual arrangements, or joint ventures designed to gather market information and important learning experiences, as a precursor to majority-owned or wholly owned foreign direct investment activities.

4.3 Expansion Paths in the Manufacturing Sector

4.3.1 Propositions

The argument of this chapter rests on four propositions.

Proposition 1: The whole channel must be considered in making market servicing decisions. Firms will be aiming at servicing their final customers with appropriate products. This entails the necessity to meet customer needs. 'Closeness to the customer' entails the optimum mix of location and internalization decisions throughout the channel.

Proposition 2: Once a part of the channel is externalized, downstream activities (towards the consumer) will not be internalized.

Proposition 3: Once a part of the channel is located abroad, there will be a tendency for downstream activities to be also located abroad.

Proposition 4: Control and monitoring of information is vital to the success of international channel management. The control and direction of information will be a major reason for internalization of key functions.

4.3.2 Qualifications

The above propositions are fairly strong assertions on the pattern of international market servicing and channel management. Proposition 2 is particularly strong. It would be disproved if the pattern in figure 4.2 occurred with any regularity.

A similar disproof would apply to proposition 3, although there are likely to be exceptions to this rule. The first exception applies to multi-product firms. The channel for one individual product within a given product portfolio may include downstream activities located at home after upstream activities are foreign based, if that facility were fundamentally designed for a separate product. The channel system of one product taken separately can thus 'piggy-back' on another product's channel. The second exception concerns the subcontracting ('putting

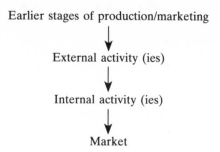

Earlier stages of production/marketing

External activity (ies)

Internal activity (ies)

Market

Figure 4.2   Pattern leading to the disproof of proposition 2: market servicing channel

out') of routine production abroad for cost reasons – often this is termed 'offshore production'. This basic production can then be reintegrated into a channel which may have a domestic location. Third, there are important complementarities between functions which do not exist as totally independent entities (see section 4.3.3 below).

4.3.3   Examples

Figure 4.3 shows possible market servicing modes highlighting potential downstream expansion paths. In general, the location of production predetermines the location of stockholding. Consequently, only in the case of exporting can firms choose to locate their stockholding activities domestically. On the issue of internalization versus externalization, the choice of using independent organisations at a particular stage in the process generally determines that all activities further down the chain will also be externalized. This interdependence between functions suggests that firms must treat the channel as a *whole* rather than as a series of independent units when foreign market servicing strategies are developed. Although the diagrams show decisions apparently emanating from the form of market servicing (i.e., exporting, licensing and foreign direct investment), important issues related to stockholding and retailing may, in turn, impinge on the location of production, determining the mode to be employed. It should be noted that particular factors specific to the firm and the market may result in certain levels of the channel being bypassed.

What follows is an attempt to distinguish the factors which determine the decisions of location and internalization at the various stages in the process. Section 4.4 begins by discussing the basic concepts. Sections

(a) Exporting

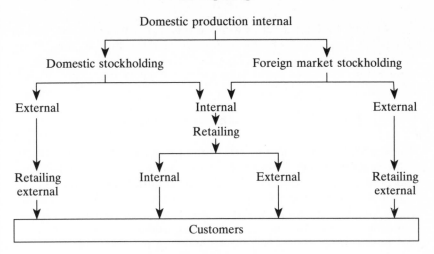

(b) Foreign direct investment

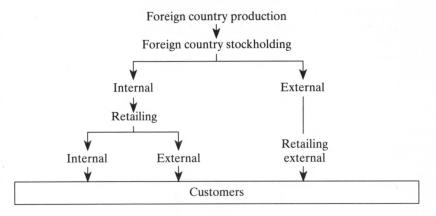

(c) Licensing

Figure 4.3   Schematic diagrams of typical product flow

4.5, 4.6 and 4.7 look at the various levels in the process. For ease of discussion they are dealt with independently. The final section, therefore, presents an overview of the channel as a whole, highlighting the information flows essential to planning an integrated channel system.

4.4   Expansion Paths in the Service Sector

The functional interrelationships in the service sector may be viewed somewhat differently. Only where service commodities are distinct from the production process (viz. Boddewyn, Halbrich and Perry's (1986) classification) will the picture for services emulate that for manufactured goods. The inseparability factor associated with many service industries dictates that production and consumption take place simultaneously – *in the same location*. Additionally, many services cannot be stored or transported and thus the wholesaling and distribution functions do not figure in the channel. Alternatively 'retailing' – the point of sale or service delivery takes on greater significance for many service firms due to the inextricable nature of production and consumption. Expansion paths pertaining to location bound services are presented in figure 4.4.

4.5   An Exposition of Basic Concepts

4.5.1   Internalization

We can begin by envisaging the firm as an internalized bundle of resources which can be allocated (1) between product groups (in which changes are identified as conglomerate diversification) and (2) between national markets (expansion in this direction is multinational diversification). The growth of the firm *relative to markets* is determined by its internalization decisions. The firm grows by replacing or creating neighbouring markets according to the (positive) balance between the benefits of internalization versus the costs in each instance. The growth of the firm, in this analysis, is determined by the superiority of the firm over the market (Buckley and Casson (1976 and 1985), Buckley (1983a) Casson (1987), Buckley (1988)). In a shorter run, strategic context, internalization can be a weapon. Internalizing the market in key inputs (including technology) can represent a significant barrier to entry to the industry. The ability to use discriminatory pricing in an internal market, allows a firm to cross subsidize highly competitive markets where there is a fear of entry. Elimination of bilateral bargaining may further

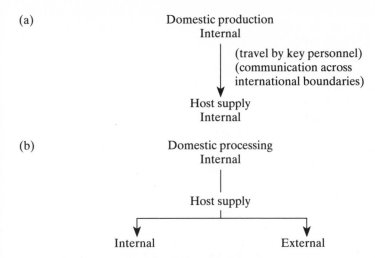

Figure 4.4 Schematic diagrams of service 'flow'

strengthen a firm relative to others faced with bargaining instability. Further, internalization of markets across international frontiers allows the reduction of the firm's overall tax bill relative to firms who trade at arm's length. Consequently, internalisation decisions can be a strategic weapon versus other firms in certain contexts. It is undeniable that certain managements will see internalization opportunities faster than others and may be more skilled at the evaluation of such opportunities. This will create differentials in the relative scope of firms, with cost penalties for those with non-optimal scope (at a given point of time).

In information intensive sectors, where information is tacit and costly to produce, but where it can be replicated with ease, there are advantages of internalizing such competitive assets and protecting leakage of firm-specific knowledge derived from these assets. In such instances, there is greater likelihood of firms pursuing foreign direct investment strategies as opposed to licensing contracts. As many service industries can be characterized as highly information intensive, a high degree of inter-nalization may be expected (Dunning (1989), Enderwick (1989)).

Licensing may also be discounted on the grounds that there is no identifiable 'technology' or 'managerial' element in the service which can be packaged in such a way that it becomes saleable. If firm-specific advantages are embodied in the experience and knowledge of firms' pool of personnel, licensing becomes a non-viable option. Costs of market transactions in services may also be higher than manufacturing. Dunning (1989) highlights five major reasons for this:

1   Tailoring services to individual customer needs is an important factor in many sectors and production highly idiosyncratic;
2   The human element in services results in variability of quality;
3   Until recently information gathering and the knowledge and experience required to evaluate and interpret information was tacit and non-codifiable;
4   As certain information may be inexpensive to replicate, the possibility of its use outside formalized contracts and its dissipation throughout the market, poses a real threat;
5   Markets for many services are highly segmented and opportunities exist for price discrimination within internal systems.

4.5.2   Location theory

Standard location theory assumes constant returns to scale, freely available and standardized technology, and that firms are price takers in all factor markets. Given such assumptions, firms choose their optimal location for each stage of production by evaluating regional production costs and choosing the set of locations for which the overall average cost of production is minimized. Regional production costs vary only according to regional differentials in non-tradeable goods (as the price of tradeables is standardized by trade), the relative prices of tradeables and non-tradeables, and elasticities of substitution between pairs of non-tradeables and between tradeables and non-tradeables. Overall average production costs are minimized by the correct choice of the least cost 'route' from the location of raw materials through to the final market (Buckley and Casson (1976 and 1979)).

For the purpose of explaining market-servicing policies, the location of marketing services is crucial. Marketing may be considered to have four main constituents: stockholding, distribution, generating new customers and promotion. The location of stockholding depends on the balance between the better quality of service provided by decentralized stockholding and the declining costs per unit of large, centralized warehouses. Only above a certain market size is local stockholding efficient. Routine advertising and distribution are usually located in the final market. However, there is growing emphasis, in theory at least, on global advertizing. Here, as elsewhere, there is a balance in the cost advantages of standardization versus the revenue advantages of adaptation to individual markets.

Unlike the manufacturing sector where location of production is heavily dependent on relative production and transportation costs and tariff barriers, location of many services is more determined by closeness to customers. Hirsch (1986) alludes to personal contact as being the most expensive element for firms trading their services across international frontiers, involving both time, and the high cost of international travel. To a degree, this can be equated with transportation costs of manufactured goods, although rather than the physical goods being transported to the market, the production (personified in key personnel) moves to the customer. However, Hirsch goes on to suggest that modern communication technology is reducing the need for face-to-face contact, making it possible for some service firms to centralize their activities and 'export' services internationally.

4.6 The Manufacturing Sector: Production

4.6.1 The location of production

At its most simple, exporting can be differentiated from licensing and foreign direct investment by the location effect. As with exports, the bulk of value adding activity takes place in the home country, whilst the other two methods transfer much of value adding activity to the host country. Arising out of standard location theory, much of the literature on choice of foreign market servicing mode (which is generally biased towards the location of production) is predominantly cost based. A number of theoretical models of the foreign market servicing strategy of firms are extant. They are almost entirely concerned with the switch from exporting to a foreign market to investing in it, including the Product Cycle approach (Vernon (1966), see also Hirsh (1976), Horst (1971, 1972 and 1974)).

4.6.2 Internal versus external production

Licensing can be differentiated from exporting and foreign direct investment by the externalization effect. (Davies (1977), Buckley and Davies (1986)). Licensing represents a market sale of intermediate goods or corporate assets by the firm. In licensing, the firm sells rights and the use of assets to a licensee. In exporting and foreign investment, such activities are internalized (Buckley and Casson (1976 and 1985)). Licensing generally takes place when firms possessing transferable competitive advantages are unable to exploit the technology themselves – either due to limited available assets for foreign investment, or limited capacity to produce domestically for export, or a combination of both these factors. Alternatively, licensing may be the only available strategy where markets are protected by high tariffs, and limitations on investment.

Subcontracting of production is a clearly defined market relationship covering an agreement of one firm to purchase from another. Although such arrangements are, in ideal type, purely market based (externalized), linking purchaser to producer, in practice there is often an input from the purchaser to ensure that quality standards meet specification and often advice on methods of production is given. The factor means that violations to 'hypothesis 2' are not absolute. Such 'production sharing' agreements usually involve sales in the purchasing firm's home market. Often, these arrangements are related to the tariff regulations in developed countries where producers from less developed countries, often located in free-trade zones, carry out externalized production (Buckley (1983b), Watanabe (1971 and 1972)). Examples of international externalized production exist in textiles and electronic equipment including computers.

4.7 The Manufacturing Sector: Wholesaler/ Distributor Functions

4.7.1 The need for wholesaler/distributor functions in the channel

In international markets, the need to include stockholding and physical distribution in the channel is generally perceived to be a result of manufacturer remoteness from the target market, both in physical and cultural terms, in addition to the more generally accepted functions of building bulk/breaking bulk, which characterizes domestic channel issues. The international perspective tends to suggest location of stockholding in a proximate location to the target market in order to minimize lead times and promote more efficient monitoring of demand through operating within the market where information gathering is facilitated. The latter point relates to product and target market characteristics widely discussed in channel management literature (for an example, see Christopher (1972)).

4.7.2 The location of wholesaler/distributor functions

The location of wholesaling/distributing, like that of production, is discussed in the international business literature in relation to costs.

The optimum *location* of inventory is dependent on (1) the ratio of stock to sales required to maintain a given quality of service to the customer (for example, the time taken for a delivery from stock) is likely to decline as the warehouse turnover increases and (2) the technology of warehouse design favours the larger warehouse (for example, the ratio of cubic capacity to surface area increases with size). These factors encourage the concentration of stockholding at just one location. Against these factors must be set the additional costs of distributing to the customer from a location remote from the market. The interplay of inventory and distribution costs will make local stockholding optimal for any volume of sales above a given critical level (Buckley and Casson (1976)). A critical assumption of this analysis is that the quality of service to the customer is fixed. In certain circumstances of product/market conditions such an assumption cannot be justified. Remoteness may mean being out of touch with market needs. This may also be a factor in choosing a local stockholder who may be more in touch with local stockholding regulations and market needs. An alternative formulation of this problem is that of Berg (1971), who maps cost against time of delivery to give a total cost function including cost of lost sales, which is an increasing function of time.

The location of stockholding activities is inextricably interlinked with the location of production. Where foreign direct investment and licensing strategies are followed, then stockholding will necessarily be located in the host market. However, where exporting strategies are followed, i.e., production is based in the domestic market, the choice of location is not pre-determined. The firm may choose to ship goods from domestically held stock, wherein the wholesaling/retailing function is internalized in the case of direct exporting (where the firm controls the exporting tasks) or, perhaps, externalized when indirect exporting modes are employed (stock being held by trading companies, joint export associations or the 'carrier' in piggyback exporting ventures (Terpstra 1983)). Alternatively, the firm may export goods to their own wholesaler/distributor in the host market (which may be tied in with a sales/marketing investment).

This is not to say, however, that the choice of production location is made independently of that of wholesaling/distributor location. Where competitive success relies on rapid delivery or 'just in time' delivery to retailers, the essential decision to stock goods abroad may have repercussions on the choice of production location. It is dangerous to assume that the multinational firm has an unrestricted choice of mode and location of its wholesaler/dealer functions. Such activities face entry barriers such as the existence of established networks of dealers, the capital costs of establishments and external (including governmental) restriction on entry.

4.7.3 Internalization versus externalization of wholesaler/ distribution functions

Like production, stock can be held internally or externalized to an independent wholesaler, distributor or stockholder. The choice of which form to follow depends primarily on five factors (1) the relative costs of operation (2) importance of market intelligence (3) the perceived needs of the manufacturer to control operations (4) host market infrastructure (5) distinct competencies of the firm.

Relative costs   The balance between internalizing wholesaler/distributor functions rests on the heavy investment required to set up such functions versus the problems of constant renegotiation on price with existing external wholesalers. This can be resolved by examining the relative fixed and variable costs of each type of arrangement. The heavy fixed costs may deter firms from fully internalizing the function, particularly those firms sensitive to share-price maintenance demands. However a quasi-internalized channel may be a viable alternative when transaction costs can be reduced by the exercise of power within an administered channel by a dominant member (Brown (1984), Diamontopoulos (1987)).

Market intelligence   In international operations, sensitivity to cultural and business differences in host markets is generally considered to be a key factor for success. An ability to understand and plan for these differences stems from the quality of market intelligence available to firms and the success with which it flows back to the decision-making locus within the manufacturing organization. Alternatively, successful implementation of business plans relies on forward information flows through the channel concerning strategic direction and product (differential advantages both actual and perceived). The wholesaler may then be seen as either a facilitator or a bottle-neck for the flow of information through the channel, providing a link between the retailer/dealer and the manufacturer, and indirectly between consumers and manufacturers. Information on demand fluctuations, retailer buyer behaviour, packaging, pricing and competitor activity may be directly available to wholesalers, and information on consumer behaviour, reactions to promotion and product adaptation indirectly gathered through retailers. In addition, the linkage between the manufacturer and wholesaler should allow the effective organization of inventory and production schedules.

Host-country management who have experience in the particular foreign market may better understand the scope of information pertinent to decision making within their sector. There are three options facing manufacturers in this respect (1) buying up this expertise through forward integration (2) buying in this knowledge from outside in the event of greenfield operations, and (3) utilizing the expertise of independents in relation to cultural and market understanding, perhaps at the expense of high quality information.

Manufacturer control   The major advantage of operating through an independent wholesaler is that the management of inventories and distribution is passed on, thus lowering manufacturer management costs (although costs will be incurred using this system in relation to monitoring of activities). One of the fundamental disadvantages is that the producer in passing on the responsibility of these activities, also passes on control over them. Thus, he must rely on the wholesaler/distributor stocking enough volume to serve retail demand, maintaining the quality of products in transit and storage and also selling to the right retailers/ dealers, that is, those who serve the market at which the manufacturer's product is targeted. To some extent these problems may be overcome by the drawing up of contracts and agreements, although others, often those arising from cultural distance and differences in management approach, may require the provision of additional support services, which Munro and Beamish (1987) perceive as being a preferable alternative to increased compensation or threats. The expense incurred through providing support to intermediaries may diminish the cost-saving advantages of operating in this way.

Other factors may also impinge on the desire of manufacturers to control their own distribution operations. Firms may be more likely to invest resources when the product is a major contributor to their overall sales in order to enhance contact with clients/customers in the pursuit of additional sales (Davidson and McFetridge (1985)). Alternatively, where firms wish to protect patents in order to sustain a competitive advantage through technology or differentiation, they may be reluctant to operate via independent wholesalers, perceiving them as a potential source of 'leakage' (Anderson and Coughlan (1987)). Such issues are not, however, specific to international operations.

Host-market infrastructure   The nature of the host market, particularly its political and economic stability, may pre-determine the form of channel to be employed. Government pressure on multinational firms to use indigenous channels, and legal restrictions on foreign direct investment may diminish the choice of options available to firms. Indeed, firms may have no choice being compelled by host governments to employ available resources in the form of independent wholesalers/ distributors.

Competencies of the firm   Established distribution channels tend to determine the mode of distribution employed for the introduction of new products, i.e., if an integrated channel is already in place, the product will be sold through the existing arrangement, and independents will continue to be used where they are traditionally employed (Davidson and McFetridge (1985)). This also applies, to some extent, across borders. This is due to the management skills and competencies of head-office personnel who, through their experience in managing either integrated or independent wholesale/distribution operations, will tend towards similar operations elsewhere in order to exploit existing skills.

4.8   The Manufacturing Sector: Retailing

4.8.1   The need for retailing in the channel

In consumer markets the need for retailing operations is generally determined by the wide geographic spread of consumers and the low value/high volume nature of purchases. In certain industrial markets, the need for a dealer network is determined by similar issues. However, in the case of high value 'big ticket' manufactures, this level of channel intermediary may be bypassed in favour of selling directly to customers or shipping straight to customers ex-wholesale stock. These issues apply equally at both domestic and international levels. In an international context, the important consideration is the form of channel traditionally employed in various overseas markets which tends to determine buyer behaviour. Where products are traditionally sold through a retailer/ dealer network, bypassing this stage in the channel will necessitate customer 're-education' and specific benefits of purchasing offered by the alternative mode. This can prove a costly exercise, although may prove favourable to competing head-on in highly competitive retail markets.

4.8.2   Internal versus external retail operations

The large number of outlets and the wide geographic spread necessary to serve retail demand make internalization of such operations costly and difficult to manage centrally. In addition, the growing trend towards 'one-stop-shopping' in the consumer goods sector which originated in the USA but which is now spreading throughout the developed world, means that single manufacturers cannot provide the width of product range necessary to cater for this kind of buyer behaviour. In this respect, ownership of retail activities is rare in the area of consumer goods. In industrial markets, specialist dealers are perhaps more easily integrated by manufacturers, particularly those who manufacture a complementary range of products. Geographic dispersal of outlets may be less important for goods, as consumers are prepared to travel further for specialist equipment.

The level of product differentiation may affect the decision to internalize retail activities. It raises the need for specialised sales/marketing and servicing capabilities best served through integrated retail outlets. Anderson and Coughlan (1987) suggest that where products are highly differentiated and not perceived as substitutes by the consumer, retail internalization is desirable, as alternative products do not compete directly: 'In contrast, non-differentiated products do compete directly, creating price-wars that drain the manufacturers' profits in integrated channels,' (Anderson and Coughlan, (1987), p.73).

Franchising retail distribution is a separate case, being an alternative mode of tying retailers to the manufacturer, particularly where perceived differentiation is important to success. Here, ownership relates to patents, know-how, management style, brand-name, form and decor of retail outlets, etc. It permits manufacturers a certain degree of control over their franchisees, who are bound to work for the benefit of the producer, whilst minimizing investment outlay. The franchiser's compensation – a one-off fee, royalty on sales, rental/lease on equipment and fixtures, regular license fee or share of profits (Kotler (1984)) – may mean that income per unit sales is lower than if they were to operate through alternative forms of market servicing. However, the opportunity to maximize the number and regional spread of their operations means that a wider market can be served, and thus the volume of sales compensates for low unit value. One of the major problems of operating a franchise system is that it relies on independent organizations to maintain the standards and quality designated by the manufacturer or service organization.

Another alternative way of tying 'retail' operations to the manufacturer is through catalogue sales. This is growing in importance in both consumer and industrial markets. In international markets this relies on establishing regional wholesalers or employing independents with a well-dispersed wholesale network, and the availability of, or resources to establish, a transport operation to ensure rapid delivery.

The flow of information through the channel may be greatly assisted through integrating retail operations. As manufacturers are provided with an opportunity to interface directly with their customers, detailed information on the specific needs and wants of the market, and scope for segmentation and adaptation, becomes easier to gather and assess. In the case of franchising, these benefits will be diluted, as the successful flow of information depends on the adeptness of franchise managers to gather relevant information and pass it on to the manufacturer. With catalogue sales, although manufacturers may deal directly with consumers, the lack of face-to-face contact may similarly dilute the amount and quality of information. To what extent this factor determines, the decision to integrate retail operations is not clear, although it would appear a secondary issue in the light of the limited number of manufacturers who have integrated forwards into retailing in the consumer sector, which is traditionally motivated by market research.

4.9   The Manufacturing Sector: Associated Channel Functions

Agents' functions, promotion and transport, traverse the integrated model, feeding directly into the strategic decisions facing firms at different levels in the channel.

4.9.1   Agent functions

In most marketing channel systems there is a need, at some stage in the channel, for agents, whose primary function is to generate new business contacts. Typically, agents and other similar intermediaries, do not take title to the goods, they simply generate contacts. They may be used at the stage of the wholesaler/distributor to generate new retail customers or end-users or at the level of the manufacturer contacting end-users direct or finding new wholesalers to handle their products.

Internalization versus externalization of agents   The relative advantages/disadvantages of operating using independent agents, as opposed to a company-controlled sales force, are well documented in the literature. In this context, then, a brief resume will suffice. In terms of cost: 'The fixed costs of engaging a sales agency are lower than those of establishing a company sales office. But costs rise faster through a sales agency because sales agents get a larger commission than company sales people,' (Kotler (1984), p.556).

The decision to use company-employed salesmen/agents may be influenced by the problems associated with dealing with agents. The problem of control of agents is a classic dilemma in economics, leading to the whole of the literature on principal-agent problems and agency theory, which is capable of a wide range of applications (for a review see Thompson (1988); the most influential model is that of Jensen and Meckling (1976)).

The monitoring of the performance of salesmanship is fraught with difficulties (Nicholas (1983 and 1986)). Ways of bonding the agent to the principal, through exclusive contracts, reward system, etc., are measured as incentive systems against internal direction and provide a classic instance of contracts versus the market as the most efficient motivation. Means of holding hostages against good performance, and systems for punishing bad performance in an external market must be set against internal systems of control (promotion, special increments, etc.).

In an international context, the International Product Life Cycle proposes that, as firms gain experience from operating abroad through using independent intermediaries, they are likely to invest in overseas facilities including sales and marketing functions (Vernon (1966)). This argument is derived from an assumed lack of knowledge on the part of manufacturers relating to cultural and business practices in the foreign market. However, independent agencies will have (often location specific) skills and contacts with key purchasers. Local knowledge may not be available by buying in key individuals, who may already be selling their services packaged into an agency. The reward for these individuals may be greater in selling their services to a number of principals rather than tied to the internal market of one (multinational) firm. In the long term, then, continuing to operate via independent firms may prove the optimal mode of generating new customers.

4.9.2 Promotion

Like the function of agents/salesmen, promotion can take place at different levels in the channel, and by different channel members. It is often assumed that promotion is only directed at consumers at the end of the channel. Within standard marketing systems, where channel functions are externalized, manufacturers operating through two-stage channels (i.e., giving title to wholesalers who sell on to retailers who in turn sell to final customers) may find the need to target four different sets of promotional literature:

1 Information directed at wholesalers aimed at persuading them to stock their products.
2 Information for wholesalers to use in their agents/sales-forces sales to retailers.
3 Promotional literature for retail outlets designed to persuade end-users to purchase their goods (as opposed to substitute products).
4 Direct advertising to end-users designed to generate demand.

The second and third elements in this list may be passed on to wholesalers and retailers in the transfer of title. The decision to pass on such responsibility may depend on the need to promote a standardized brand image, or the need to convey specialist information on technology or differential advantages to all members of the channel and the final customer. The coordination of promotion with the performance of other functions is crucial to competitive success. This process is highly information intensive, and gathering relevant information on which promotional campaigns may be based is often perceived as facilitated by internalizing functions (i.e., production, wholesaling, retailing and sales/marketing).

4.9.3 Transport

The management of the transport function requires great skill and sensitivity because, uniquely, at some point it involves the transnational transfer of goods and usually of rights (see, in another context, Buckley (1987). This may be when the final product is transferred to a foreign warehouse or where a domestic (central) warehouse exports to a foreign distributor or else where a direct distribution sale is made from home. The national boundary can impinge at any of these stages as can the change of ownership (see also Graham (1972)).

Information flow is also of great importance to the planning of transportation modes: information on the modes of transport available, relative costings, feedback from drivers and shippers, and also consumers concerning their level of satisfaction with quality and delivery schedules. Once again, this kind of information is perhaps easier to collect where certain areas of the transport function are internalized. The propensity of firms to integrate their transport functions will be influenced by the transport infrastructure available. In some less-developed countries, poor indigenous transport facilities may determine that the manufacturer establishes some kind of network of their own.

4.10 The Service Sector: Production

For those services which require some form of direct interaction between the supplier and customer, that is (according to Boddewyn, Halbrich and Perry's classification), those in which there is no tangible (exportable) product element or where there is a mix of tangible and non-tangible elements, firms need to establish structures that facilitate producer and customer interaction. For these services, the expansion paths of the various business activities may be viewed differently.

4.10.1 The location of production

Services in which interaction between suppliers and customers is essential are frequently referred to in the literature as 'location-bound' services indicating that a foreign presence is a pre-requisite for doing business on an international scale. For some services this may entail the establishment of a foreign subsidiary or branch office, whilst for others staff may be sent out to visit customers on an ad-hoc basis. This suggests, therefore, that it is interaction in the foreign market which is the critical element of 'location bound' services as opposed to the domestic or host country place of production. Arguably, however, the interaction may be an integral part of the production, which raises the question of what constitutes the 'production' element in the service sector. Although a full discussion of this question is beyond the scope of this chapter, some elements can be highlighted. Firstly, certain services (notably legal, consulting, design and architecture and some areas of banking) contain a degree of information gathering and/or utilization of knowledge. The dissemination of such information and knowledge can be through documentation and correspondence or via face-to-face discussion. Second, there are those services (such as entertainment, travel and hotel accommodation) which involve the right to use a particular resource. Here the production not only involves the physical facilities (the hotel, the aeroplane, the theatre) but also the additional service elements such as cleaning of the hotel room, provision of in-flight food and drink and the theatrical production being staged. To some degree, retail services may be similarly categorized, as they involve both the provision of the physical outlet, along with the additional elements of range and quality of goods, store 'ambience', choice of methods of payment, etc.

Given these categorizations of service 'production', it may be useful to consider services according to whether or not a physical 'outlet' or place of provision is necessary. In this respect, knowledge/information-based services emerge as those in which a physical foreign presence is not essential (although in some cases it may be desirable). In the latter instances, 'production' may take place domestically, interaction between supplier and customer being facilitated by telecommunications or visits to the customer by key personnel. In the former case, Vandermerwe and Chadwick (1989) found that information technology is emerging as a 'new' form of market servicing in the services sector, with the following characteristics:

1 Transactions are classified as exports as there is no physical movement by the service provider; transactions require an infrastructure in the foreign market – provided by host-market third parties – which may include customers.
2 A market 'presence' is achieved through locating the technology abroad. Control is achieved via ownership of the technology, systems procedures and management arrangements.

There is also cause to believe that information technology is growing in importance as a mode of market servicing. For the period 1975 to 1983, the percentage of foreign sales of British non-manufacturing firms arising from export sales (*vis-à-vis* licensing and FDI) showed a marked increased from 15 to 38 per cent.

In the latter case, where firm personnel are required to travel to the customer, the high cost of international travel may put the firm at a cost disadvantage *vis-à-vis* foreign competitors. This factor, like the cost of transporting goods in the manufacturing sector, may make firms more likely to invest in the foreign market as the volume of business increases. Although the cost of international communication may also be considered as putting the firm at a disadvantage in relation to foreign competitors, the nature of information technology being taken up by firms according to Vandermerwe and Chadwick's survey demonstrates a sharing of costs between the supplier and third party or customer. Not only does this minimize the cost disadvantage, it also demonstrates a commitment to a long-term working relationship, which acts as a barrier to entry to local competitors.

4.10.2 Internal versus external production

It has already been suggested that externalization in the service sector is limited due to the problems of controlling the quality of people-supplied services. In addition, we have identified a group of service firms in which information is a critical factor in the production process. Here, the capability to gather, store, monitor, interpret and analyse information at the least possible cost can be the key intangible asset providing firm-specific advantages (Dunning (1989)). Enderwick (1989) points to the economies of learning in the scale and scope of information gathering and use, and the often high investment requirements for such indivisible assets. This reinforces the idea of specialization by service firms and economies of integration throughout the production process. Such economies can also provide first-mover advantages, firms willing to invest in information accruing short-term benefits from its use and longer-term benefits from scale and scope economies. Coupled with information is knowledge which can be derived from investment in information, or which accrues as a result of the experience gained by the firm's personnel. When the knowledge is invested in the personnel of the firm it can be produced and sustained over time, the firm capitalizing on their innate firm-specific knowledge.

Clearly, in information intensive sectors where information is tacit and costly to produce, but where it can be replicated with ease, there are advantages to internalizing such competitive assets and protecting leakage of firm-specific knowledge derived from these assets. In addition, where imparted knowledge is an important element in the delivered service, the role of service provider includes educating the consumer, best achieved through vertical integration of production and sales (Enderwick (1989)).

4.10.3   Production – a summary

Unlike in the manufacturing sector, where 'production' refers to the manufacture of tangible goods, 'production' in services is a more abstract concept. This makes categorization of services into sectoral groups which distinguish between different patterns of location of the productive process, a difficult task. Due to the inseparability factor inherent in some services, it is almost impossible to differentiate between 'production' and delivery. However, by identifying specific elements within the 'production' function, we can distinguish between those which demand a physical 'outlet' or place of delivery and those in which information forms the key element in the process, which can be transferred via more remote modes of supplier–customer interaction. This latter group of information-intensive services is more likely to be internalized than those requiring the provision of physical facilities. This is, in part, a result of the information/knowledge content, which is potentially the key source of firm-specific advantage, and also as a result of the problems of controlling the quality of the service when it is linked to the skills in information gathering, monitoring and interpretation, and knowledge accumulation, by the firm's personnel. Alternatively, in those sectors where part of the 'service' depends on the physical facilities, there is greater scope to control the quality of the service through owner-ship or control of the tangible 'trappings'. International retail franchising, for example, whilst involving externalized management of individual outlets, can permit a high degree of quality control through the provision of standardized physical facilities, goods and management training.

4.11   The Service Sector: Wholesaler/Distribution Functions

Wholesaling is characteristically a function for building/breaking bulk. In the service sector, the 'tangible' element of the service is often some form of documentation (for example, tickets, insurance documents), which clearly cannot be construed as requiring wholesaling facilities in the same way as physical products. Indeed, they can be sent directly to customers via postal services without handling by intermediaries. Thus, even for those services which include a tangible 'product' distinct from the service, the likelihood of wholesaling being included in the channel is small.

4.12   The Service Sector: Retailing

Whereas in the manufacturing sector the propensity of firms to control retailing activities through vertical integration is small, for many service firms establishing 'retail' outlets, wherein the supplier and customer can interact, systems to facilitate such interaction can be a prerequisite of foreign business due to the inseparability factor. This places much greater emphasis on retailing as a critical business function in the service sector. Related to the manufacturing sector, it was noted how the large number of outlets and the wide geographic spread necessary to serve retail demand makes internalization costly and hard to manage centrally. These problems apply equally in the service sector and are compounded in the case of 'localized' services (for example, shoe repairs, restaurants, retail banking) where the catchment area of customers is small. This raises several implications. First, global coverage on a similar scale to international manufacturing firms demands multiple representation (Enderwick (1989)). This is costly to achieve through vertical integration, and may partly explain why the most well-known international service firms (for example McDonalds and Kentucky Fried Chicken) are those which can successfully externalize their activities through franchise networks. Second, this factor may contribute to the low levels of international expansion in certain sectors. Third, it raises the importance of mergers, takeovers and joint ventures, as all three forms of market servicing provide access to established retail facilities.

Alternatively, services which have a wide catchment area (notably, specialist consulting services) can attain a high degree of internationalization from a centralized location. Customers are often prepared to seek out their services either because no alternative is available locally or because the reputation of the foreign firm outweighs their 'foreignness', or are introduced to the services of a foreign firm through local agents.

4.13   The Service Sector: Associated Channel Functions

4.13.1   Agent functions

Generating business contacts by agents in the host market also assumes an important role in the service sector. This is particularly true for those firms operating at arm's length from the market (for example, consultants, insurers). As is typical of agents, they do not take title to the goods, but generate business on behalf of the principal (the service firm).

Internalization vs externalization of agents   The problems associated with controlling agents may be similarly applied to those acting on behalf of service firms. Similarly, the cost arguments advanced to stress the benefits of utilizing agents as opposed to establishing a company sales office, also apply in the service sector. Where services differ from manufactured goods is in the role played by agents in intermediating between the supplier and customer. In many ways, the agent may be viewed as a personification of the firm. Although this is true, to some extent, of agents operating on behalf of manufacturers, whereas customers of manufactured goods are able to support their purchase decision with a close assessment of technical information, and in some instances product testing, service customers rely on perceptions and expectations developed by agents. This, therefore, raises additional problems when operating via external agents, who, not aware of the company's culture and ethos, may potentially give the wrong signals to customers or, indeed, foster the wrong 'types' of customer. One may expect, therefore, a greater propensity to internalize the agent function in services, agents being considered as a first-step 'market-testing' option or a strategy of last resort.

4.13.2   Promotion

Because of the intangibility of services, promotion can play a key role in conveying information about what the service constitutes. Although this is, of course, true for manufactured goods, services cannot be described in the same clear technical way as products. Consequently, the challenge of promoting services can be viewed differently. 'When a consumer attempts to judge a service, particularly before using or buying it, that service is 'known' by the tangible clues, the tangible evidence that surrounds it'. Shostack (1977)

Promotion plays an important role in providing tangible clues. Relating promotion efforts to physical features (a photograph of the hotel room, a photograph of the scene of a play) or drawing the attention of the customer to the service provider (the consultant, the personal banker) helps to focus the customers mind on elements of the service which provide tangible clues about expected performance.

Another important challenge facing service promoters is capitalizing on word-of-mouth endorsement. Consumers generally accept that purchasing services involves higher risks than purchasing goods as a result of their intangibility, and consequently place a lot of importance on personal recommendations. In order for firms to achieve this, it is essential

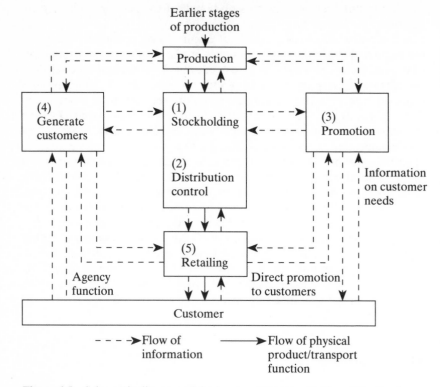

Figure 4.5 Schematic diagram of the key constituent activities of the firm's activities: manufacturing
Source: Developed from Buckley and Casson, 1976, p.51.

that they meet customer expectations and not overstate the benefits. Underperformance will not lead to personal endorsement and can therefore be very damaging for business.

4.14 Synthesis of Functions

Figure 4.5 is an attempt to encompass the key elements of the market servicing decision. The key functions for the manufacturing sectors are shown: production, which may be a multi-stage process, stockholding, distribution control, promotion, generating customers, transport and retailing. The flow of physical product runs through the production stages, distribution control and (possibly) retailing to the customer. These functions are linked therefore by flows of physical product but equally crucial are the flows of information between the functions which also tie in promotion and the generation of customers. These flows are difficult to ensure and secure in an externalized environment. Worries about secrecy, creating competitors, and misinformation argue for internalization. However, the local knowledge of agents (and their contacts) performing the role of generating customers, and of external promotional agencies, may counterbalance these arguments. Moreover, agents and promoters may have specialized skills unavailable to (foreign) entrants. Consequently the internal/external decision must be taken on a case-by-case basis. It is, however, crucial to recognize the interdependence between the various functions shown in figure 4.5. It is also the case that imperfect competition (monopoly, monopsony, bilateral monopoly) at one stage of production induces price distortions in this multi-stage process and creates an incentive for backward or forward integration (Buckley and Casson (1976), Casson (1985)).

In the service sector, given the greater propensity for firms to interact directly with their customers, there is likely to be less distortion in the flow of information, except in cases where external agents interface between the firm and its customers. In many instances, the physical flow is restricted to paperwork and contracts, and the lack of 'physical product' means that stockholding is absent from the picture. The establishing of business systems is consequently more concerned with providing for supplier/customer interaction than the movement of the product through the channel. Equally, distribution control is likely to be dominated more by database marketing practices (monitoring the customer base and extending the consumer franchise) than traditional logistics management tasks. These differences are highlighted in figure 4.6.

Consequently, any analysis of the foreign market servicing decision must consider all the activities listed and the key elements determining their location and internal versus external performance. The activities cannot and should not be considered in isolation. It is the interrelationships and interdependencies between the activities which make the market servicing decision so complex. Because of the many factors affecting the configuration of activities, policies should be constantly under review.

4.14.1 Flows of information

The flows of information in the diagram are vital sources of competitive advantage. For instance, the flow of information from the retail/customer interface can be the source of data on consumer tastes, preferences and selection between closely competing products. The retailer in the manufacturing channel, then, may act as a facilitator or bottle-neck

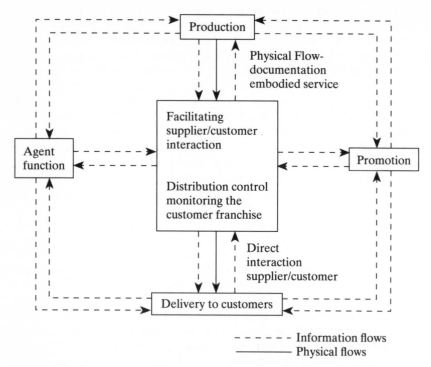

Figure 4.6   Schematic diagram of the interrelationships between functions: services

for the flow of such information. The willingness to gather and forward relevant data depends, in part, upon the importance of the manufacturer's brand within the product range he offers and the contribution it makes to turnover. The flow back of information from the interface with the customer to distribution control, stockholding and eventually production, is a fundamental input to a marketing information system.

In the service sector, the more direct interaction between suppliers and customers makes the gathering of market information an easier task. Because of the systems imposed upon them by the nature of the service being provided, service firms, in one form or another (whether through personnel visiting the customer, face-to-face interaction, tele-communication, or post), interface directly with their customers. Thus, adaption to individual needs and tailoring promotional efforts are fa-cilitated by more direct information flows. The exception is where firms utilize the services of external agents. Here, as with wholesalers in the manufacturing sector, firms must work to develop good relations with their agents in order to encourage their passing relevant information back to the firm.

Nevertheless, due to the multirepresentation factor alluded to earlier, the dispersed nature of business activities demands well-developed communication networks in order to maximize the benefits accruing from direct interaction with the market. Furthermore, regional variations in consumer tastes and buying behaviour may make it difficult for firms to standardize their response to market information and autonomy of subsidiaries may prove desirable, the head office merely reinforcing the general direction of the company and its culture.

4.15 Conclusion

The view expressed in this chapter is that the categorization of foreign market servicing strategies into exporting, licensing and foreign investment, is too crude a division because it ignores the crucial role of channel management. Marketing costs cannot simply be aggregated as a lump: costs of distribution, stockholding, transport, promotion, retailing and generating new customers are radically different. The location and internalize/externalize (do or buy) decisions are as crucial for each of these functions as they are for production. An integrated treatment recognizing the interdependencies and cost implications of each function is essential for a complete conceptualization of the foreign market servicing decision. This necessitates an analysis of the crucial role of information flows between and among channel members, be they internal or external, foreign and domestic, and of possibilities for information blockage in the channel.

5

The Impact of Foreign Market Servicing Strategy on Competitiveness

5.1 Introduction

This chapter presents the results of the empirical investigation into the impact of foreign market servicing strategies on the competitiveness of UK firms. The first part of the chapter examines foreign market servicing strategy and considers whether, in practice, the firms in the sample have such a coherent strategy. The second part of the chapter examines the relationship between the separate strategic moves analysed and the outcome in terms of competitiveness.

The central hypothesis tested in this chapter is that the competitiveness of firms is dependent on an appropriate set of foreign market servicing strategies.

The model we envisage is shown as figure 5.1. The change in market servicing strategy may impact upon (1) competitive performance (2) competitive potential and (3) management process. There is also a potential dynamic interaction or feedback between each of these inter-related measures of competitiveness.

5.2 Policies on Foreign Market Servicing

The difference in international orientation between manufacturing firms and retail financial service firms means that the target markets for the two groups of firms differed. For manufacturing, we examine market servicing moves in France, Germany,[1] USA, Japan and Australia. In retail financial services, international experience is much more restricted

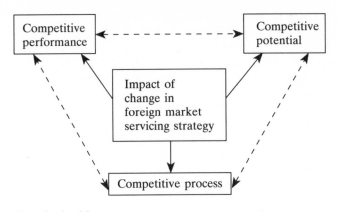

———— Hypothesized impact
– – – – Feedback/interactive potential

Figure 5.1 Hypothesized impact of foreign market servicing changes on competitiveness

and the foreign markets examined are restricted to Continental Europe. In practice, this means France, Germany, Spain and Italy.

In the manufacturing sector, in-depth interviews were conducted with 15 manufacturing firms across five industry groups: glass, industrial gases, pharmaceuticals, scientific instruments and consumer paint (glass and industrial gases are grouped together as 'national champions'), who made 25 strategic foreign market servicing mode changes. The fifteen manufacturing firms are coded as follows to preserve anonymity:

> National Champions (1.1, 1.2)
> Pharmaceutical Firms (2.1 to 2.5)
> Instrument Engineering Firms (3.1 to 3.5)
> Paint Firms (4.1 to 4.3)

The firms varied greatly by size. It is useful to categorise them by scale factors. Four distinct groups emerge (1) Small firms with a primarily national orientation, targeting maybe one or two international markets as a first step to reaching a wider international market. The turnover of firms within this group rises to approximately £25 million. (2) Medium sized firms in a comparatively early stage of internationalization, seeking a more consolidated approach to their overseas investment, often involving capital investment for the first time. The turnover range for this group is £25M to £100M. (3) International firms who are players in most, if not all, of the significant national and regional markets in their industry. There may be significant gaps in the global coverage of these firms who may be dominant in one or two regions and weak in others. The turnover range of this group is £100–1000 million. (4) Global firms who are major players in oligopolistic world markets and whose turnover exceeds £1000 million.

Classifying the firms by turnover and international orientation results in a conflict in the positioning of some firms who, despite low levels of turnover, showed quite a high level of international orientation. Incidence of such conflict was particularly high in the scientific instruments industry. Several reasons for this exist. The industry is highly fragmented, consisting of a large number of small players operating in specialist areas. Domestic markets are too small to sustain production and a degree of internationalization is consequently essential to survival. In one case, the firm was a subsidiary of a larger parent company, international operations being conducted by 'sister' companies abroad. As a result, turnover *relative to the industry* was also used as a determining factor, which raises the rankings of certain firms not lying within the above stated turnover bands. Generally, however, divisional firms are ranked by size of division.

A considerable industry effect exists in the scale coding. Both national champions are rated 4. The pharmaceutical sample includes two global players, one international firm and two small nationally-orientated companies who manufacture generics. Scientific Instruments has one international firm, three medium-sized firms and one small firm. The paint sample contains one global firm and two medium firms. These ratings reflect the nature of competition and technical factors such as economies of scale and nature of the product. It also, to some extent, yields a macro picture of UK manufacturing strengths in the various industry sectors. In the scientific instruments industry, no firms achieve a 'global' ranking, which may be indicative of their lack of comparative advantage and low-tech orientation. Global manufacturers in the other industry sectors suggest a buoyancy of UK manufacturing in these industries acting as role-models for competitive success to all players.

In the financial services sector, interviews were conducted with six banks, eight building societies and ten insurance companies. The twenty-four financial service firms are coded as follows to preserve anonymity:

> Banks (5.1 to 5.6)
> Building Societies (6.1 to 6.8)
> Insurance Companies (7.1 to 7.10)

A clear picture of size categories based on both financial data and European orientation proved impossible within this sector, partly as a result of compatibility of data (asset size appearing relevant to banks and building societies, although clearly not to insurance companies where premium income would have been more appropriate) and partly due to the diversity of opinion across the whole sample as to the major benefits of being a Continental European player. Given that all firms within these sectors (with one exception) can perhaps be regarded as 'large', attention is focused towards European orientation. Four groups of firms were identified:

1　Firms with a UK orientation planning defensive strategies in the light of possible threat to the UK market from European financial liberalization after 1992. Included here are also those firms showing some vague (unformulated) interest in niche marketing in Europe in the future.
2　Firms scanning Europe for opportunities.
3　Firms who have identified target markets and are in the process of establishing operations.
4　Firms with established operations in one or more European markets.

Clearly, within the financial service sector the experience of many firms is skewed more towards first-time expansion than strategies for consolidation of international activities. Only ten of the 24 firms (three banks and seven insurance companies) fall into category four. When coupled with four firms in category 3 (one bank, one building society and two insurance companies), it may be seen that a relatively large proportion of the sample has *no* experience of operating in Europe.

None of the firms in the manufacturing sector have a set, formalized policy on foreign market servicing despite the fact that 14 of the 15 managers contacted commented on the importance of operating internationally to maximize returns and generate growth. The major reasons behind this reluctance to formalize policies on foreign operations lie in the distinct differences between countries (including competitive structure, legal and political regulations and market size), product characteristics and financial constraints within the firm. The manufacturers can, therefore, be divided into three groups. Firstly, there are firms whose limited resources currently preclude choice, and generally compel them to consider only modes of exporting which require minimal capital outlay and enable returns to be generated more quickly. Secondly, there are those firms who are forced to manufacture abroad due to the bulky nature of their product offering. Thirdly, there are those firms who have relatively free choice over preferred modes of operation, dependent only on the constraints of individual markets.

Firms falling into the first category include three instrument engineering (3.2, 3.3, 3.4) and two pharmaceutical manufacturers (2.1, 2.2). For them, generating scale economies in domestic manufacturing is an important part of their striving for competitive advantage. In addition, generating rapid returns in order to satisfy shareholders or for reinvestment in new technology dictate the use of the most economical mode of market servicing, i.e., exporting through agents/distributors. Exporting through this channel mode is not, however, perceived to be a satisfactory form of market servicing. All of the firms recognize the benefits offered by establishing sales/marketing subsidiaries. The advantages mentioned include increased control over sales activities, more credible delivery and after sales service and better understanding of consumer needs gained through more direct contact with the market. For these five companies, therefore, the unwritten 'policy' is to generate a customer base through current export operations which is large enough to justify investment in sales/marketing subsidiaries in specific target markets. For most, this kind of strategy will be actionable in the short to medium term.

Both national champions fall into the second category (1.1, 1.2). They are constrained in their choice of foreign market servicing by the nature of their product offering. The bulk of their products, and the need to be close to the market in order effectively to manage distribution, necessitates local production in order to compete in foreign markets. Both firms strive for a geographic balance of activities but approach foreign market servicing in notably different ways. One firm's aim (1.2) is to maximize returns through the retention of technological property, which results in their establishing foreign production plants in all markets where operations can become viable, and substantial returns can be achieved over 'a reasonable period of time'. Conversely, the other firm (1.1) has a more dualistic approach to foreign market servicing. In markets where demand is great enough, and the company believes it can efficiently manage the operation, or where foreign governments have persuaded them, they have set up or acquired foreign manufacturing plants. Where, however, they perceive cultural and business practices would make it difficult to invest, they license their technology to local manufacturers. The philosophy behind this approach is to prevent firms without the technology pursuing price-cutting strategies, damaging to all players, leaving firms with no money to invest in R&D. Both firms, however, did not construe their general aims as 'policies'. Within their overall objective of achieving a global balance of activities there is a certain degree of flexibility, which allows different approaches not only in different markets, but also across different products in the companies portfolios. Where opportunities arise, take-over of existing firms may be considered over greenfield investment, for example, and in some 'specialist' product areas exporting is preferred as the level of value-added can bear the cost of transportation whilst generating scale economies in domestic production.

To some extent, one of the paint manufacturers also falls into this category (4.1). In the past, the commodity nature of paint, and the low margins per unit meant that exporting was not considered a viable option. Hence, the firm established overseas manufacturing bases from which to service foreign markets. Although today, as paint has become more expensive and sophisticated, and exporting has become a more attractive proposition, the firm continues to manufacture abroad as a result of its historical development. The change in the product 'image' does, however, mean that future policies may be developed whereby longer transportation runs from regionally located manufacturing bases may be considered more efficient and strategically effective.

The remaining seven manufacturing firms fall into the final category. Of these, three pharmaceutical firms have a widely understood direction for foreign market servicing which they follow where market conditions allow. For two pharmaceutical companies (2.4, 2.5), where a market presence is desired, their aim is to be there with a company on the ground. This is the case except where the market is too small to sustain an investment, or in centrally planned economies and politically unstable markets, which are either served by exporting, or ignored as not being worthy of attention. For one of these firms (2.4), foreign 'manufacturing' entails putting the active ingredients into capsules and tablets and packaging (secondary production). The manufacture of bulk actives, the active ingredients (primary manufacture), is conducted domestically and exported to the foreign manufacturing plants. This strategy is followed for two reasons. Firstly, control over the manufacture of actives is more easily managed domestically, and economies of scale in primary manufacturing can more easily be achieved. Secondly, overseas 'packaging' activities gives a closeness to the market which enables them to tailor products to the needs of consumers. Marketing traditions are generally considered as being very different, particularly in terms of package size and design.

For the other pharmaceutical firm (2.3), central manufacturing is normally retained unless there are commercial grounds for not doing so. For example, in Latin American countries, finished products cannot be imported and this prevents the market being served through exports. In some countries (for example, France), price reimbursement on pharmaceutical manufactures persuades them to produce there as it gives bargaining strength. In markets which are served by exports, sales/ marketing support is frequently located in the market for the purpose of understanding consumer and business practices in overseas locations.

The remaining four manufacturing firms, two instrument engineering (3.3, 3.5) and two paint manufacturers (4.2, 4.3), have an 'open book' approach to foreign market servicing. One scientific instrument producer (3.5) is forced, by the diverse nature of its product range, to remain open to various possibilities. As different products are best served in different ways, various strategies are often employed simultaneously. The other scientific instrument firm (3.1) operates on a very opportunistic basis based on guesswork by the owner manager. One paint manufacturer (4.2) has a purposefully flexible approach, for fear of their operations being damaged by adverse market fluctuations. The other (4.3) also operates in an opportunistic fashion, although in this case, strategies based on such opportunities are more rationally worked through.

Of the 24 banks, building societies and insurance companies interviewed, 14 revealed that they have or are contemplating operations in Continental European markets and six that they are contemplating establishing operations. The remaining firms had made a conscious decision not to enter mainland Europe. They are concerned with defending their position/expanding operations in the domestic retail market. This group includes two banks whose European objectives relate only to wholesale and corporate banking. These four firms are excluded from further analysis as they are not concerned with the consideration of foreign market servicing strategies.

Objectives for Europe fall into 4 principal categories:

1   Identification and exploitation of niche opportunities;
2   Exploitation of core strengths;
3   Broadening of business horizons to the extent that Europe is viewed as the domestic market;
4   Adaptation of overall company approach to facilitate overseas operations.

Those firms exploiting niche opportunities (5.2, 6.5, 6.8, 7.2, 7.5, 7.10) are concerned with opportunistic ventures in which they can generate additional profits. Although firms seeking to exploit core strengths are also financially motivated (6.2, 6.3, 6.8) the strategic focus is on longer-term commitment to international operations. At face value, those firms viewing Continental Europe as an extension of the domestic market (5.5, 5.6, 7.1, 7.3, 7.7, 7.9) are planning a more grandiose expansion across Europe. However, these firms accept that some markets offer greater advantages than others, and sequential targeting of successive markets – securing a substantial position in each in turn – is generally viewed as more advantageous than 'dabbling' in several markets at once. This objective is, again, partly financially motivated, although it heralds a concern for spreading risks geographically. The final groups of firms (5.2, 6.4, 7.4, 7.7) are concerned with reassessing organisation forms and product ranges for individual markets. This adaptive approach includes: making organizational changes at divisional level to encompass European operations; raising the degree of autonomy and discretion for foreign managers; adapting business practices for specific markets; tailoring product ranges to cater for various local demand conditions.

A sectoral breakdown reveals that the intention to exploit core strengths was only mentioned by building societies, who view the uniqueness of the UK mortgage market, as offering competitive advantages in certain European markets, which have, in the past, been heavily regulated by governments. Although this will undoubtedly continue to be the case after '1992', UK building societies have the ability to offer different types of mortgage products, based on more flexible instruments and this can constitute a competitive advantage. No building societies currently view Europe as an extension of the domestic market. This could be explained by their historical 'regional' orientation, and although many have emerged from a traditional 'parochial' outlook to develop a strong national network, one interviewee suggested that there remains a general reluctance amongst building society personnel to extend their geographic outlook. No banks identified the search for and exploitation of niche opportunities. Recent strategies of extensive product diversification and pursuit of cross-selling opportunities are apparently being transferred to Europe.

Within these four groups of objectives little consistency was shown in the strategies for foreign market entry or continued market servicing planned to achieve these ends. Five distinct 'policies' for foreign market servicing were adduced:

1 the designing of strategies on a market-by-market basis, dependent on local business practices and cultural environments (7.7, 7.8, 6.2, 7.1, 7.4)
2 expansion on an opportunistic basis, (6.5, 7.3, 7.10)
3 market entry dependent on gaining access to distribution networks (5.2, 5.6, 6.4, 6.5, 6.8, 7.1, 7.5)
4 pursuit of strategies which allow the maintenance of control of head office (5.2, 7.2, 7.4, 7.6, 7.7, 7.9)
5 choices of strategy which offer a high level of autonomous management by local personnel invested with market knowledge (5.6, 7.6).

No single strategy for foreign market entry/market servicing emerged as a general policy of the sampled organizations (although some interviewees clearly indicated that some strategies are considered to be more beneficial than others) and the responses are not mutually exclusive. The divergence of strategic approach across markets is highlighted in table 5.1 which shows the activities of banks, building societies and insurance companies in four Continental European markets (France, Germany, Spain and Italy) at the end of 1989. In the case of 7.6 (an insurance company), the firm has a wholly-owned subsidiary in France,

Table 5.1 Modes of foreign market servicing of UK retail financial firms, end 1989

	Agency	*Branch*	*Wholly owned subsidiary*	*Joint venture*
France	7.7	5.1	5.2	7.10
			7.2	
			7.6	
			7.7	
			7.9	
Germany	7.2	5.1	7.8	5.2
	7.4			5.5
	7.5			5.6
				7.6
Spain	7.7	5.1	7.3	5.5
		7.2		7.4
		7.9		7.9
Italy	7.5	5.1	7.2	5.6
		7.9	7.4	6.8
			7.7	7.6
			7.6	

a joint-venture in Germany, a wholly-owned subsidiary for general insurance and a joint-venture in life assurance in Italy. Insurance company 7.2 has wholly-owned subsidiaries in France and Italy, an agency in Germany and a branch in Spain. Consequently, market specific factors and opportunities appear to have had more bearing on strategic choice.

The 'choice' of foreign market servicing is often severely limited due to constraints imposed on firms by their products, host markets, or their own financial constraints. This results in firms not always being able to take the optimum route to foreign markets, but rather being required to manage most efficiently the alternatives available to them. In terms of competitiveness, product and market constraints affect all firms across different industry groups to relatively the same degree, excepting manufacturers in their home markets. It is, therefore, only financial constraints which give firms a strategic disadvantage. However, from our sample, even where firms are not limited financially, organizations within the same sector show markedly different approaches to foreign market servicing. This may be due to the character of individual organizations and the diverse nature of management structures and styles from which differing strategic approaches emerge.

Three distinct areas of commonality did, however, emerge. Firstly, even where firms have a well-defined approach to foreign market servicing, the need for flexibility is still considered important. Peculiar quirks of market structure, politics and competition in individual countries, make firms aware of the necessity to approach each market separately – looking for the optimum mode of servicing individual markets rather than attempting to establish an holistic, global approach. Many firms commented that a strategy which works successfully in one market is not necessarily so effective in another. Secondly, across the manufacturing sector except in the case of one national champion and one instrument engineer, firms are averse to licensing. For many, this is due to the fact that their technology is an important part of their competitive advantage. For others, it is seen as producing inadequate returns in relation to the management time and effort required to service and police the licensing agreement.

Finally, there is a general consensus of opinion that some form of market presence is required to serve effectively overseas markets. For manufacturing firms who choose not to manufacture abroad, the nature of the ideal presence is a sales/marketing subsidiary. The major benefit offered by pursuing this kind of strategy is 'closeness to customers' which is perceived by all managers as a way of overcoming problems of cultural and business naivety when selling abroad, allowing firms a better understanding of consumers and competition in world markets.

For financial service firms it is a presence in the form of retail outlets (or sales representation in the case of some insurance companies) which is deemed essential for securing a customer base in the foreign market.

5.3   The Impact of Strategic Moves on Competitiveness

The basic hypothesis of this research can be presented as:

Competitiveness of British firms	is a function of	appropriate market servicing strategies and other variables

From this, using our definition of competitiveness, this becomes:

Competitive Performance	Competitive Potential	Competitive Process	$= f$ (Market servicing strategies and other variables)

A priori, we can postulate that both host country and industry variables will affect the outcome of a strategic move. Further, the *type* of strategic move, for example, from no foreign involvement to exporting through an agent, or from exporting through a distributor to a foreign direct investment, is likely to have an impact on the components of competitiveness. The hypothesis now becomes:

Competitive   Competitive   Competitive = f (Type of market
Performance   Potential   Process   servicing change,
                                                 industry factors,
                                                 host country factors
                                                 and other variables)

As far as possible, other variables are to be held constant and so are assumed to have no impact on the elements of competitiveness. Further, we take each of the elements of competitiveness separately before attempting to combine the impact as figures 1.1 and 1.3 show (chapter 1, pp.5 and 9.) In the manufacturing sector, this artificial division can be justified to some degree by the fact that the three groups of dependent variables have been shown to operate at different levels. Our key measure of competitive performance, profitable market share seems to apply widely across firms and industries, whilst competitive potential, technological advance and investment strategy are largely industry specific. Finally, management process, as measured by internal and external relationships, functional integration and communication, is largely idiosyncratic to individual firms. We can thus expect the impact of market servicing policies to be felt differentially because of the level of impact.

This kind of distinction is not apparent in the financial service sector. This may be partly due to the blurring of traditional boundaries between the three sectors, which has occurred in response to the deregulation of financial markets. As firms are now offering a wide range of products across the traditional business sectors, the diversity of measures identified in each sector may result from the diversity of products being offered.

There is considerable variability in each of the explanatory factors. Table 5.2 shows the country and industry variation for manufacturing firms and table 5.3 those in the financial service sector.

It is clear that a large number of variables are involved: industry, target market, nature of strategic move, size of firm, nature of competition are amongst the most important. Further, the issue of comparator arises. Here, we are comparing the situation before and after the strategic move on a with/without basis. We do not answer the question of whether a better alternative could have been found. In several cases, the firms themselves felt that *in the target market itself* a better form of market servicing existed to which they should move. One scientific instrument maker actually identified its market servicing stance as a

Table 5.2 The 25 strategic moves of manufacturing firms: host country and industry variation

Host country		Industry	Firms	Moves
USA	9	National Champion	2	4
France	5	Pharmaceuticals	5	7
Japan	4	Scientific Inst.	5	9
Germany	3	Paint	3	5
Sweden	2	Total	15	25
Australia	1			
Small Export	1			
Total	25			

Table 5.3 Strategic moves by financial service firms: host country and industry variation

Host country		Industry	Firms	Moves
France	4	Banks	4	4
Germany	2	Building Socs	6	1
Spain	4	Insurance Cos	10	9
Italy	4	Total	20	14
Total	14			

strategic disadvantage. One firm, in generic pharmaceuticals, has no foreign ventures and is included as a no-strategic-involvement benchmark.

The impact of the strategic moves analysed varies enormously. Some are clearly and unequivocally positive in their short and long-run impact on competitiveness, improving performance, competitive potential and having a stimulating effect on management processes. Others are generally negative, the firms having to search (unsuccessfully) for any positive impact. A third group involves the trade off between positive and negative impacts on different parts of our multiple competitiveness model. In some cases, this can be reconciled by a short-run versus long-run dichotomy. This can be further rationalized by examining time horizons and trade offs in time. It is not without risk for a firm, particularly a publicly quoted firm, to trade off short-run performance in favour of long-run potential. Capital market constraints on behaviour of this kind were frequently quoted.

Table 5.4   The 25 strategic moves in the manufacturing sector by type

(1)	Minimal	1	
(2)	Minimal to export	5	First move	11
(3)	Minimal to license	1	
(4)	Minimal to FDI	4	
(5)	Change in export form	5	Export adjustment	5
(6)	Export to FDI	5	
(7)	License to FDI	1	Move to FDI	9
(8)	Sales subsidiary to FDI	3	
Total		25		25

5.4   Impact on Competitiveness: The Manufacturing Sector

The variation in the exact type of market servicing move in the manufacturing sample is enormous as table 5.4 shows but it is possible to simplify types as the table demonstrates. Three classes of move are identified: first move, export adjustment and move to a foreign direct investment in production.

First move   In all cases the first move is the first significant attempt to penetrate the foreign market. In one case, although no real attempt to penetrate a single market had been made, sporadic halfhearted exporting had taken place in response to individual foreign orders. Five cases involved a move to exporting in various forms (through an agent or distributor), one to a license and four to foreign direct investment. This proportion moving to a full involvement from little or no market penetration is unusual (compare Buckley, Newbould and Thurwell (1988), table 4.1, p.46). This category covers 11 of the 25 moves.

Change in export form   Within mode changes can often be as significant as changes in mode. Of the four firms who adjusted their mode of exporting, one changed from an export distributor to an agent; one changed from a distributor to direct export to the end user; one changed the form of agent from an independent to company employed representative; one firm made two seperate export adjustments one from direct sales to a joint venture sales subsidiary; one changed to a wholly owned sales subsidiary from an agency agreement.

Move to FDI   Like the former group, nine firms had an operational form of market servicing prior to the strategic move analysed. These firms, however, all changed to foreign direct investment with production facilities. Five firms changed from exporting, one from licensing and three converted a sales subsidiary into a production facility.

We now go on to analyse the strategic moves by type, recognizing both that there are other influences on competitiveness other than type of move and that competitiveness is multi-faceted.

5.4.1 First moves

The most simple case is that of the small pharmaceutical company which had made no concerted attempt to internationalize (2.1), only filling occasional export orders, which it did not seek in a proactive fashion. Naturally, the impact of such a null strategy on competitive performance was negligible. The effects on competitive potential could actually be said to be negative in that opportunities were being missed and (foreign) competitors were beginning to erode domestic market share. Management process, too, was inward looking and not orientated to international markets. The firm was attempting to innovate and build market share in the UK, whilst creating niches by R&D spending. If, however, competitive potential is created by such a strategy, the firm will find it difficult to achieve the rapid market penetration necessary to capitalize on a technological lead, and recoup the costs of R&D, as the managerial know-how and distribution network will not be in place. Thus, a mismatch between potential and distribution capacity can be predicted.

Our sample contains six cases of a typical first market servicing move from a standing start to an initial concerted export venture. These ventures were diverse: a pharmaceutical company in the USA (2.2), a scientific instrument company in France (3.3) and one in Germany (3.4), and paint companies in Sweden (4.1), Germany (4.2) and the USA (4.3). The impact of these strategic moves on the competitive process of the individual firms is presented in table 5.5. Across all firms, and all elements of competitiveness, the impact of this kind of strategic move is marginal. For the pharmaceutical company in America (2.2), operating through an agent, the major benefit accrued by this form of market servicing was the learning process involved concerning the American market and business practices. The size of the operation is too small for it to make a significant effect on the overall performance of the business, although turnover is increasing steadily, and little effect occurred on competitive potential. By contrast, the scientific instrument makers entry into France (3.3), via a distributor led to a deterioration in performance because of fragmentation of effort in a small market and a negative impact on potential because the firm recognized that the form of market servicing was sub-optimal – a sales subsidiary would have concentrated

Table 5.5   Strategic moves from no presence to exporting

Firm code and market	Performance	Potential	Process
USA (2.2)	Positive (better but not significantly so)	Little effect	Learning about US environment and management
France (3.3)	Decline because fragmentation of capital	Limited – as strategy considered inappropriate	–
Germany (3.4)	Poor profit and turnover	Wide product range but no presence to exploit	Realization of opportunity
Sweden (4.1)	Positive – market share and profitability	Mode of access bypassed previously closed channels	Communication problems reduced benefit
Germany (4.2)	Minimal	Minimal	–
USA (4.3)	Too early to judge but income increased	Outlet for R&D	Improvement in marketing/ promotion

the effort and would enhance future potential. The scientific instrument company in Germany (3.4) frustrated by arms-length operations and a perceived stockholding limitation, felt unable to capitalize on potential. Performance was consequently poor, and their competitive advantages not exploited. The three paint companies had contrasting results. One firm with an export venture to Sweden (4.1), supported by a local office, experienced positive effects on performance (market share and profitability) as a result of its tying in with a leading local retailer, allowing it to exploit the benefits and increase its potential in a market previously closed by limited access to predominantly manufacturer-owned distribution channels. Distance from their local office, however, has meant poor communication, which is considered to dilute the benefits. The second paint company, exporting to Germany through an agent (4.2), experienced a minimal effect on performance and potential, partly as a result of the market (somewhat surprisingly) being far more backward than that in the UK. The third paint company, which established agency and distributorship in the USA (4.3), experienced some early increases in income and felt that the venture had potential to exploit

Table 5.6   No market presence to a licensing agreement

Firm code and market	Performance	Potential	Process
Japan (1.1)	Substantial because large inflow of cash	Danger of technology leakage	Learning about Japanese culture and management

R&D and that marketing and promotion would improve. Overall it is a little early to judge the effects of the move.

This collection of six of a typical type of initial market servicing move shows that the outcome of the move is contingent on the choice of target market, product/market fit and the timing of the move. It is also indicative of companies' experience in international dealings and the ability of organizational structures to offer support to overseas activities. For example, the paint company exporting to Germany (4.2) in their own words, is a 'trading company' in which strategic approach to foreign operations is less important than selling wherever they can. Conversely, the paint company exporting to Sweden (4.1) is an internationally experienced company, which carefully weighed up the strategic pros and cons of entering the market in this way. Whatever the reasons, our sample illustrates the contrary and even opposing impact such moves can have on the different elements of competitiveness.

One firm (1.1), dependent on a strategy of licensing technology abroad entered the Japanese market through a series of licenses to rival producers. The outcome of this move is presented in table 5.6.

The large inflow of cash resulting from the licenses, enhancing company performance, has to be offset, in terms of competitive potential by the danger of a technology leak, which may be partly compensated for by a small inflow of technology through stipulation in the license that improvements must be handed back to the licensor. The firm also recognizes the benefits of learning about the Japanese market and culture, essential should they decide in the future to look for joint-venture investment options.

Our sample includes a high number of first ventures which took the form of a foreign direct investment. One of the national champions (1.2) entered the American market and Japan by this method, a scientific instrument manufacturer entered the USA (3.3) and a paint manufacturer entered Germany (4.1). Table 5.7 represents the impact of these moves on the firms' competitiveness.

The national champion (1.2) was constrained by the nature of its

Table 5.7 No presence to foreign direct investment

Firm code and market	Performance	Potential	Process
America (1.2)	Better returns due to lower manufacturing costs and a wider customer base	Bought in new technology with the takeover	Global outlook
Japan (1.2)	Minimal, because small venture	Market under-standing feeds into future potential	Understanding of Japanese market and culture
America (3.3)	Minimal	–	Poor management – not capitalized on the benefits
Germany (4.1)	Poor profitability	Regionally located product development	Poor tactics spoilt opportunities

product to invest in order to penetrate foreign markets. The product is not exportable and licensing is not possible because of the scale of investment necessary to exploit the technology in production. The two investment moves contrast sharply.

In the USA, competitive performance was enhanced because the cost of manufacturing was reduced and the number of consumer outlets increased. Competitive potential improved as new technology was bought-in as part of the takeover package. Management process was also enhanced because the venture brought a more balanced global outlook to the firm. In Japan, the same firm's joint venture had a minimal impact on performance because it is small relative to its competition. Management processes were enhanced because there was an effort to understand the initially strange business culture of Japan and it is believed that this will enhance the firm's overall long run potential. These two cases from the same firm throw into relief the long-term versus short-term considerations which a full analysis of competitiveness must encompass. The scientific instrument manufacturer investing in the USA (3.3) felt only a trivial impact on competitive performance, and because of the poor management processes (poor communication, conflict of direction between them and the company they took over) they have failed to capitalize on the benefit of having a presence in this market.

In terms of sustainability of competitiveness, it is essential that they have a significant presence in the USA but the foundation for this success is not in place at the moment. Finally, the paint manufacturer which made a takeover in Germany (4.1), undermined by poor tactics and lack of strategic direction, suffered poor profitability. There has been a positive impact on competitive potential because investment allows product development to be conducted in local markets. The latter two cases illustrate the importance of the management process element in interacting with and underpinning the other components of competitiveness.

5.4.2 Export adjustments

Five changes in market servicing are 'within mode' rather than 'between mode' involving an adjustment to the firm's exporting arrangements. The results show that significant changes in competitiveness can be brought about by relatively minor adjustments. Four cases involve the same firms twice – both are scientific instrument makers. One (3.2) altered its exporting arrangements in France from a distributor to an agent and in the USA from exporting through an agent direct to the end user. The other (3.1) changed its French operation from direct sales to a joint venture sales subsidiary and its German operation from an agency to a wholly owned sales subsidiary(s). The other case involves a paint firm in France (4.2), which moved from an independent agent to a company employed representative. The outcomes of these moves are presented in table 5.8.

In both cases, the first scientific instrument manufacturer (3.2) experienced positive impacts on all three classificatory elements of competitiveness. The French move stimulated performance by increasing effective demand and economies of scale. This reduction in production costs has improved the company's potential along with enhanced global experience. Improved external ties with the agent has had positive impact on the management process, although this benefit has been dulled by poor market intelligence. In the case of the USA, the move brought high-term returns and enhanced economies of scale, specialization and flexibility. In management process terms, customer-firm interaction increased and costs fell. However, the firm feels that this form of market servicing is still suboptimal and that it should move to establishing a direct presence. For the paint company in France (4.2), the move has improved marginal profits and extended the customer base. Potential improved because the firm could buy in bulk from the UK and market knowledge has increased. However, because of management problems, poor communications resulted in longer delivery times. Again the firm

Table 5.8 Export adjustments

Firm code and market	Performance	Potential	Process
France (3.2)	Significantly positive – increased demand and economies of scale	Gained global experience	Improved external ties with agents (dulled by poor market intelligence)
USA (3.2)	Significantly positive – high short-term returns and economies of scale	Costs fell	Customer–firm interaction improved
France (4.2)	Improved marginal profit and extended customer base	Able to exploit bulk buying in the UK	Improved market knowledge
France (3.1)	Early days: costs increased but so did volume	Control of own destiny	Management problems (not specifically international)
Germany (3.1)	Losing money but pull out costs are high	Local presence important	Management problems (not specially international)

recognizes the need to move to a deeper presence in the market. This case, from an independent agent to a company employed agent is, in some ways, more akin to a sales/marketing subsidiary investment than an export venture.

The second scientific instrument maker's (3.1) export adjustments in Europe were mixed blessings, to say the least. The French venture has increased costs as well as volumes but this is perhaps to be expected in the early days of the venture. The major benefit in terms of potential is felt to be central to the firm's own destiny. Both this venture and the German one, which the same firm made, were plagued by management difficulties. These were not specifically international problems but were the result of autocratic, centralized and personalized management in the UK by the 'owners' of the private firm. Indeed, the wholly owned German sales subsidiary was having difficulties in recouping its investment in the highly competitive German market. The potential of the venture was the control of local sales but this would not be realized unless the management problems were solved.

Surprisingly, considering the number of respondents who indicated the value of establishing a sales/marketing subsidiary, or even retrenching to this form of market servicing from a production subsidiary, only two examples emerged of extending export activities to sales/marketing. Why this should be the case is unclear. Perhaps increased focus on international operations initiated by The Single European Market Act has persuaded firms that increased market presence is important to increase competitiveness abroad, and thus the timing of the survey is partly responsible for the incidence of cases which have revealed intentions to establish sales/marketing activities.

Overall, the amount of success apparent by firms following 'intra mode' strategic changes may be partly attributable to the fact that company structure (including export departments and individuals experienced in export operations) is already in place and thus the incremental change can be easily incorporated within the companies' management processes. The exception to this is the privately owned scientific instrument maker, which is plagued by management difficulties.

5.4.3 The move to foreign direct investment

The sample includes nine cases where the firm moved to a direct investment in production: five from exporting: a pharmaceutical company in the USA (2.4) and one in France (2.5), two scientific instrument engineering companies in the USA (3.1, 3.5) and a national champion in Sweden (1.1); one from licensing (a pharmaceutical company entering a joint venture in Japan (2.3)) and three firms moving from a sales/marketing subsidiary to production facilities (two pharmaceutical companies, one in Australia (2.3) and one in Japan (2.4) and a scientific instrument manufacturer in the USA (3.4)). The impact on competitiveness of these strategic moves is shown in table 5.9.

Both pharmaceutical companies experienced positive effects on all elements of competitiveness. For the first, (2.4), the move from exporting through an agent to a wholly-owned production investment through takeover, resulted in fast growth in market share and profitability combined with improved manufacturing and marketing and better R&D invested with USA technical know-how. The high quality of management in the USA which the firm described as 'technically advanced' had a beneficial effect throughout the firm. For the second firm (2.5), the move from exporting through an agent to a wholly owned greenfield venture increased market share and profitability, improved R&D potential and led to wider opportunities for management training, in that

Table 5.9 Moves to foreign direct investment

Firm code and market	Performance	Potential	Process
USA (2.4)	Very positive, market share and profitability	Improved R&D	Improved marketing
USA (3.5)	Improved turnover profits and market share	Economies of scale in the UK piggy-backed on success of US venture	Improved market understanding but communication problems dulled impact
Sweden (1.1)	ROI was positive but ensuing price war cut profit margins	Local supply improved and lead times fell	Understanding of foreign management styles
France (2.5)	Improved market share and profitability	Improved R&D potential	Wider opportunities for management training
Japan (2.3)	Consistent and growing profit	Potential enhanced by management learning	Management understanding of culture
Australia (2.3)	Profits not improved	No significant benefits	No significant benefits
Japan (2.4)	Increased market share	R&D in Japan	Better cultural understanding
USA (3.4)	Increased turnover	Diseconomies of scale although increased tech. competence	Improved market focus but marketing still poor
USA (3.1)	Losing money but pull out costs high	Local presence	US management good but UK problems

staff could be moved to the French plant and learn from French technicians and managers. The national champion (1.1) moved from exporting to a greenfield investment in Sweden. The rate of return of the venture was enhanced but a price war ensued as competitors indulged in an 'exchange of threat'. Potential was enhanced because local supply improved and lead times declined. Benefits to management process were felt through the opportunities of learning about management and styles and approaches in Sweden. The scientific instrument manufacturer (3.5) which moved from exporting to a distributor to foreign direct investment through a takeover in the US, improved turnover, profits and market share. In terms of potential, economies of scale in the UK were 'piggy backed' on the US success as increased turnover of products in the UK resulted from exporting domestically produced parts of the company's portfolio through the new foreign operation. Management process benefits arose as a result of better knowledge of the US market and by specialization and concentration, marred only by communication problems with the new subsidiary. The other scientific instrument maker (3.1) moved from an agency to a wholly owned manufacturing subsidiary and was losing money although the pull-out costs were too high to contemplate withdrawal. The potential of the local presence and the good quality of the US management was to a large extent being undermined by management problems in the UK. This is the private firm with highly centralized management.

The pharmaceutical company, which changed its Japanese market servicing mode from licensing (2.3) to a joint venture, achieved consistent and growing profits as a result of it gaining in its management's understanding of the culture. However, it does not regard the joint venture as the ideal stance and as its learning progresses, it plans to move to a wholly owned subsidiary.

The final category is a type of within mode shift – from a sales subsidiary to a production subsidiary. The only Australian venture in our sample, (2.3), made by a pharmaceutical company, is in this category. The move has not really enhanced competitiveness at all, largely due to market conditions, principally the problems imposed by the government over pricing and sale of pharmaceuticals. In contrast, the pharmaceutical company, which added production to its sales subsidiary in Japan (2.4) whilst remaining a joint venture, increased its market share and benefited from establishing a research and development facility in the Japanese market. This has enabled the firm to focus on product development specifically for Japanese consumers and enabled the firm to gain knowledge of Japanese market-development techniques, which are considered to be advanced. In addition, they have learned much about Japanese management styles. Finally the scientific instruments company which moved into production in the USA via a takeover (3.4), improved performance by increasing turnover, but felt the effects of diseconomies of scale by adding a production unit to its business resulting in their plants working under-capacity. However, with the influx of American managers and technical staff, their technological competence improved and their market focus was clarified. However, the success of the venture, is considered to be marred by poor marketing.

If any one conclusion can be drawn from the strategic moves to foreign direct investment, (and, considering the diverse nature of companies and markets, it is necessarily a very loose conclusion) it is the importance placed on the benefits of increased market and management understanding resulting from this kind of presence in the market. The knock-on effects of such learning are also important to competitive potential.

5.5   Impact on Competitiveness: The Financial Service Sector

Given many service products cannot be transported (exported) and require production in contact with consumers, nearness to the consumer emerges as a critical element in market servicing. This restricts the choice of foreign market servicing options – specifically resulting in exporting being a far less important alternative than is the case in manufacturing. Its use is principally restricted to the sale of insurance products through host market intermediaries. Moreover, licensing may be ruled out on the grounds that product advantages are easy to copy and technology is often bought-in from specialist computer and telecommunications manufacturers, and is therefore available to all. Consequently, it is not surprising that a different picture emerges of strategic adaptations in the financial services sector. Three types of strategic move can be identified: first moves (market entry); shifts between mode and 'additions' to existing business.

First move   Unlike in the manufacturing sector, the first move for many financial service firms can *only* be to some form of foreign investment due to the need to be close to customers. Our sample includes seven examples of a first move, but in only one instance is this a move to 'exporting' (using the services of an agent in the foreign market). The remaining six moves include four to joint ventures and two to greenfield subsidiaries. Table 5.10 summarizes the results.

Shifts in mode   Three shifts between mode were identified, one move from an agent to a subsidiary and two from a branch to a subsidiary.

Additions   These are situations in which firms add new types of operation (that is, new forms of market servicing) to existing activities. Two types of additions emerged from the research, accounting for four strategic moves. Firstly, there are those which involve establishing new types of activity to support the introduction of additional product groups to foreign operations. Three cases follow this form. The final case involves a firm which has incrementally added branches to those that were acquired through the takeover of a foreign bank.

Table 5.10   The 14 strategic moves in the financial service sector

(1)	No activity to agent	1	
(2)	No activity to joint venture	4	First Move 7
(3)	No activity to greenfield subsidiary	2	
(4)	Agent to subsidiary	1	Shifts in Mode 3
(5)	Branch to subsidiary	2	
(6)	New forms for new products	3	Additions 4
(7)	Incremental branch expansion	1	
TOTAL		14	14

5.5.1   First moves

The smallest incremental step, moving from no activity to operating via an agent, was followed by an insurance company in Italy (7.5). The limited degree of commitment stems primarily from financial constraints, and past experience in other markets wherein a critical mass proved difficult to achieve through acquired branches. Nevertheless, as table 5.11 summarizes, despite the financial benefits accruing to the firm through operating through market intermediaries, there are few other positive impacts on the elements of the competitive process. The benefits to company performance have been minimal and control of agents has proved difficult as a result of conflicting objectives. The agents are motivated by market share, whereas the company is more concerned about the quality of customers. Those firms moving from no involvement to a joint venture include a bank in Spain (5.6), a bank in Germany (5.5), an insurance company in France (7.10), and a building society in Italy (6.8). In these instances the impact on firm competitiveness was rather more favourable. The bank in Spain experienced good profit performance and gained access to key personnel in the guise of the managing director of its partner, a key figure in industry policy making, which facilitated the development of products for the market. Although the distribution network accessed through the arrangement was seen as offering short-term benefits, particularly in terms of exploiting an existing customer base, as it remains in the hands of the Spanish partner future potential is critically dependent on the success of the joint venture. Consequently, securing their own distribution network was viewed as offering greater long-term potential. The bank in Germany has a joint venture arrangement with a Spanish bank in Germany. As the activities lie in an independent third market, conflict was thought to be less of a problem than if they were encroaching on each other's markets. Although

Table 5.11   Strategic moves for financial firms from no presence to first venture

Firm code and market	Performance	Potential	Process
Italy (7.5) Agent	Minimal	Low Cost Entry	Control of agents difficult, particularly customer quality.
Spain (5.6) J.V.	Good profits	Access to distribution in the short-term.	Access to key personnel
Germany (5.5) J.V.	Too early to judge	Joint capital – risk sharing and search for opportunities.	
France (7.10)	Too early to judge	Market learning opportunities	Access to local knowledge
Germany (7.8) Greenfield Subsid.	Positive ROI and Profitability	International net-work minimizes risk.	Minimal
Spain (7.3) Greenfield Subsid.	Too early to judge	Extended network to exploit product development skills.	Freedom of personnel choice
Italy (6.8) J.V.	Too early to judge	Market access	Problems of controlling agents, particularly customer quality

it was too early to judge performance, a positive impact on potential was viewed as arising from joint capital investment, risk sharing and search for European opportunities. No clear positive effect was ascribed to the management process. The insurance company in France similarly felt it was too early to comment on performance, but highlighted the positive impact of market knowledge gained through operating with a local partner, which not only facilitates current decision making (process) but also impacts on future potential and establishing their own independent opportunities.

The building society in Italy principally chose a joint venture as the only option offering potential competitive market access. As building societies cannot set up branches, and subsidiaries are considered too costly and high risk, only agents and joint ventures remain viable options. This approach is a mixture of both – a joint venture with an exclusive agent. Although it is too early to assess performance, they expect favourable returns. Conversely, they are prepared for management problems – particularly protecting the quality of customers contacted by the agents. In response to this, they have centralized their underwriting operations so they have ultimate power to accept or reject customers.

Those two firms moving from no-involvement to a greenfield subsidiary include an insurance company in Germany (7.8) and one in Spain (7.3). In the former case, the major impact on the competitive process lies in the potential offered to the firm by having an international network which allows it to minimize risk from individual country economic fluctuations. Performance has generally been favourable, with positive Return on Investment and profitability, although management benefits have proved minimal. In the latter case, the operation has not been operating long enough to comment on performance, but it is hoped that the venture will offer the potential to exploit their product development skills across a wide geographical market. Also, it is believed that by establishing a greenfield subsidiary there is much greater control over choice of personnel, which enables them to choose staff who not only operate in line with head-office policies and ethics, but also have the right personal attributes, which they believe is as important, if not more so, than experience in the insurance industry.

5.5.2 Between mode shifts

This group covers two insurance companies in France (7.2, 7.6) and one in Spain (7.7). The summarized findings are presented in table 5.12. One insurance company in France has very recently moved from an agent to a subsidiary in the area of non-life insurance. They are very confident that this move will have a positive impact on all elements of the competitive process. Performance is expected to improve in the medium-term as the company had, in the past, been constrained in the volume of business handled by their agents and had thus failed to meet demand for some time.

By acquiring a firm, they were not only able to secure a strong distribution network and thus greater potential for market penetration, but they are now also in a position to control their own destiny in the market rather than be reliant on the efforts of intermediaries. The other insurance company in France moved from a branch to a subsidiary, setting up their own operation from scratch. Although they experienced a small increase in market share, organic growth is limited due to the

Table 5.12   Strategic moves for financial firms for switches between mode

Firm code and market	Performance	Potential	Process
France (7.2) Agent → Subsid	Confident can satisfy demand	Secured a strong distribution network	Can control their own destiny
France (7.6) Branch → Subsid	Small increase in market share but limited organic growth	Gained a local image	Staff have market but not company knowledge
Spain (7.7) Branch → Subsid	Negative – drain on resources	Greater potential for market penetration	Lost scale economies through devolvement of activities to subsidiary

highly competitive nature of the market. They have been able to secure a local image in the market, but are finding it difficult to control the operation. Although the indigenous managers have a high degree of local knowledge, they lack understanding of the parent company's culture and ethos. Such management conflicts have diluted the competitive impact of the shift. Finally, the insurance company in Spain has also moved from a branch to a subsidiary. In many ways, this has proved a bad strategic move. The company's performance has suffered as the subsidiary has proved to be a drain on resources. As product margins are very tight, it is necessary for the company to generate large volumes. Nevertheless, the company did view a subsidiary as offering greater potential for future penetration. Lost economies of scale were also seen as resulting from devolvement of all activities to the subsidiary. In the future, deciding which functions should be centralized and which left under autonomous control was viewed as crucial to the efficient management of the operation.

5.5.3   Additions

The four firms in this category include two banks, one in France (5.1) and one in Spain (5.2) and two insurance companies, one in Italy (7.4) and one in Spain (7.9) (see table 5.13). The bank in France has added retail branch networks to an existing corporate banking operation by

Table 5.13 Strategic moves for financial firms adding to existing operations

Firm code and market	Performance	Potential	Process
France (5.1)	Rapid returns and increased income	Acquisition gives access to distribution networks	Access to local market knowledge
Spain (5.2)	Improved profitability	Access to 'closed market'	Local market knowledge
Italy (7.4)	Improved income exceeding expectations	Access to distribution network	Conflict with partner in some business areas
Spain (7.9)	Improved growth and profitability	Extended distribution base	Access to local knowledge

acquiring branches across the major regions of the country. By incrementally adding retail operations to its existing business, the firm has been able to capitalize on its knowledge of the market to develop a strategy which clearly has a favourable impact on all elements of the competitive process. Although costs have increased, so has income performance, not least because the acquisition of branches has allowed rapid returns to be made from existing customer bases. In turn, acquisition of such consumer networks impacts positively on potential, and indigenous management of these branches add to the knowledge base of the organization and its understanding of the French market. The insurance company in Italy has recently added a joint venture to its subsidiary. The major motivation, and positive impact on competitiveness derived from this approach, was access to a distribution network. Through this, the firm's performance (in terms of income) has been two and a half to three times better than the original feasibility study led them to expect. However, the effects on competitiveness have not all been positive. The joint venture is not without management conflicts, particularly in those product areas which require a dedicated selling effort. The insurance company in Italy has recently entered into a joint venture with a local bank, where they can access mortgage customers requiring housing insurance. This operation complements their branches offering commercial insurance. The strategy has impacted favourably on all elements of the competitive process. Profitability and growth have improved through their extended distribution base, and through indigenous managers with a comprehensive understanding of the local market they are able to capitalize on the opportunities for personal lines which had grown apparent to the managers handling commercial insurance. Finally, the bank in Spain has incrementally expanded its branch network out of an earlier acquisition of a small local bank. By buying a local bank, they were able to gain access to an otherwise 'closed' market. From this point of access they have utilized this competitive potential and have built up a strong branch network through greenfield start-ups.

As they sought to maximize returns from existing customers through cross-selling (involving training 'back-room' administrative staff for 'front office' sales roles) they have increased profitability, and by drawing on the local knowledge of indigenous managers, they have successfully adapted products for the Spanish market.

5.6   Conclusion

Several conclusions are in order. Firstly, the choice of market servicing policy in any one case is highly constrained. The choice is constrained by the nature of the product, the firm's previous involvement with the market, the actions of competitors, demand conditions in the market, financial considerations and cost conditions.

Secondly, even after making allowance for the impact of constraints, a range of choice is available as demonstrated by the different choices made by similar firms (and the choices made by competitor firms not directly considered here). Therefore, it is possible to have a policy on foreign market servicing, recognizing the constraints on choice. Firms have an approach to market servicing rather than a strategy. In many cases the market servicing stance is reactive rather than proactive. Thirdly, the choices made do not have a universally positive impact on the competitiveness of firms. In each of the categories (performance, potential and management process) there are examples of changes in market servicing stance which had negative impacts. The pattern of these impacts must be further investigated but two particularly problematical areas appear to be entry via exporting through a foreign distributor and the take-over of a foreign company. Interestingly, these are the opposite ends of the size and involvement spectrum.

Fourthly, we are able to discern definite causal relations between market servicing mode and competitive outcome. The choice of foreign market servicing stance is an important component of the competitiveness of UK firms.

Notes

1   Although West Germany and East Germany were unified in October 1990, most of the statistical data and primary research predates this and consequently relates to W. Germany.

6

The Impact of the Single European Market Act on the Foreign Market Servicing Strategies of British Firms

6.1 Introduction

The Single European Market Act, 1986, extended the principles enshrined in the founding legislation of the European Community (the Treaty of Rome) with the objective of creating a 'single market' (by 1992 if possible) by the removal of various internal obstacles to the free movement of goods, services, capital and persons between the 12 member states of the Community. Under the Act, the European Commission has, to date, submitted around 400 Directives for eliminating disparities between members in respect of physical, technical and fiscal rules and regulations, so as to create a unified Community-wide set of practices; for example, common technical specifications are to be introduced related to product descriptions and design, health and safety standards; VAT and other sales taxes are to be applied on a uniform basis; persons and freight transport will be able to move across national frontiers without undergoing passport and customs checks, etc.

As 1992 approaches, the divergence of opinion as to the likely impact of the Single European Market Act on British industry grows more severe. There are those theorists and policy makers who claim that the Act will herald the establishment of an homogeneous Europe in which product standardization will provide European firms with massive scale economy advantages in a wider market. Diametrically opposed to this line of thought are those who believe that the Act, while providing easier access into Europe, will emphasize the need for British firms to better understand the political, historical, economic and consumer differences between the 12 member states, if they are to penetrate successfully the European market and defend their position domestically.

This chapter, which addresses the strategic policies of firms in relation to their foreign market servicing, highlights the attitudes and opinions of a group of British managers towards the Act. It focuses on a broad section of British companies across six industries: pharmaceuticals, scientific instruments, paint, glass, industrial gases and retail financial services. Within the latter sector, banks, building societies and insurance companies are dealt with separately because of the different regulations and industry structures pertaining to each group. Firstly, it presents an assessment of industry specific factors and emergent strategies which have characterized the industries to date. This is followed by a discussion of how managers from our sample of firms view the likely impact of the 1992 Act on their industry, and the implications of such changes on market servicing in the different industry sectors. We can thus highlight factors which affect switches between different modes of foreign market servicing and within alternative servicing strategies.

From this industry level approach, we go on to make a firm-specific assessment of strategic approaches to a single European market which can be expected by British companies. From this, some of the important opportunities and threats facing British firms in the wake of 1992 are discussed.

Finally, the chapter looks at some of the wider implications of the Single European Market Act, presenting some managers' speculations on how the Act will affect global business activities both in and out of Europe.

6.2 The Character of Foreign Market Servicing to Date

6.2.1 Manufacturing

Pharmaceuticals Pharmaceuticals can be divided into two groups, branded pharmaceuticals, i.e., those products which are protected by patents, and generic pharmaceuticals, those products for which the patent has expired. National governments' drug approval and procurement practices have had a pervasive influence on the industry, tending to produce fragmented national markets and differential pricing levels. The customary policy of governments, the main purchasers of pharmaceuticals, to place their orders with indigenous producers, has encouraged international companies to invest in local plant. The need to recoup R&D costs over the short patent life remaining to firms once the long process of testing and registration has been completed (a process which is estimated to cut the life of the patent from 20 to eight years) determines the need for manufacturers to operate internationally, and also deters firms from licensing technology.

Once a drug goes 'off-patent', competition tends to shift towards a greater emphasis on efficient mass production achievable by the smaller firms due to their lower overheads resulting from the absence of expensive research and development commitments. Price competition in this sector, and governments' desire to moderate their spending on pharmaceuticals can allow foreign producers advantages over indigenous manufacturers. This, to some extent, negates the need for firms to manufacturer abroad.

Distribution channels of pharmaceuticals can be divided into two distinct types. Ethical pharmaceuticals (drugs used for clinical treatment of heart, respiratory, nervous system, etc., disorders – more frequently prescription medicines) are usually supplied direct to large buyers (for example, hospitals). Other prescription and over the counter (OTC) drugs (for treatment of minor ailments such as headaches, coughs and colds) are supplied through wholesaler and retailer networks.

Scientific instruments 'Scientific Instruments' covers a broad spectrum of product categories ranging from high-technology products such as sophisticated thermoanalysis equipment down to low-technology items such as pipettes and glass beakers. Market servicing strategies are therefore diverse, although some generalizations are possible.

The market is highly fragmented, and because of the diverse nature of products, lack of synergy between various ranges tends to limit firms to specific markets or market niches. As the UK market in many of these sectors is too small to make solely domestic operations economically viable, firms have been compelled to operate on an international scale. The limited resources of many firms has meant that European markets have been penetrated through exporting. At the low technology, commodity, end of the market, competition is driven by price. Firms are thus concerned with generating scale economies in domestic production, and exporting through the most cost-effective channel available – wholesalers/distributors – to reach what are geographically highly dispersed markets. At the other end of the scale 'big-ticket' technically sophisticated products, of which only a handful may be sold each year, are generally exported direct to end users. Such products can bear the cost of exporting arising from the high level of value-added. For these products, specialist sales and service support may be necessary and thus many firms operating in these sectors have established sales/marketing offices abroad. In the area of medium-technology products, where both wide geographical distribution and specialist sales/servicing skills are required, the establishing of sales/

marketing offices or the employment of specialist agents in conjunction with indigenous wholesalers/distributors is often the mode of market servicing employed.

British scientific instrument manufacturers are skewed more towards the low-technology end of the market, which explains to some extent the lack of overseas investment. Those operating in more technologically sophisticated sectors are beginning to appreciate the importance of sales/marketing offices in the successful penetration of overseas markets, although for many, resource limitations or the short-term profit constraints within which they are bound, prevent them from implementing such strategies.

Consumer paints Local production of paint has been the predominant form of foreign market servicing rather than exporting because of the high transportation costs. The setting up of manufacturing operations was dependent on extensive market penetration to generate a critical mass of production which was achievable by few. Consequently, the market players became entrenched domestically. Today, however, paint has emerged as a more sophisticated quality product backed by large advertising budgets. As this change took place, successful firms were those which were able to invest in research and development and advertising, which resulted in a concentration of the industry. For example, in the UK, there were 250 manufacturers twenty years ago, whereas today there are only four major players.

With this increase in added value, it has become possible to export paint profitably, and to establish overseas manufacturing facilities and therefore the industry is becoming more globalised. However, the long-term effects of strong indigenous manufacturing in foreign markets means that they are difficult to penetrate successfully when operating at arms length. Consequently, even when selling through independent wholesalers/distributors, manufacturers see the need to have their own agents 'on the ground' in foreign locations.

The well-developed retail distribution network in DIY outlets in the UK is considered to offer British manufacturers advantages over their European counterparts who lack experience in dealing through such outlets as the 'DIY supermarket' a retailing approach which is in its infancy in many European countries – particularly France. This trend in consumer behaviour also has implications for low-cost, non-advertising 'own-label' specialists, who have the potential ability to take Europe by storm as DIY purchasing of 'own-label' products begins to emerge as an important sector.

Flat glass Flat glass is used predominantly in the building and construction industries for glazing into house, factory and office windows, doors, roofs and more recently exterior 'walls'. Other applications include mirror manufacturer, picture framing, photographic plates and lenses and clock faces. In the period since 1945, with the expansion of the motor vehicles industry, a large demand for safety glass has developed for glazing into windscreens and rear and side windows.

Originally, exporting was the principal method of serving international markets, as the massive economies of scale demanded for competitiveness in glass manufacture meant that producers concentrated on developing efficient domestic manufacturing plants. In their search for more effective ways to penetrate international markets, leading global manufacturers looked to take-over opportunities and licensing to extend their operations. As a consequence, the industry developed a global character, with technology developed by multinationals being exploited in less economically developed countries. To some extent, however, the traditional market structure of dominant indigenous manufacturers still prevails in developed economies.

The revolutionary float glass process invented by Pilkington and protected by patent rights became a commercial reality in the early 1960s with the building of a new flat glass plant in the UK. As to the worldwide exploitation of the invention, two broad strategic options faced Pilkington (1) it could either license glass, or (2) it could itself invest in new float glass capacity abroad. In the event, the foreign investment option was rejected on both financial and strategic grounds. Financially, the development of the process had drained the then private, family-owned business of funds limiting capital for investment. Strategically, there was the likely reaction of local producers to the entry of Pilkington into their established markets bringing with it the threat of cut-throat competition and also the likelihood that the invention would be 'pirated' raising attendant 'policing' costs. The option of licensing, therefore, appeared to be far more appealing, while at the same time leaving Pilkington room for foreign investment initiatives at some future time as its finances improved.

Economies of scale on the whole dictate centralized production with physical distribution being undertaken to regionally dispersed customers through a network of independent and producer-owned warehousing facilities, or in the case of large users, direct drops. In some instances, centralized production can be combined with proximity to customers so as to capitalize on producer–buyer synergies.

Industrial gases   The industrial gases industry supplies a range of gases to a diverse spread of customers, including the steel, chemical, food, beverages, metallurgy, electronics and oil industries.

Industrial gases are difficult and expensive to transport and this has tended to produce local monopolies. Foreign direct investment by the main international companies, together with more 'portable' technologies has increased competition in the industry, but the logistics of gas distribution and established contractual practices mitigate against widespread competitive encroachment. Many high volume users of oxygen and nitrogen are tied to manufacturers by pipelines running to on-site air separation units, operations running for specified contractual periods of 10–15 years. Lower volume users are supplied by merchants who again work through contracts of 3–5 years. Competition, which occurs largely on the boundaries of a merchant plant's economic radius of supply, tends to be more intensive than in the tonnage market, reflecting the shorter duration of contracts and the greater variability of demand both in terms of existing volumes and new customers. Very small volumes of gas, particularly speciality gases, are supplied in cylinders, customers contracting to take supplies on a rental basis. There is a small export trade in this market.

6.2.2   Retail financial services

Banks   De-regulation of financial markets in the UK has had two important effects for UK banks:

1   The opening up of markets has led to intense competition which has forced banks to pursue a path of innovation and diversification. Consequently,
2   There has been a blurring of traditional boundaries between banks, building societies and insurance companies, as banks have extended their operations beyond traditional banking activities – current accounts, deposit accounts, unsecured loans and more recently credit cards – into mortgage and insurance markets and high net-worth banking activities targeted at affluent customers. The result is that banks today may be regarded as financial supermarkets rather than providers of a restricted selection of financial services; This has led to linkages being formed between banks and insurance companies, wherein the banks benefit from the economies of scope accruing from offering a wide range of financial products within their branches, and the insurance companies gain access to well-developed distribution networks and customer bases of the extensive banking branch networks.

The banking market in the UK is considered by many observers to be highly saturated. This is partly as a result of it being the most open market in Europe which has resulted in a high level of penetration by foreign institutions, and partly due to the intense competition resulting from deregulation. In retail banking activities, this places a lot of emphasis on the development of extensive branch networks and a strong brand image, which can only be developed over a long period of time. The existing European coverage of UK banks is not well developed.

Initially, one of the major motivational factors for banks to establish branches and subsidiaries abroad was following UK multinational enterprises into overseas markets. Thus, the direction of much of the outward investment by banks tended to be Commonwealth countries and other English speaking nations, notably the USA. European expansion of this sort was limited, and that which did take place concentrated on corporate, not retail customers, although some retail services were offered to expatriate managers of the multinational enterprises. Although the intention was not to develop international retail networks, the establishing of branches and subsidiaries has given these institutions a presence in certain markets from which it is possible to develop retail activities.

Building societies   The building society sector has been similarly affected by de-regulation of financial markets. In the face of increased competition, the societies have extended their activities to include current accounts, credit cards, and unsecured loans. Furthermore, in response to the threat to their mortgage business posed by the banks, they have extended into estate-agency business and associated services in order to tie customers into their business at an early stage in the house purchase process. This form of backward integration has not always proved profitable, and although some firms fear that such development has resulted in a drain on resources, others are keen to maintain the momentum of the strategy, in the opinion that such ties are an important way of securing sales in the increasingly competitive mortgage market. Associated services such as removals, transit insurance and property insurance have also been explored and developed by some institutions keen to cross-sell services to 'captive' house buyers. Stemming from this, there is also evidence that some building societies are aware of the natural synergies between housing finance and insurance, and the establishing of ties between insurance companies and building societies has become a feature of the financial service industry. For some building societies this has meant the establishing of partnerships with life companies, whereby the life company provides the know-how and administration for the insurance contract, the banks the distribution network and investment; for others it has meant becoming representatives of life companies whereby the life company is responsible for the marketing by the building society and the staff involved.

The building society industry, until very recently, has expressed a continuing commitment to mutuality, wherein the societies are owned by their savers and borrowers and not by outside shareholders. Abbey National, however, in an attempt to provide itself with a strong foothold for European development, broke the mould by floating its shares on the stock market. It argued that in order to compete on equal terms with the rest of the market and offer customers a full range of financial services on a large scale, it was necessary to raise money in this fashion.

It is only the very largest societies who have the means to offer a diverse services portfolio. The medium-sized and small mutual firms are likely to find it hard competing in the open market with equity based institutions. Thus, many medium size and small players are concentrating on a small number of services or are opting to remain niche players in the mortgage market. Whether or not other societies will follow Abbey National's lead and covert to public limited company (plc) status is debatable. Their ability to survive as independent institutions after the five-year protection from takeover after conversion means that conversion may merely indicate an acceptance of takeover after the five-year period is up.

Unlike banks, building societies have only recently been given permission to sell financial services in Europe. Consequently many are at an early stage of development, in the throes of considering possible options rather than actually implementing strategies.

Insurance companies   Until the 1986 Financial Services Act, the UK insurance market was a relatively open sector, with considerably less regulation than other markets in Continental Europe. For many years, therefore, British insurance firms were exposed to intense competition in their domestic market, which resulted in their becoming relatively efficient. However, since the 1986 Financial Services Act, much time and management attention has been directed towards complying with the new legislation. A major upheaval was brought about by the polarization requirement which dictated that intermediaries marketing life-assurance products had to become either completely independent, dealing with the whole of the market rather than a selection of suppliers, or become a representative of a single life company. For the smaller life companies who were heavily reliant on independent intermediaries, their traditional channel of distribution came under threat as many intermediaries became sole agents for the larger firms. Therefore, it became necessary to develop their distribution outlets to secure their new business. As consumers showed little concern regarding the status of the representative they dealt with, the possibility of setting up in-house specialist life-insurance divisions became a reality for the banks. Barclays and Lloyds therefore set up from scratch a life-insurance division, branch staff becoming representatives of the in-house life company. Midland, however, went into partnership with an established life-insurance company, Commercial Union, on the grounds that it takes time to set up the necessary administration system and product expertise to support such a business. Midland provides the retail network, Commercial Union the product expertise and administration systems. Other banks and building societies, aware of the potential scope economies to be earned from such a strategy have followed suit, resulting in a change in competitive focus in which access to the extensive distribution networks of the banks and building societies is an important way of securing business in the highly competitive marketplace. As a consequence, some analysts argue that these developments will lead to a demise of the highly fragmented life-insurance industry in the UK as the industry is taken over by the banks and building societies. This raises questions about the ability of mutual companies to survive in the long term. Restricted in their ability to raise capital outside of that which can be generated internally from their own resources, and as non-mutuals become subsumed in the banking sector and are thus potentially protected by the financial assets of the large retail houses, the ability of mutuals to actively compete with the new financial conglomerates is in doubt.

In 1973, freedom of establishment in any EC Member State was granted to European non-life insurance companies. This was followed in 1979 by a similar directive for life insurance. However, significant restrictions on cross-border business still remain. For example, Germany does not permit insurance firms from other countries to conduct business without establishing a branch or subsidiary. Although some UK insurers took advantage of these directives, the majority have not established significant business in Europe. For life companies, this is partly due to the highly fragmented nature of the UK life-assurance market, which means that many firms lack the resources to consider European expansion. More recently, the radical changes resulting from the Financial Services Act, have turned the attention of UK life companies away from European expansion. Furthermore, the introduction of personal pensions has consumed much management time and financial resources. As a result, UK life companies have little representation in Continental Europe and many have no operations at all. Conversely, although the non-life companies were less hard hit by the 1986 Financial Services Act, expansion abroad has principally been into Commonwealth countries and the USA, leaving many companies less well represented across the EC than many of their European counterparts.

6.3   The Impact of the Single European Market Act (1992)

6.3.1   Manufacturing

Pharmaceuticals   The aims of the 1992 directive in the field of pharmaceuticals are:

1   A community-wide application procedure for drug licensing
2   Harmonization of testing, licensing, packaging and pricing of drugs

3   Limited marketing of dangerous drugs
4   To open up publicly financed health authorities to contracts with
    non-national suppliers.

The details of how these will be achieved have not yet been settled
on by the European Commission, and talks are still in progress concerning the standards which are to be set in relation to testing, licensing
and pricing in particular.

The opinion of managers concerning these issues shows a general
consensus. The Community-wide application procedure for drug licensing
and the harmonization of testing and licensing is a long-awaited development. If it is achieved (and there is much scepticism about the
ability of licensing and drug testing authorities to come to an agreement
on the Community-wide standards to employ), it will reduce costs and
work loads. This should, to some extent, ease the difficulties of recouping
R&D costs over the short marketable patent lives of research intensive
pharmaceuticals (branded ethical medicines) by giving ease of access to
what may become the largest global market for pharmaceuticals.

Conversely, the plan to harmonize pricing in the Community is not
welcomed by British manufacturers. Traditionally, pricing levels set by
the British government have been favourable to manufacturers in the
branded ethical pharmaceutical sector, recognizing the need for producers to earn continual profits for reinvestment in R&D. Other governments have not been so understanding. As they have been faced
with increasing costs of healthcare, due to demographic changes, the
legislation they have imposed to control the cost of pharmaceuticals has
become a threat to firms doing business abroad. Following 1992, these
controls, it is feared, will affect all member-state manufacturers, as the
price harmonization will be based on the 'lowest common denominator'
of all members.

The effects will also be marked for generic drug manufacturers.
Currently, the margins to be earned in the generics sector are considerably higher in Continental Europe than they are in the UK. For example,
in Germany, UK manufacturers currently have an advantage over indigenous manufacturers for whereas in the UK generic drugs retail at
around 20 per cent of the brand-leader price, in Germany they retail at
between 70–80 per cent of that price. With price standardization based
on the UK margin, British firms operating in Europe will lose this
advantage. Furthermore, heavy competition in the UK generic drugs
market has resulted in price-cutting strategies which have cut margins
to an even greater extent in the domestic market. This has had knock-
on effects in terms of the reimbursement drug tariff, which is also on a
downward spiral. This lowering of margins has reduced profits (despite
increased scale economies and improved manufacturing efficiency), which

has reduced the capital available for overseas investment in the run up to 1992.

The attainment of product and pack standardization post 1992 was considered by all managers as unlikely. For example, the need for special warnings on the packs of some pharmaceutical products in certain countries such as France, the colouring and flavours, the information required, the form in which the drugs are presented (capsule or tablet, liquid or solid, etc.) and the size of prescription doses (the number of tablets sold in each pack, or the weight of pack) vary from country to country depending on consumer tastes developed over a long period of time. Such adaptation requirements are not considered likely to alter post 1992, as they are entrenched in consumers' attitudes in the various member states.

Access to contracts of foreign publicly-financed health authorities has already been achieved by many multinational companies who have invested in manufacturing facilities or sales/marketing facilities abroad. For these manufacturers, this therefore provides no advantage. Indeed, due to the new pricing structure after 1992, British manufacturers, having lost their differential advantage, may find it difficult to set competitive prices when bidding for contracts.

Absent from the 1992 recommendations are issues related to distribution, marketing and selling, which are also currently controlled by government regulations. British managers believe that such controls will not change in the wake of 1992. As with product standardization, adaptation of strategies to individual markets in the Community will continue to be important. The idea that Community-wide strategies can be implemented after the 1992 Act is conceived as an affectation brought on by cultural ignorance. There was no suggestion made that firms could retrench to centralized production in the UK and exploit increased scale economies in a wider market. Conversely, increased investment abroad is considered by all firms as an important way ahead in the future; production investment to cater for the different tastes of consumers in different member states, and sales marketing investment to better understand the needs and requirements of health authorities, drug distributors and retail outlets in the various markets. There was some suggestion, however, that 'regionally' sited manufacturing plants could serve more than one market, in order that market proximity and economies of scale may be optimized.

Scientific instruments   The Single European Market Act plans to implement the following changes in all manufacturing sectors:

1   Harmonization of technical standards and specifications
2   Reduction of restrictive public procurement
3   Approximation of VAT
4   Freer access to the Communities' markets.

On the first point, the advantages expected to be offered to manufacturers in the wake of 1992 are greater scale economies in both manufacturing and R&D. The general consensus of managers in the scientific instrument industry is that such benefits are overstated. At the commodity end of the scale, products are already standardized to a large extent and thus there will be little change in this business post-1992. At the other end of the scale, big-ticket items are often customized for individual clients and this will necessarily continue. In the 'mid-tech' range, standardization may potentially have the greatest impact, although here too, there are many 'global' products already in production. Furthermore, where laboratories require equipment compatible with that already in use, the scope of standardization may be dulled. Overall, however, the unification of test standards/electrical safety standards will undoubtedly make international trade in Europe easier to manage, reducing costs and man-hours involved in paperwork.

Experience in product standardization in the industry has revealed certain problems which the Act which, it is suggested, will not diminish. In conjunction with extending scale economies in manufacturing by standardizing products, firms have also sought to maximize scale economies in promotion by standardizing brand names and advertising. The cultural and language difficulties they encounter are sometimes difficult to overcome. Journals in instrument engineering are, for the most part, international. This makes targeting of advertising difficult. What is appealing to the British often does not have the same impact on other nations. This will not change after the establishing of a Single European market, as preferences and perceptions of different national markets cannot be standardized.

Cultural and business practice differences between member states also extend to distribution and customers in the different markets. For instance, the French market differs from the UK market in the type of research laboratories. The health-care laboratories in France require different products to the Department of Health in the UK, as they are smaller scale private commercial concerns. Such established practices cannot be assumed away with Community-wide policies. As a result, the way to compete successfully in Europe is perceived by all manufacturers as operating through a wholly-owned sales/marketing subsidiary which combines central control and closeness to the customer. This allows adaption to the specific needs of the market and high levels of after-sales support and servicing, which is particularly important with technically complex products. They need to offer credible servicing benefits, which requires training of technical staff and engineers, an operation which is perceived as more effectively internalized. For many UK manufacturers, this will require a reassessment of approach. Short-term profits will necessarily be sacrificed for long-term gains. Certain firms are beginning to take steps in this direction. In the run up to 1992, they have seen the need to strengthen their European production and have begun employing linguists, establishing sales/marketing offices or employing specialist agents, aware of the importance to sustain or develop their operations in the community to gain access to public procurement contracts and protect themselves from the potential threats of increased competition.

At the commodity end of the market the need for investment is less marked, and exporting through widely dispersed distributors is still perceived to be the optimum way of selling large volumes to a widely dispersed target market. There is a trend, however, towards international distributors demanding higher levels of service. Tight delivery schedules are vital, as are immediate technical support, monitoring of stock levels by the supplier, regular visits and high levels of product quality. Following such a strategy therefore requires careful management and control. It is not, as is sometimes believed, a strategy whereby all activities and responsibilities are passed on to an independent organization.

In general, the managers interviewed believe that the benefits of 1992 will be felt by those players already established in Europe by 1992. In the lead up to 1992 manufacturers have begun to consolidate their positions in Europe. Many of the largest firms are integrating forwards, tying up well-developed market networks throughout the Community. Market entry will become more difficult, and firms without a European presence by 1992 are considered to be disadvantaged.

Consumer paints   As consumer paints falls into the generic class of 'chemicals' the 1992 directive which covers pharmaceuticals and chemicals applies. Specifically:

1   Freer access to and passage through Europe
2   Harmonization of technical standards, packaging and pricing.

On the first issue, the effects of 1992 should bring advantages to all manufacturers in the Community. Currently, the major barriers of operating in Europe are the restrictions on trucking and cross borders. At present, market opportunities past a certain level of business have been closed to exporters, forcing the more serious international players into acquisition or greenfield manufacturing ventures in what are, in some cases, more expensive production locations. Post-1992, freer movement of products across borders and in unlimited quantities should provide firms with the opportunity to locate their manufacturing operations in a small number of production sites in low-cost areas from which they can economically serve more than one market. For multinational companies who currently operate in many member states this may mean a retrenching of activities into a small number of larger plants, which will add weight to their manufacturing cost-cutting strategies by increasing economies of scale. For smaller producers, who currently concentrate on exports to Europe, this will necessitate investment or take-over of a manufacturer in a centrally located European area. This will allow them to reduce their transport costs and more efficiently serve some of the outlying markets within the Community. How far this is an effect of lowering of barriers in 1992 as opposed to seeking more effective ways to penetrate Europe is questionable, particularly in the light of the comparability of production costs in certain EC countries, and the fact that raw materials are cheaper to transport than the final product.

Aside from production location issues, most managers feel that sales/marketing operations should be sited in all markets. The only way to create national brands is perceived to be a local operation run by local people. It enables firms to understand what product adaptations are necessary to meet the needs of local customers. Internalized stockholding facilities are also viewed as advantageous. A wholly-owned stockholding capability is believed to dispel the fears of host-market customers of the ability of foreign suppliers to meet delivery schedules. Regionally centred warehousing with large-scale economy advantages, may therefore become a feature of the market post 1992.

One of the effects of increased European expansion in the run up to 1992 on the paint industry is being felt through the global migration of some of their leading customers – DIY retailers. Their well-developed ties with these customers will enable them to extend their transnational customer base across Europe. This knock-on effect of internationalizing distribution should serve British manufacturers well as the UK DIY retail industry is more developed than in most EC markets and consequently is expected to develop extensively across Europe.

On the second issue, there is a divergence of opinion between the managers interviewed. Although the actual consistency of paint sold across Europe cannot be standardized, due to different building materials, different applications and climates, one opinion is that global branding and advertising is an important way ahead in the future. The major motivating factor behind pursuing this form of standardization is to achieve greater scale economies in promotion. Conversely, the opinion is that even in a Single Europe different brands should be tailored to the tastes of individual countries, and product ranges tailored accordingly. In terms of price harmonization, opinion is divided according to the form of market servicing currently pursued by firms. For firms with manufacturing facilities abroad, price standardization is expected to bring greater profits. For firms exporting to Europe, however, managers fear that the higher transport costs charged in Europe will become the standard, which will undermine the cost advantages accrued by using

British transporters, and outweigh the benefits of increased profits from the harmonized price of paint. This adds further weight to the importance of increased European production investment after 1992.

Glass   The manufacturing industry recommendations also apply to glass. However, in this sector the implications of 1992 on foreign market servicing are not perceived to be so great. Overall, an investment on the ground is considered to be a constant source of advantage providing favourable lead times on delivery. Closeness to the customer means levels of service should be high, and quality control is easier. This will not change in the wake of 1992. Increased centralization of production in regional locations does not emerge as a viable strategy due to the increased transport costs that this would incur. Regionally sited locations to serve more than one small market have already been established. Furthermore, the well-entrenched competition in particular markets, for instance St Gobain in France, precludes much competition in these countries, a factor which, it is believed, 1992 cannot overcome.

Product standardization, in terms of make-up, already exists. Conversely, user-applications differ widely across Europe due to differences in building materials, architectural design and climate. For instance, Norway and Denmark's building industry has set mandatory legislation to ensure all buildings are double glazed. In Finland, legislation demands triple glazing. These legislations will prevail after 1992 as they are not merely a cultural quirk, but are necessary measures in the face of the adverse climate.

Theoretically, it is believed that 1992 will put Europe into a position of power. However, the wider implications of such, particularly the reaction of the United States who, it is feared, will become protectionist in its international dealings, may have important implications on global business *per se* (see section 5). Another peripheral effect of 1992 is considered to be the greater exposure to European business practices, something which has already begun to play a part in their European dealings. Facing issues such as Worker Directors in Sweden has prompted a reassessment of business practices and greater awareness of business cultures prevailing in different national markets.

The high concentration of manufacturers in the glass industry and recent investment in more efficient production by all leading players has resulted in comparable costs and pricing across Europe. Consequently, price harmonization is not perceived to pose a threat to profitability.

Industrial gases   Industrial gases come under the heading of chemicals. As with glass, however, the effects of The Single European Market Act are not considered to be of significance. It is not possible to export in most product groups within the industry, production investment proximate to the target market being a necessary requisite of doing business in all markets. All global players have been compelled to take this course, and additionally develop extensive channels of distribution in all markets in order to compete. The pattern of trade will not, therefore, change as a consequence of the 1992 Act.

The market is changing, however, as heavy industry is declining and new user applications in light industry are being sought. Marketing is therefore becoming an increasingly important business function in the industry, firms being assisted in developing marketing strategies by their presence in geographical markets. Although this is not an effect of the forthcoming Single European Market, firms may experience knock-on effects of their new clients, particularly in the retail trade, globalizing their activities. Product adaptation is not a feature of the business, and therefore standardization will have no impact.

6.3.2 Retail financial services

There are four major directives concerned with the establishing of a single market in retail financial services:

1 Freer access to establish branches and sell services in other member states
2 Some harmonization of activities (for example, the form of public accounts, reserve ratios) and mutual recognition of home country control
3 The introduction of a single banking license
4 Reciprocity provisions by non-EC financial institutions operating in Europe.

Although freedom of establishment has been available to European financial service firms for some time, the ability to offer services across borders provides an important development in the international expansion of banks, building societies and insurance companies. In turn, this has important implications for the regulation of financial services across Europe. The decision to implement a policy of home country control is partly due to the difficulty of harmonizing standards across Member States, which have traditionally had very different regulatory regimes. Thus, supervision will be the responsibility of the country in which the head office of the organization is based. While a degree of harmonization of basic requirements will be established, the mutual recognition of standards set by each Member State demands a considerable degree of mutual trust and acceptance, if the system is to work successfully. Although in the short-term those companies operating out of less regulated markets may experience competitive advantages, in the longer term it is expected that these differences will be ironed out by increasing pressure to harmonize standards.

The single banking license is designed to allow banks to operate freely across Europe on the strength of their having their head office or a subsidiary in an EC Member State. This, therefore, applies to both European and non-European institutions. However, the Commission is keen to prevent non-EC banks who do not allow reciprocal access to their domestic markets from operating freely across Europe. Although some Member States, particularly the UK, are against this proposal on the grounds that such measures are protectionist and work against the idea of a free market economy, the Commission has asked some Member States to implement this provision ahead of time.

These Directives are expected to result in greater competition and thus greater market efficiency leading to lower prices and higher rates of growth. However, the costs of achieving these benefits should not be overlooked. As a result of 'non-tariff barriers', which are an important impediment to free trade, there are major hurdles which firms will need to overcome to take advantage of the new European market. Most notably, language barriers will require investment in language training, and cultural differences will require firms to invest in personnel with an understanding of other EC markets. Increased investment overseas, start-up and acquisition costs will also weigh heavily on the financial burden of firms expanding across Europe, which could impact on employment as firms pursue greater efficiency through rationalization of their workforce.

Banks Theoretically UK banks have a lot to gain from the single European market operating as they do out of a highly competitive market place, which has resulted in their being relatively efficient and at the forefront of the development towards maximizing returns from economies of scope. As much of their product range is covered by the single banking license, their scope for Europeanization is vast. Furthermore, the relative sophistication of UK products which has resulted from the highly de-regulated market environment in the UK gives firms a leading edge over new-product developments in European markets.

Following the implementation of the 1992 Directives, firms will be faced with six major strategic options for market entry and development of European business:

1   Greenfield establishment of subsidiaries in other Member States
2   Greenfield establishment of branches in other Member States
3   Takeover of firms in other Member States to convert to subsidiary status
4   Takeover of existing operations in other Member States under branch status

5   Joint ventures with either majority or minority stakes with firms in other Member States
6   Offering products to indigenous customers in other EC markets from a domestic base.

The first five of these options are currently available to European financial institutions, and thus the only major difference arising from the implementation of policies for the Single European Market will be freedom to offer financial services across borders. The question therefore arises, why, in the light of the apparent advantages possessed by UK banks, and the freedom of establishment which has already been granted to them, have banks been reluctant to establish pan-European networks before this time? The answer to this question lies partly in the nature of retail banking which, as has been noted, is critically dependent on an extensive branch network and brand image. As much of Europe is considered to be overbranched, the scope for greenfield establishment is limited due to the time it would take to build up a distribution network and customer base in the foreign market and the necessity of operating on thinner margins that their competitors in order to penetrate the market. Alternatively, acquisition strategies, whilst a possibility, would be expensive and require large good-will right-offs at a time when the banks have redressed the balance of their capital ratios to an acceptable level. Although this does not rule out establishing overseas branches and subsidiaries, it suggests that identification of niche sectors, or targeting of a small number of markets which are considered to be less developed in terms of branch and product coverage, notably Spain and Italy, is a more likely approach. This has characterized European expansion to date – banks already having established operations in niche sectors which offer profitable returns and future growth prospects.

In terms of cross-border trade, as has been suggested by Boddewyn, Halbrich and Perry's classification of services, not all products are tradeable across international boundaries, and thus cross border delivery is only possible in a small number of product areas which do not require direct interaction between producer and consumer. Trade in a restricted set of services which can be distributed by electronic means, via intermediaries, or through direct marketing techniques is likely. Within this ambit, credit cards may provide an important source of future growth for British banking institutions, for although the UK market for credit cards has reached a stage of maturity, it is relatively undeveloped in other Continental European markets, particularly Germany. However, underlying cultural attitudes towards credit may slow down the process of product acceptance, and require a considerable period of consumer education before substantial market penetration can be achieved. This may prove costly, although the long-term benefits which accrue could be substantial. Insurance may provide another area of opportunity as products can be issued and administered centrally and distributed through intermediaries. However, the highly competitive nature of insurance markets in many Member States and the ties being established between foreign insurers and banking institutions, which provides them with extensive distribution networks for the supply of insurance, may make this market equally difficult to penetrate for UK banks lacking foreign branch networks. For products which can be offered from a central location, firms will be able to take advantage of scale economies in central processing and production.

There are two critical factors implicit in the above discussion. Firstly, barriers to entry have less to do with regulations than with access to distribution networks. As retail banking services are traditionally sold through branch networks, the lack of distribution systems abroad mitigates against European expansion in many product areas. Secondly, although some product markets are less developed in certain EC countries than in the UK, the ability of British banks to exploit these products in other Member States depends upon the national or cultural preferences of foreign consumers. It is tempting to assume that the relative sophistication of UK banks' products automatically offers competitive advantages over and above their European competitors. But caution must be exercised when making these assumptions, and consideration taken of the needs and wants of consumers in different countries. In the short term, it is possible that such products are *too sophisticated* for the target market, wherein customers may show reluctance to purchase services which are so far removed from those with which they are familiar. This problem may particularly apply to firms offering service at arms-length. The lack of presence in the market limits their ability to establish themselves as a credible suppliers.

Joint ventures offer a possible mode of market servicing which would allow firms to minimize these difficulties, the host country partner providing the necessary distribution channel, established customer network and credibility in the market place, the UK producer the competitive product. Such an approach depends on the identification of an appropriate joint-venture partner. Whilst there are obvious benefits to be gained by both partners, this task is not as straightforward as it may first appear. With the underlying awareness that the Single European Market is likely to result in a degree of rationalization within the European banking sector, firms are likely to be wary of entering into ventures which could result in their being taken over by a stronger partner in the long-term. Furthermore, whilst UK products may be competitive in the short-term, financial service products are non-patentable and easy to replicate, and therefore the benefits offered to the foreign partner are short-lived. Therefore, it is likely that foreign partners will seek some form of reciprocal access into the UK banking market, which dramatically alters the stakes being considered.

With the increasing importance of electronic modes of financial service delivery, banks could potentially gain access to customers, not through the establishment of 'bricks and mortar' distribution systems, but through automatic teller machine (ATM) networks. Alternatively, gaining access to existing networks could be an important method of tapping into existing customer bases and informing customers of available products and services. Although many ATM networks in the UK are run independently, in other European countries, notably Germany and France, banks operate through shared networks. As a result, joint-venture agreements may be difficult to initiate, being dependent on acceptance by more than one institution. Furthermore, the sharing of networks restricts the freedom of institutions to innovate their services and the nature and scope of the ATM systems.

Building societies European mortgage markets are highly localized. The small degree of penetration of mortgage markets by institutions based in other Member States demonstrates the importance of specialized local systems and legislation, and cultural difference and preferences. As mortgages represent the largest loan and investment made by most individuals, it is not surprising that consumers are inclined to use a known and trusted indigenous institution. European expansion has also been restricted to date by the highly protectionist nature of many EC markets who are concerned with the impact on economic and monetary policy, and social and housing policy. Consequently it is likely that true freedom to sell services overseas may not be achievable given the desire of local authorities to impose their own regulations. Although there are apparent advantages for UK institutions willing to offer finance up to 100 per cent of valuation in markets which currently restrict the loan to valuation ratio at a much lower level, the opportunities may never be realized if country legislators can convince the European Commission that such provision would work against public interest in their country.

Currently, building societies are not permitted to set up branches in Europe, and thus they are limited to foreign subsidiary establishment for European expansion. However, there is little evidence of firms establishing, or considering the possibilities of establishing, greenfield operations or acquiring indigenous institutions. Whilst these strategies cannot be ruled out, it is unlikely that many of the mutual companies have the resources to invest such large amounts of capital in overseas operations. It is more likely that firms will identify profitable niche markets which are inadequately served by local institutions, or develop activities on a small scale in Member States where margins are high (for example, Spain), or where the market is highly fragmented or geographically restricted (for example, Germany). This may yield a number of small acquisitions or start-ups in certain less-developed locations or potentially profitable regions.

As with the banking sector, opportunities for expansion are restricted by the lack of distribution network and cultural barriers to product acceptance, and the most successful approach may be to develop joint ventures with indigenous firms who can provide a distribution network and customer base and help to ease cultural resistance. Although the same problems of securing joint-ventures with appropriate partners applies in the mortgage sector, due to the differences in funding mortgages across Member States, greater advantages may be offered to joint-venture partners whose funding is more restrictive and prevents product differentiation to the same degree as in the UK market.

Opportunities for providing services across borders in the short-term are limited in the mortgage sector, due to the tradition of offering mortgages through branch networks. Customers in most Member States are thus used to the 'personal element' in the supply of mortgages, and given the importance of the service within the household budget, offering mortgages from a domestic rather than local base is unlikely to earn consumer acceptance. In the longer-term, however, utilizing the services of financial advisers, estate agents and solicitors may provide UK institutions with possible modes of access into foreign markets as systems become more sophisticated with increased competition. It is also possible that the three stages of granting housing finance – origination, funding and administration – will be segregated and performed by different institutions. This kind of division is growing in evidence in the UK where some foreign firms have entered the market in funding only, relying on other institutions to supply the marketing and administration services. This fragmentation of functions may provide further access opportunities at a later date for UK building societies contemplating European expansion.

Insurance companies   Again, distribution is a key issue. Whilst UK companies may have advantages over their European competitors in terms of greater efficiency and more innovative products resulting from high levels of competition in the UK market, ultimately success will depend on their ability to generate substantial customer bases in other Member States. This can principally be achieved in five ways:

1   Establishing a sales force/agent network in the foreign market
2   Purchasing an insurance company invested with a sales force/agent network in the Member State
3   Utilizing the services of foreign intermediaries
4   Establishing joint ventures with overseas institutions (banks, mortgage companies, or retail outlets)
5   Direct marketing methods.

The differences between these options and those available to banks and building societies reflect the importance of the sales function in the provision of insurance and also the ability in the field of insurance services to distinguish between the sales function and the provision of the actual product which is embodied in the service contract.

Establishing a dedicated sales/agent network from scratch is both expensive and time consuming. In the face of stiff competition from indigenous organizations, particularly the banking organizations now offering insurance services through their branch networks, it may also be difficult to generate a substantial customer base. Alternatively, firms may opt to purchase existing companies with an established sales force or agency network. Whilst this may not be possible for some of the small UK life companies, this approach cannot be discounted for the larger institutions, particularly those operating in non-life mass risk markets less affected by the recent upheavals caused by the Financial Services Act. Independent intermediaries, whilst offering a well-dispersed market coverage, fail to provide the same dedicated effort on behalf of the company as is the case with agents and sales representatives who are controlled by the supplier, and this approach may limit the extent of market penetration.

The recent trend towards the development of links between insurance firms and banks, mortgage institutions and retail outlets with branch networks, opens up the possibility for foreign insurance companies to gain access to foreign markets by providing the necessary product know-how and administrative systems which the traditional banking, mortgage and retail organizations lack. However, local insurers may be better placed to develop links with indigenous companies due to their knowledge of the market, cultural understanding and the innate nationalistic tendencies of firms seeking protection from outside competition. The success of direct marketing options obviously depends on the accept-ance of such techniques in the various Member States.

Although there is great scope for insurance companies to take advant-age of the opportunities offered by cross-border delivery of insurance products, due to the tradeability of insurance contracts across national boundaries, the existing strategies of UK firms in Europe show a marked preference for acquisition and greenfield methods of market servicing. This is partly due to the protectionist nature of many EC countries, which hampers this kind of activity but also reflects the importance of controlling the sales effort, which is such an important part of securing insurance business. Coupled with this, the establishing of a dedicated company salesforce or agency network does not prevent the adminis-trative element of insurance provision being centralized in the domestic market, reflecting the combined nature of insurance products which include some location-bound elements (the sales function) and some goods-embodied elements (the contract). By combining activities in this way, it is possible for insurance companies to reap the benefits of scale economies in central administration and 'manufacture' in a way which location bound services cannot.

As the highly regulated markets, such as Germany, France and Italy come under new regulatory controls, the perceived threat to their domestic markets by competitors from less regulated markets may result in their seeking to protect their domestic market positions by grouping together to form larger international groups. In response, it may be necessary for UK institutions to follow suit, for although they may be more efficient as a result of their long history of operation in a competitive domestic environment, the size and resultant deep pocket advantages of the new groups, may place UK insurers under threat of takeover. Complacency at this stage by UK insurance companies may lead to their demise in the longer-term.

6.4 Strategic Approaches

6.4.1 Manufacturing

The preceeding section has revealed different implications of 1992 across five industry sectors and our major service sector. In terms of the traditional theory of foreign market servicing, that is, the decision to export to, license or invest in manufacturing in the host country, the Single European Market Act will have limited impact on manufacturing firms' approach to international dealings. Where the bulky nature of products, difficult handleability and high unit costs of exporting prevail, manufacturing abroad or licensing local manufacturers will continue to be the preferred strategy. Conversely, where high volumes are destined for widely dispersed geographical markets, and economies of scale in domestic production are important factors for success, firms will continue to pursue export strategies.

The only major changes in production location to emerge was the opportunity, in some industry sectors, to rationalize production to take advantage of greater scale economies in attractive, low-cost production locations which will be able to serve wider markets as a result of freer movement of goods across Europe. For those countries from which production will be withdrawn, sales/marketing operations will, however, remain. In other sectors, increasing internationalization of activities across Europe is to be expected in the future in order to by-pass higher costs of transportation, which 1992 is expected to bring, and achieve closeness to the customer. This goes against the notion that 1992 will enable firms to serve the whole of Europe from a domestic manufacturing base. The need to establish 'regional' manufacturing sites as central bases to serve more effectively European markets (for firms who currently export) and the need to maintain a certain level of European manufacturing (by firms currently operating through production investment in Europe) emerged from our research. The motivation for such approaches is the need to protect levels of European business or extend EC activities in order to defend operations domestically or across Europe in general.

The notion of developing activities which allow firms to be 'close to their customers' is perceived as an important factor for success across *all* the manufacturing industries we have researched. 'Closeness to the customer' has become a stock phrase in much of the international business literature. It is, however, an issue which is rarely analysed, and deserves some comment. In the context of our sample of firms, many managers noted problems of generating commitment among wholesalers/distributors, the need to adapt marketing strategies to cater for cultural differences in foreign markets and the need for rapid delivery to secure contracts, as factors influencing the establishment of some form of overseas presence. Sales/marketing operations were generally cited as the essential form of such a presence. Sales/marketing offices can perform several functions: stockholding, distribution, generating new customers, promotion and market research. Therefore, we may assume that firms view the internalization of certain, if not all, of these activities as accruing maximum benefits.

Thus, beyond the idea that 1992 will permit rationalization of production, the 'follow up' functions of stockholding sales, marketing, promotion and market research are continuing to internationalize through Europe. The lowering of physical barriers, therefore, whilst reducing time and costs of crossing borders, will not persuade firms to reduce their investments in the EC at this level.

The flow-back of market/customer information to the decision-making locus of the organization is essential, if the manufacturer is to tap most effectively and efficiently the opportunities available. This information provides a basis on which strategic decisions can be made. For example, who are the key decision makers in purchasing; how can we gain access to them; exactly what do they want in terms of product and service; what kind of promotion would appeal to them; what adaptations are required in our product and service offerings to meet their needs and expectations? The 1992 directives which are aimed at providing manufacturers with the opportunity of standardizing products and product strategies across Europe, in all of our targeted industry sectors is regarded as a fallacious opportunity. Consumer tastes, business practices and environments all differ between the member states and require adaptations of strategy and in some instances products in order to compete successfully. This is considered to be facilitated by internalizing operations and establishing foreign offices. The flows of the physical product may, therefore, be superseded by the flow of information in the level of importance perceived by managers.

Whatever form sales/marketing investments may take, the general consensus that such operations will be maintained by those firms who have already established them, and greater investment in this direction by firms without, is seen as an important part of operating in Europe post-1992. The words of one manager neatly describes the necessary approach:

> One of the major issues we are constantly confronted with is the need to reap the benefits of being a global manufacturer whilst maintaining our sensitivities to local markets.

Even where global branding and products are sought, adaptation of strategy to local markets is always considered as necessary, with or without 1992.

6.4.2 Retail financial services

Despite the stated aim of the Directives of the Single European Market to develop a 'level playing field' for financial services, there are problems of achieving such commonality as a result of the divergence of approach towards national monetary and housing policy between the twelve Member States. It is likely, therefore, that regulations will prevail past 1992 which will protect particular Member States. Notably, continuance of state aids, resistance of resource reallocation and a protectionist attitude to third country firms are likely to reduce the potential gains which would be achievable given a fully integrated market. Furthermore, the theoretical freedoms, whilst providing some opportunities for exploiting advantages in a wider European market, are constrained by the nature of financial service products and the structure of financial service markets. Whereas one of the conclusions drawn in the manufacturing sector was the need for firms to develop a local market presence in order to be close to their customers to facilitate adaptation to local market conditions and cultural differences, for many financial services, a market presence is a prerequisite of operating abroad. As the production and supply of many services takes place simultaneously, the ability to extract the sales and marketing element from the production process is not feasible, and thus full 'production investment' a necessary condition for foreign business. The exceptions to this relate to services which are embodied in tradeable goods which can be managed from a central location. These include products which can be sold by either company-employed representatives or independent intermediaries based in the market, through direct mail or electronic means. Insurance services and plastic cards are the most obvious services to which this applies, although it is likely that firms will experiment with selling other services in this way, particularly mortgages.

Compounding the difficulties of foreign establishment for location-bound services is the need in many financial service sectors to develop, or gain access to, a wide distribution network, which requires fragmented establishment of subsidiaries/branches or sales force/agent networks (or access to the same) across numerous regional centres. Due to the highly overbranched nature of much of northern Europe, and the difficulties of finding appropriate joint-venture partners, the ability for financial service firms to gain a pan-European coverage are severely limited. For those products which are tradeable across international borders, opportunities for market penetration may be restricted by cultural differences which impede acceptance of the innovative services characteristic of this sector.

The major similarity with the manufacturing sector is the importance of catering for cultural and business differences across the twelve Member States. This is particularly important for UK firms contemplating expansion across Europe, as the highly competitive nature of retail financial service markets in the UK has resulted in a sustained period of product innovation. Although seemingly offering UK producers competitive advantages, the products are at risk of being too sophisticated for markets which have for so long been highly regulated and in which product standardization and price competition is the norm. Consequently careful assessment of the needs and wants of indigenous consumers is an important requirement for firms assessing potential product opportunities.

Although the basic product requirements may be similar between different Member States (that is, life insurance, finance for house purchases, current bank accounts) the differences in the format and specific nature of the services delivered (for example, life-insurance packages which provide for longer female life expectancy and non-smokers, low start mortgage plans for young, upwardly mobile first-time buyers, and interest bearing bank accounts with fixed banking charges) should reflect the adaptations necessary to satisfy local market requirements. Sensitivity to local cultures and consumer preferences is necessary to gain access to markets and it is probable that firms will enter markets with products which are familiar, although in the longer-term it will be possible to educate consumers and offer more innovative services. The standardization of income differences is resulting in growth in particular markets, particularly insurance, which has increased potential opportunities particularly in those markets where increasing affluence of consumers means a great upsurge in demand for a wide variety of financial services. Although business practices and marketing systems currently differ widely between the Member States, it is possible that some convergence will take place in the future as firms seek to exploit all possible channels to gain access to highly competitive markets. It could be suggested that 1992 has merely rushed the process of international expansion, which would have taken place when competition in the delivery and marketing of financial services had resulted in an exploration of the systems utilized in other Member States, leading to a degree of similarity between the methods of marketing and distribution across the EC. The final motivation for international expansion suggested, the growing importance of communication and technology and the resultant scale economies to be earned, is only relevant for certain services in which the production of the service and its consumption can be separated.

The benefits of freedom of cross-border delivery are limited in financial services due to the location bound nature of many services, which makes establishment a prerequisite of selling abroad. Few financial firms are likely to pursue a strategy of pan-European expansion, and thus the degree to which competition will be stimulated and efficiency of markets promoted is constrained by the already highly competitive nature of many financial service markets. The greater freedom of firms to generate economies of scale and further promote efficiency is also limited to some extent by the restricted number of service groups which are tradeable across international boundaries. For location-bound services, the need for a local presence means the fragmentation of effort across numerous regional locations as opposed to the centralization of activities in large 'production' sites. This reduces the economies of scale benefits and resultant efficiencies available to many financial service firms. Greater efficiencies are, however, being achieved through the pursuit of scope economies as firms are exploiting the advantages of cross-selling within branch networks. This has resulted, in the UK at least, from the liberalization of financial markets, and although 1992 will further impact on this process, it has less to do with the Directives for the Single European Market than liberalization on a domestic scale. This further impinges on the importance of distribution networks in the supply of financial services and further promotes the idea that, unless a strategy of acquisition is chosen, which is often a preclusively expensive option, joint ventures will become the most widely exploited strategy for financial firms seeking to gain access to overseas distribution systems.

6.5   Wider Implications

The wider implications of 1992 mentioned by managers relate to three distinct areas: increased penetration of foreign firms in Europe, increases in take-over and merger activity and greater protectionist measures by the USA and Japan.

6.5.1   Increased market penetration from outside Europe

Firms who have establishments in the Community before 1992 will be free to take the opportunity of the Single Market of 320 million people. Hence, since the announcement of the Single European Market Act in 1982, there has been increased investment in the EC, particularly by Japanese firms. The motivation to invest for the Japanese has been provided by increased anti-dumping actions against exporters. Thus, investment in Europe is partly a result of their fears that entry into Europe will be difficult after 1992 and partly due to European legislation. The effects of this are twofold. Firstly, it should make a valuable contribution to employment, technology and manufacturing efficiency. Secondly, it will increase competition. The fear of British managers is that competition will be intensive and internal EC competitive battles will become more extreme. The suggestion that Japanese firms will lose their cost advantages when forced to perform a greater amount of value-adding activity in Europe is approached sceptically. Their business practices, particularly production management, coupled with plant technology make their encroachment on Europe a real threat. Their growing ability in technological research and their strengths in product development and marketing make even some of the small investments which exist today a potential threat of tomorrow. The attitude of several managers interviewed towards British marketing and product development which are considered to be areas of weakness act as confirmation. Indeed, one manager described British Marketers as: 'a bunch of willing amateurs'. This gives further weight to the importance of sales/ marketing offices across Europe if markets are to be protected against Japanese efficiency!

One manager from the manufacturing sector suggested that the best defence against Japanese encroachment is attack. Rather than solely concentrating their efforts in Europe for the marginal benefits which will ultimately be achieved, firms should be targeting their interests in the Pacific Basin. He proposed this is much more important than 'getting together in an incestuous huddle in Europe.'

When coupled with the opinion of a second manager, that increased competition in Europe will cause firms to 'cut each others' throats' in their efforts to survive, making non-EC firms stronger and more competitive, European concentration is perceived by some as damaging in the long-term.

For many British firms, however, available resources to launch this kind of attack cannot be generated. This results from the short-termism of the City which works against the desire of manufacturers to make long-term investments, and makes the climate for British manufacturing very unfavourable. Also at issue is the fact that academic research is being starved of funds and this limits the pool of resources on which technology-driven companies can draw. This is a particularly important issue for pharmaceutical companies, although it is not restricted to this sector. The quality and added value to 'GB Ltd' generated by investment is critical, but something which firms feel governing bodies often do not recognize.

It should be noted, that despite the theoretical opportunities offered by the Single European Market Directives for financial service firms, it is likely that many firms will take a defensive rather than proactive stance. Although the UK market has been open to competition for a long time, increased competition may be expected as 1992 catalyses a period of reassessment of European opportunities. In the banking sector, major threats will depend on acquisition of a leading financial service company as this is the only way in which a foreign firm can penetrate the highly saturated UK market. Thus, only leading European players (possibly one of the leading German banks) with extensive capital backing are expected to pose any real threat. Interest is therefore being shown in vulnerable UK banks (particularly those with exposure to Latin American markets) and building societies which now look more feasible takeover targets than ever before as a result of possible conversion to plc status.

Third country banks with branches in EC markets will not benefit from the single banking license as a result of the principle of home country supervisory control for head offices and subsidiaries. Approximately three quarters of non-EC institutions with activities in London operate through a branch, not a subsidiary, and therefore firms who wish to benefit from the single banking license may change their status in the run up to 1992. Japanese banks, despite their financial muscle, are not expected to become a major threat in the short-term, as a result of their preoccupation with de-regulation of their own financial markets, adaptation to which is taking up much of their time and management resources. Furthermore, their familiarity with Europe is relatively limited and it is likely that they will continue to pursue activities in the USA and Asia before they make a serious play for the European market.

The same restrictions on European expansion apply equally to Continental European firms as they do to UK-based building societies. The highly diverse nature of the European mortgage sector is likely to limit the extent to which firms penetrate other Member States. However, the most likely development is that large EC banks and financial service companies will take advantage of the growing fragmentation of the UK mortgage market, establishing links with institutions wherein they will provide funds to companies who are able to generate and administer mortgage services.

The growth in insurance business across the EC is likely to stimulate increased penetration into the European Community of non-EC insurers. Both US and Japanese firms are showing an interest in the possibilities of developing European operations, although the potential returns to be made will necessarily be weighed carefully against US and Pacific Rim market potential. As the selling of insurance depends heavily on well-developed distribution networks, it will be necessary for institutions to either establish networks or initiate cooperative ventures with European institutions. However, some suggestion that atypical channels of distribution are being considered may be assumed in the light of the recent acquisition by US and Japanese firms of stakes in insurance companies, banks and other non-insurance financial organizations.

6.5.2 Mergers and take-overs

The expectation of many managers is that 1992 will prove to be a catalyst for increased take-overs and mergers, despite new Community-wide policies to control more effectively such activities. This will result from many bids being made by companies seeking to grow in order to compete more effectively in global markets – specifically with Japanese and American giants. This has two potential implications for certain of our targeted firms in all sectors. Firstly, small independent firms may be absorbed into the big groups for the purpose of acquiring technology and absorbing competitors. For many firms this is a real threat they expect to face in the near future. The only way to protect oneself against this kind of threat is through counter-attack. This, however, is only a viable option for the major multinational firms with 'deep pocket' advantages, and even this can be difficult due to the short-termism of the City. Secondly, the knock-on effect of firms' growing through merger/take-over in terms of increased scale economies in production and research and development may, in certain sectors, result in firms capturing market share on price. This may force the smaller independents to cut their prices below that required to generate profits either forcing them out of the market, or making them more vulnerable to take-over/merger bids.

In the manufacturing sector forward integration by manufacturers into channel functions – wholesaling and retailing, is also expected to be a feature of increased merger/acquisition activity. This tying up of traditionally implemented routes to markets gives further emphasis to the need to establish company-owned channel activities. As more and more channel intermediaries become tied to manufacturers, access to the market may only be achievable for firms prepared to establish their own market networks. The fear of some manufacturers is that later take-over of some of the channels through which they currently operate, will have extremely damaging effects on their business, excluding them from channels, or increasing the cost of operating beyond levels of profitability. Some companies are developing their own networks before such adverse effects can damage their operations. For others, the preferred course is to 'wait and see'.

6.5.3 Protectionism

A common attitude to the Single European Market of businessmen and academics, both in and out of Europe, is that in the final analysis, the effect will be that of developing 'Fortress Europe'. The outcome of this, while 'protecting' European firms, is ultimately considered to be highly damaging. The principal effects of this kind of 'wall-building' are two-fold. Firstly, countries outside Europe are thought likely to become more protectionist. Thus, global business *per se* may become more difficult to manage.

Increased tariffs, tighter restrictions on take-over and investment and tighter control on overseas investment, particularly by the USA and Japan, pose a great threat to firms seeking a global balance in their business. For many companies, strong activities in all three major global markets (Europe, America and Japan) are necessary to generate the level of return for continual investment in R&D activities and scale economies. Restricted access outside Europe may distort the geographical balance of some firms, ultimately reducing their world market share by making it hard to tap global opportunities.

Secondly, protectionism is considered by many managers and theorists alike to stem the development of competitiveness. Countries with an 'open-door' policy are thought to be faced with extensive competition which results in them battling hard, producing a vigourous and dynamic economy. On the other hand, countries with stringent protectionist measures shelter their companies from competition and they consequently become in the words of one manager, 'fat and lazy' and uncompetitive globally. On a world scale, increased benefits offered in Europe by the 1992 Act may result in reduced opportunities elsewhere.

Only time will tell what the true impact on firms' global competition will be. However, it seems certain that leading multinational firms will be persuaded to lobby the European Commission if they feel that they are being 'pampered' in Europe to the detriment of global business elsewhere.

6.6 Conclusions

In conclusion, our findings suggest that the latter opinion of the Single European Market Act, cited in the introduction to this chapter, best describes the attitude of managers. That is, while providing easier access into Europe, 1992 emphasizes the need for British firms to better understand the political, historical, economic and consumer differences between the 12 member states.

This attitude is reflected in the proposed market servicing strategies of firms in the wake of 1992. The firms in our sample fall into three principal categories. Firstly, there are those firms who have widespread production facilities across Europe and who need to be close to the market because of the difficulties and expense of transporting their products. As proximity to the market in production and stockholding outweighs the advantages of increased scale economies in centralized production, no rationalization will be affected. Secondly, there are those firms for whom increased mobility will allow greater benefits to be achieved from rationalizing production in centralized 'regional' production sites, maintaining only a sales/marketing presence in certain countries where production formerly took place. Finally, there are those firms who are currently establishing centralized 'regional' production facilities to take advantage of increased mobility or who plan this strategy in the long-term when an extended consumer base has been established across Europe. General to all these firms is the need to establish or maintain some form of sales/marketing facility in all nations. This is due to the different cultures which dominate the various markets and the need to gather information to adapt marketing strategy and promotion to cater for different customers and different consumer tastes.

In the retail financial service sector, as retailing of products is as critical a function as administrative handlings, gaining access to distribution networks outweighs all other factors in planning for European expansion or strengthening market position. Foreign market servicing options are thus, for the most part, limited to those which provide access to an existing customer base. As much of Europe is overbranched, greenfield establishment is not deemed feasible by all but the small niche players. As 1992 has catalysed a high degree of interest in European expansion, many potential takeover targets are overpriced, concentrating management focus on joint ventures as the most preferred mode of market servicing. However, as the frenetic pace of expansion dies down, takeovers may, in the future re-emerge as an important strategic option for firms seeking to strengthen their European coverage.

Overall, it is proposed that while the lowering of physical barriers may have an important impact on European business, what are traditionally referred to as non-tariff barriers, that is, culture and specific business practices peculiar to different nations, will prevail, despite suggestions that 1992 will somehow eliminate them. Indeed, European countries wishing to protect themselves against greater competition within the EC may deliberately encourage such non-tariff barriers after 1992, becoming more nationalistic in their business practices. What is required is that British managers become more sensitive to European markets, exploiting their diversities rather than searching for commonalties which may prove ephemeral.

7

British and Foreign Firms Compared

7.1 Introduction

This chapter presents the findings from a series of interviews conducted with foreign firms. The main objective of this strand of research was to provide a 'yardstick' for analysis. Comparisons of competitiveness and foreign market servicing have, up until now, been made between UK firms and within UK firms on an historical basis (that is, before and after a particular foreign market servicing mode change). Whilst this has allowed us to identify particular factors within the various industry sectors which shape foreign market servicing decisions and competitiveness it is not possible to conclude whether these factors are specific to UK firms or whether they are applicable to all competitors in each industry sector. Given that one of the objectives of this research is to determine what British firms need to do to enhance their competitiveness, it is essential to isolate those factors which are peculiarly 'British' and which may, therefore, put British firms at an advantage or disadvantage *vis-à-vis* their major competitors.

By comparing the British findings with the comments of managers from firms across a broad array of foreign markets, some idea of universally applicable and UK specific factors within each sector can be adduced. Although the sample size in the four industries analysed in this chapter (pharmaceuticals, scientific instruments, industry champions and retail financial services) is relatively small, some tentative conclusions may be drawn.

The comparator firms are shown in table 7.1. Firms in manufacturing are taken from the UK firm's major competitors; those in retail financial services are European, as this is the major theatre of expansion for UK companies.

Table 7.1 Comparisons of competitiveness – firms by nationality and industry

Manufacturing	France	Germany	Japan	US	Total
Pharmaceuticals	1	1	2	–	4
Scientific Instruments	1	2	–	1	4
National Champions	1	–	–	–	1
Retail Financial Services					
Banks	–	2			2
Housing Finance	1	1			2
Insurance	1	–			1
Total	5	6	2	1	14

All of these firms are close competitors of at least one firm in the UK sample. Unfortunately, no competitors in paint could be included.

7.2   Competitiveness

The important measures of competitiveness used by UK managers in each industry sector were identified in chapter 3. This section builds on those findings, identifying the measures used by international competitor firms and comparing them with those for the UK sample. The intention is to reveal any differences which may be attributable to firms based in the UK.

7.2.1   Pharmaceuticals

The UK interviews revealed that the branded pharmaceutical industry is dependent on research-and-development investment through which future potential for sustained competitiveness can be created. However, as investment does not equate with successful marketable products, decisions on which avenues of research to pursue form an important arm of the management process within the sector. Given this picture, it is not surprising that securing profits (for future investment) is an important performance target. In addition, market share is also an important measure for some firms. Although this is specifically product-line based, it demonstrates how important an extensive coverage is in order to recoup the heavy costs of research and development. This factor is also reflected in the importance placed on global networks (particularly sales and marketing) highlighted by several firms.

Generally, the picture revealed by the foreign firms showed a very similar overall picture. Four pharmaceutical firms were interviewed, two from Japan, one from France and one from Germany.

Performance   The potential trade-off between profits and market share was revealed by the German and French firms. The German firm, market leader in its own domestic market, suggested that return on investment was a preferable measure to market share as the latter can be bought and is therefore not a true measure of long-term success. Consequently, they concentrate on achieving as good a return as possible on their investment. The French firm, reiterating these points, suggested that whilst in the short-term return on investment and profitability are more meaningful measures, in the longer-run they aim for market share and ranking in the market. In achieving both short- and long-run objectives, they are able to sustain profitable market shares. The Japanese firms, due to their domestic market orientation, are more concerned with domestic sales-force performance.

Potential   All firms agree that future potential rests on research and development. The German firm, whose prime objective is the advancement of science, have a clearly dedicated policy of research. However, they feel to some extent, that this can be disadvantageous leading to their being more research rather than market orientated. This has knock-on effects on the direction of their research for whereas those firms with a clear market focus constantly reassess their research areas, they concentrate for longer on specific fields. Whilst there are certain cumulative research advantages, what can be gained from any particular field is regarded as finite. Thus, continually looking down the same avenue is not thought to be the key to finding the answer. They believe that the pharmaceutical industry is all about finding new areas of research – big breakthroughs – which are frequently stimulated by the market. The French firm, whilst placing equal emphasis on having new innovative products hitting the market on a regular basis, also stress the importance of having a balanced portfolio. They are wary of the dangers of relying on single 'best-sellers', or a small range of successful products. Furthermore, they regard their French national origin as being an advantage and offering potential strength for the future. As the French government sets very low prices for pharmaceutical products, the margins to be earned are low (which in many senses is a disadvantage) as compared to other nations (for example: Italy 10–15 per cent higher, UK 20 per cent higher and Germany 50 per cent higher). As a result, the company has been forced to become more efficient and improve their overall productivity. Although in terms of profitability (and funds to invest in R&D) they have been at a disadvantage, they have overcome this problem through a joint venture with a leading research based German firm. As European markets become more competitive post-1992, they are confident they will be in a strong position to compete.

The Japanese firms, in the process of increasing their international coverage, believe this will only be possible if they have unique patented products to exploit on an international scale. In addition, they also placed emphasis on distribution networks through which to sell such products. Arguably, this is a reflection of the fact that the Japanese industry is in a much earlier stage of international development. The German firm indicated that advantages are changing. Until recently the major advantages were to be had through internationalizing – securing distribution networks on a global scale and entering markets at a critical time. More recently, when international players have secured global systems to diffuse their new technologies rapidly, the emphasis has tilted more towards the development of products rather than market coverage. It is possible that the findings from the Japanese firms reflect their earlier stage in an international development process. The German firm also stressed the advantages to be gained from being a world-wide organization with a substantial presence in most major markets which provides a substantial base of experience and expertise on which to draw.

Process   Management process indicators highlighted by the German firm reflect the importance of 'backing the right horse'. Although backing the right opportunities is often chance, recruiting people with the right experience is not and thus much of the success of pharmaceutical firms can be seen to rest on the experts which firms attract to their research laboratories. The French firm referred to their policy of rationalization and organizational restructuring which has facilitated communication on both a divisional and geographic basis, generating new product and research ideas as well as management responsiveness to the needs of individual markets.

7.2.2   Scientific instruments

Competitiveness in the scientific instrument industry is characterized by creating potential, through the development of quality products which fit technological requirements, in the pursuit of profitable market share. The process by which this is managed is based on flexibility and specialization to meet varying consumer needs and wants. Four international scientific instrument firms were interviewed, two German, one French and one American.

Performance   Product-line market share again emerges as an important factor. The French firm suggested that, as more and more firms internationalize and an increasing number of competitors now exist in each international market, it is important to measure market share in order to get some feeling of comparative success. The American firm, whilst mentioning market share, highlighted the problems of getting meaningful estimates in an industry which is highly fragmented and which is poorly served by industry-wide data. However, by adding up sales of their competitors they can get some idea of their standing in the markets they serve. Both German firms reiterate the importance of market share, being cited as a single performance measure by one and in conjunction with performance/price ratio by the other. In the latter case, the firm researches the market to establish levels of competition and then decides with their agents what market share is achievable at the desired price and the best way of getting there. Consequently, performance measures are clearly a highly integral part of their overall competitive strategy. Considerably less emphasis was placed on profitability, with only the American firm mentioning that it had any significance in their management of competitiveness. However, they indicated that it is hard to measure and is highly product specific. Detailed information at individual product levels is very hard to collect.

Potential   The French firm stressed technology and the strength of their sales force as being key elements in their competitive potential. As a result, much time and effort is placed on motivation of their agents and fostering good, long-term relationships. This is critical to their strategy of offering high levels of service. They quite candidly emphasized that their products are more expensive than many of their competitors', but believe that if a company has good salesmen then price becomes less crucial and service takes on much greater significance. Levels of service were also stressed by the American firm who also added specific product features, width of product range and marketing orientation as offering the greatest potential.

The two German companies also stressed the importance of product technology and the strength of their salesforce but placed greater importance on the advantages to be gained from having a sales marketing presence in major markets. This enables them to improve their visibility in the market and generate greater customer confidence (particularly over delivery dates). They are also able to improve the levels of service they offer. Advice and guidance is believed to maintain a close contact with customers and help promote customer loyalty. Their proximity to the market means they are better placed to see the demands of the market, which means that developing products for market requirements can be done more effectively and their international experience of cultures helps them to produce high quality goods for global markets.

Process   Fostering good relationships with intermediaries was stressed by the American and French firms because they hold the key to competitive performance for the firm. This not only requires good incentives being offered to agents and distributors, but also shared problem solving and new business development. The American firm also stressed its flexibility resulting from its private status and consequent lack of red-tape as facilitating its management process. The two German firms show management of their technology/marketing interface as the key management challenge affecting their competitiveness in the market.

The major barrier to achieving competitiveness in the market was relative size, which puts small firms at a financial disadvantage *vis-à-vis* major international rivals (particularly large American firms). There were accusations made that large rivals were establishing predatory pricing campaigns and attempts were being made by the larger organizations to foster a degree of rationalization within the industry. Given the highly fragmented nature of the global scientific-instrument industry, a degree of rationalization is almost inevitable. One of the German firms, in response to this threat, highlighted the importance of growing within their means and maintaining a strong financial base.

7.2.3 Industry champions

Market share on a global scale emerged as the key performance measure for UK firms, with continued technical improvement and marketing highlighted as potential measures and global balance of activities and strong international management networks as process indicators. Only one interview was conducted with a French firm who may equally be described as an industry champion in their own domestic market.

Performance   Return on investment and market share were cited as the only really meaningful measures. The first allows the firm to judge 'internal performance' and the other its 'external performance' *vis-à-vis* its competitors in the market.

Potential   The length of time they have been established in many international markets is considered to be an advantage as it enhances their understanding of the market and the 'rules' of being a player in a global oligopoly. They are also prepared to invest a lot of the money they make in R&D and new plants which helps to sustain their potential in terms of technology and market coverage.

Process   Good decisions regarding areas of investment – new technologies, and new plants – have helped to maintain a competitive buoyancy in existing markets and opened up new markets to the firm which has allowed them to become a major world player. This process is continuing and must continue, if the firm is to continue to compete successfully with global firms who are continually growing and developing new capabilities.

7.2.4 Retail financial services: banks

UK banks were identified as being rather more financial performance orientated than building societies and insurance companies and this was reflected in the measures they use to judge their competitiveness: return on capital and return on equity. In terms of potential, a wide range of measures were identified including product innovation, customer service, and focus. Two German banks were interviewed.

Performance Profitability, market share and securities were identified by both banks as the key measures of performance. Profitability and market share are relatively recent additions to regular performance assessment. In the past, like many other banks, they were principally motivated by money management performance. However, recent market developments (not least increased domestic competition and the threat of new entrants from other European countries) have emphasized the benefits of developing a marketing focus and this has raised the issue of market share and profitability targets. Like certain UK banks, the 'profitability of customer relationships', that is, maximizing the returns to be made from their customer base through cross-selling is becoming an important issue, not only raising income, but also helping to secure long-term relationships with customers and sustaining profitability in the long-term.

Potential A good image and good contacts with the German market were cited as providing potential advantages by one bank offering an extensive data base and knowledge of market opportunities. However, outside the domestic market advantages are considered to be limited. Overall, in retail banking, the home market is seen to provide the greatest opportunities in mainline operations and beyond that there are only niche opportunities. The other bank, dedicated to its policy of cross-selling, sees advantages emanating from its recent tie with a local insurance company. As a result of offering all products under one roof, they benefit from economies of scope which adds to their drive for greater efficiency, which also involves computerization and efficient use of staff.

In relation to the Japanese, one bank proposed that it has no advantages. Given the banks fear of Japanese encroachment on European markets they consider such analysis as critically important. Raising capital in Germany is at a rate 15 per cent higher than in Japan and Dai-ichi, one of Japan's leading banks, can handle the same volume of business with one third the number of staff as a result of their intensive cost management. With 1200 Japanese affiliates in Germany and with active financial institutions in London and Germany, they are considered to be one of the real threats of the future.

Process   In terms of management process, one bank is very methodical in its planning. This, partly by chance, meant that because they were very slow to develop strategies for less developed countries they did not lose much money as did many international banks. In this respect, they regard refusing to 'jump on the bandwaggon' as often paying dividends. Firms who always seek to be first and take dramatic steps without thorough planning are thought to be those most likely to get their fingers burnt in the long-run. The other bank views communication between the various divisions as being critical to developing an overall, dedicated company policy for future business. They see the existence of a future vision as vital to creating and sustaining more business.

7.2.5   Retail financial services: building societies

Profitability was viewed by British building societies as a key measure of competitive performance, efficiency of money management as providing future potential and, in terms of their management process, many firms felt they were disadvantaged as a result of their staff having no experience of European markets. A division of a French bank and a German Bausparkasse were interviewed, and although they are rather different types of organization to British building societies, as they serve the same final market (house buyers), they are the most ideally matched comparators.

Performance   The Bausparkasse judges performance by their total receipts and their stock of contracts (which is akin to market share). Similarly, the French bank is concerned with market share – for which they have clear targets (ultimately 5 per cent in all markets in which they operate). Profitability, which was the dominant measure for the UK firms, was mentioned by neither firm.

Potential   The Bausparkasse highlighted two principal advantages of Bausparkasse over other housing finance institutions. Firstly, they offer a fixed rate of interest, which allows house buyers to plan ahead and budget their finances more efficiently. Secondly, the interest rate offered on the savings balance of the Bausparkasse account is higher than other financial institutions (4.5 per cent as compared with 3 per cent in 1989). It is also a safe way of investing money and gives the advantage of a low-rate loan later. (Bausparkasse accounts involve the customer investing with the bank for a period of time before they are granted a loan for house purchase). In relation to other Bausparkasse, they offer customers a loan from the outset of the contractual arrangement without their having to deposit money through an investment account by way of bridging loans. This brings the firm closer in line with foreign housing finance firms and housing finance divisions of the major domestic banks, which have the additional advantage of an extensive distribution network.

Distribution networks were highlighted by both firms as offering potential. The German Bausparkasse, whilst lacking a well developed branch network (having only 50 branches) employs 1800 full-time agents acting solely on the company's behalf. The French bank sells through a series of market 'professionals': estate agents, builders and banks. The French firm also highlighted new-product and system development as keeping them ahead of the competition. Developing products to adapt to changing market needs and demands and searching for new funding possibilities and constantly searching for ways of cutting administration costs or finding different administrative frameworks, all help to keep the firm competitively buoyant.

Process   In the case of the German Bausparkasse, emphasis is placed on management of the agency networks, establishing and maintaining a good market coverage and ensuring that their agents are treated well – given sufficient market areas and remunerated adequately in order that they remain motivated and committed. For the French bank, experience and good staff are thought to be the real value of a company, indeed, the sole value. Ultimately, their aim is to have nobody from France in their foreign subsidiaries. Although at the outset it is important to have staff from the head office in the subsidiaries to 'transfer' the culture of the company, ultimately it is desirable to have staff who understand the market completely.

7.2.6   Retail financial services: insurance companies

Profitability again emerged as the key measure of competitiveness among British insurance companies with potential being adjudged through product innovation, the extent of geographic networks and efficient money management. Process indicators reveal a divergence of opinion between the benefits of centralized versus autonomous management systems. One French insurance company was interviewed.

Performance   The French firms revealed that performance is currently difficult to measure as the insurance market is in a state of flux. Numerous mergers and takeovers are making it very difficult to judge where the company stands in relation to its competition. Overall, however, they are pleased with their increasing turnover and, at present, this suffices as a measure of performance.

Potential   The French market is highly fragmented with approximately 450 players. The firm compared this with the Japanese market which is more than twice the size of the French market but where there are only approximately 20 companies. Therefore, one of the key success factors for them appeared to be identifying defensible niches. Furthermore, they have good relations with their agency network. The firm referred to the problems which mergers can cause with agents – either as a result of duplication of effort and overlapping 'patches', which result in internal competition, or redundancies which lead to discontent.

Process As many agents are being approached by foreign firms and there is a lot of 'picking up of business' (i.e., agents being approached to sell products they do not currently offer in their portfolio) maintaining good relations and providing good remunerative packages is clearly essential for future competitive success.

7.3 UK and International Competitors Compared

The prevailing effect of industry-specific influences on the competitive process means that there are few differences between the findings for UK firms and their international competitors. In most, if not all, instances, the differences arising between firms may potentially be explained in terms of company management nuances rather than country-specific differences. Perhaps a key area of interest is in the obstacles to improved competitiveness where the real issues of change and development lie. The notion of 'lack of British industry competitiveness' would seem to suggest that foreign firms have a much clearer view of their competitive process and the things they need to do to attain a level of competitiveness. However, our findings suggest that they are faced with similar problems. All pharmaceutical firms are subject to a degree of 'luck' – and all depend on out-bidding competitors for key scientists. Whilst UK firms are often accused of lacking marketing skills and being poor at commercializing their technological developments, a German firm candidly refers to this as being a key issue hampering the success of their organization.

Like their international counterparts, many UK firms have secured a strong international sales and marketing network to facilitate the rapid diffusion of new products on a global scale. In this respect it is the Japanese firms who are at a disadvantage as they have been slow to respond to the internationalization of the patented pharmaceutical industry sector, which, today, is clearly a global industry.

In the scientific instrument industry, the small size of certain organizations was highlighted as a barrier to future competitiveness as firms fear losing-out to the financial muscle of large international players, who can afford to become even larger by 'market spoiling tactics' such as predatory pricing and buying up new technology by taking over smaller organizations. Due to the highly fragmented nature of the industry, this threatens many companies in various markets. The natural response for some is to shore up their financial base in an attempt to protect

themselves from takeover. Others see future competitive success relying on their merging with other firms to extend their market coverage
both in terms of geography and product range. The four international
firms interviewed fall into the former group. Conversely, two UK firms
in our sample have, since the interviews were conducted, merged in
order to strengthen their product range and become potentially more
powerful.

Industry champions, simply by their very nature, are firms which have
reached a quasi-monopoly position in their domestic markets and a
powerful position in global terms. Very little variation exists between
the strategies they follow to achieve a strong competitive position.

Finally, retail financial service firms, seriously constrained in their
ability to secure a European coverage by the difficulties of accessing
distribution networks and firms across the various markets, still show a
strong domestic orientation to their business activities. Perhaps the
exception to this is insurance companies, who, through market-based
agents, can gain market coverage with greater ease than banks and
building societies. Here, future competitiveness will depend on managing
agent networks and developing relationships with market intermediaries.
There is no reason to believe that firms in one country will be better
placed to manage this kind of development than those based in others.

Overall, the only area in which British firms appear to differ from
their international counterparts is in the lack of 'patient money' in the
British economy, highlighted as an important barrier by UK firms. This
is partly reflected in the greater emphasis placed on profit by UK firms
across various sectors – notably, scientific instruments, building societies
and insurance companies – and partly due to its absence as a inhibiting
factor for other international organizations.

7.4   Foreign Market Servicing

This section sets out to highlight the factors influencing the foreign
market servicing decisions of the non-UK based firms interviewed. In so
doing, it is possible to highlight the industry-specific and host-country
specific factors shaping foreign market servicing decisions and thus isolate factors peculiar to UK firms.

7.4.1   The pharmaceutical industry

Generally, there are perceived benefits in having a market presence in
developed countries which are large enough to sustain a critical mass in
production or which can justify investment in sales/marketing. One

German firm suggests there is an incremental process to achieving such investment. Firstly, the company establishes agents. Next, they turn agents into sales/marketing subsidiaries to which they export. Then, when the market grows big enough they set up or buy manufacturing facilities in order to exploit market opportunities. Finally, if the operations expand to a substantial level then they set up research operations overseas in order to exploit international talent and expertise – accessing a wider pool of trained scientists and researchers. Whilst the French company also stressed the internal considerations leading to greater market commitment and ultimately investment, as markets for their products have grown, they also highlighted the importance of government regulations making it essential to produce in host markets in order to gain product licenses and gain access to local procurement contracts. Although, potentially, these determinants will disappear after 1992, making it easier to sell drugs across Europe, the regulations which will permit this are not yet in place. However, the French firm, like certain British firms, only conduct secondary manufacture overseas, producing all active ingredients domestically.

Both firms stressed the importance of local sales and marketing in gaining contracts and giving buyers confidence of delivery and service. Furthermore, it also allows them to understand foreign markets and their structure (particularly key buyers and buying practices), which helps to promote sales and customer relations.

Exporting, therefore, tends to be restricted to markets which are too small to justify a production presence. Licensing is a different issue. Both firms view licensing-in of technology as a way of making up for shortfalls in the product portfolio, allowing them to generate a wider product range and benefit from scope economies. Licensing-out on the other hand allows the firms to capitalize on advantages where the company cannot do so itself. The German firm stressed that the philosophy behind licensing is to corner expertise. However, as there is so much overlap in pharmaceuticals because many firms offer very similar products at the same time, it is very difficult to corner the market and isolate drugs which can be surrounded by patents. Consequently, the firm finds few opportunities where it can benefit from licenses and thus exploiting products through their own sales/marketing networks is a preferable solution.

The Japanese firms provide a rather different case. The firms are in a very early stage of international expansion and in order to develop their international activities rapidly they see the greatest opportunities emerging from joint ventures with international firms. This process is part of their learning about foreign markets as a first step to ultimately establishing their own operations. Until recently, products developed in Japan have been licensed to other international players as the Japanese firms have not had the ability to produce and market them internationally. However, as Japanese firms develop international networks it is likely that they will become an important competitive force in the future.

7.4.2 The scientific-instrument industry

The scientific instrument sector quite clearly demonstrates a market in which incremental expansion dominates. Generally, firms begin by exporting through market intermediaries. The crucial factor here is finding the right agent or distributor to handle the product, that is, one with a satisfactory market coverage and the ability to provide a good level of service. For many firms, securing more than one agent or distributor is necessary, as the width of their product range means that there are no single intermediaries capable of handling all products. Then, if the market becomes big enough, they establish a sales/marketing presence. The two German firms in the sample appear to have reached the investment stage faster than their other international counterparts, although they have not reached this stage in all markets. Indeed one firm, whilst seeing advantages of having a sales/marketing office in some markets, feels that in others good arrangements with agents who are prepared to deal exclusively with the company and who have the ability to provide the necessary service may prove just as satisfactory. Exclusivity overcomes the difficulty of trying to ensure commitment and motivation, and the lack of investment makes this the most cost-effective way to secure successful international market coverage. A similar attitude is evident with the French firm who views company-owned sales marketing as advantageous in some countries, although others may potentially be equally well served through foreign intermediaries.

Conversely, the US firm shows no interest in establishing sales/marketing operations. They do not consider it necessary to set up their own offices in foreign markets. Rather they see choosing distributors with good service and product line and a good reputation as being the key to gaining a strong market position.

7.4.3 Industry champions

The firm is already a well-established global firm with production operations in most developed world markets. Because the product is bulky and there are little advantages to be had by exporting, they need production facilities to make a serious impression in foreign markets. Generally, they only manufacture in large markets (based on the number of people and GNP/capita) as their business depends on achieving a critical mass in order to justify production investment and generate profits. In countries they know, that is, those which they consider to be 'culturally close' they are prepared to set up greenfield operations as the risks are perceived as being minimal. In others, they pursue takeovers, although they are conscious of setting up in markets close to Europe who may be inclined to export back to the European market and provide additional competition. However, they still see areas for expansion, particularly Eastern Europe and areas of Asia. Taking over large, well-established producers is considered to be less expensive than greenfield options and enables them to grow quickly. They only invest in their core business and are not looking to diversify further. Although they do license their technology in Japan (notably their production technology) this is generally considered to be a third best option as exporting is not cost effective and investment is not possible. Basically, it is a way of making money in a market which otherwise would be closed to them. In addition, it was also thought to be a way of keeping their foot in the door. Furthermore, joint ventures were ruled out as being too risky on the grounds that Japanese firms are financially powerful and consequently pose a long-term threat to the firm through their ability to mount a takeover bid.

7.4.4 Retail financial services: banks

It is worth stressing at the outset that neither German bank views major opportunities in expansion of retail financial services across Europe. Both banks suggested that although there are potential niche opportunities which they are exploring, they are principally concerned with expanding their domestic retail activities. Both highlighted cooperation with a foreign firm as a potential option for European expansion as it opens up established retail networks. However, neither firm is over-optimistic about the option. One firm believes securing a joint venture with the right partner is very difficult. Many potential partners have 'a don't come into my country' approach to cooperation, limiting the availability of options. Even if firms do offer reciprocal access, finding partners with synergistic advantages is becoming increasingly difficult as banks have, over the past few years, followed a course of diversification resulting in a lot of overlap between firms in the various sectors. Another potential option is the acquisition of a participatory stake in a foreign firm. One bank highlighted this as a potential option offering earnings and an exchange of staff which may provide an important learning experience. The option would also provide 'a toe in the water' – an operation in which they could potentially increase their stake if further commitment to the market were deemed desirable in the future.

Finally, both firms believe that acquisition of a majority shareholding is possibly the best way of expanding retail financial activities into foreign markets. In this way they can gain access to branch networks and also benefit from full control over the operation. However, in the short-term, as they lack experience of foreign markets, it is unlikely that they will take this course. A period of learning through minority shareholdings and joint ventures is more likely to dominate their explorations in the immediate future.

7.4.5 Retail financial services: housing finance providers

The German Bausparkasse views joint ventures as providing the best option for European expansion. Greenfield establishment is ruled out on the grounds of it being too expensive and impractical to try and establish a sales network of agents in a foreign market where they have no experience and understanding. For this they would rely totally on a foreign institution who could provide the distribution network necessary to exploit a lower interest rate product (which they believe they could offer in many markets). However, the problem they face is finding a partner who would provide reciprocal access. Like the German bank identified above, they believe that foreign firms are looking for a vehicle by which to enter the German market but are reluctant to provide access to their own distribution networks. The French firm also stresses the importance of joint ventures in providing relatively cheap access to established customer bases. However, they stress that they are looking for advantages and are not constrained by any one particular option. This is borne out by the fact that although they have established joint ventures with banks in Spain and Italy, in the UK they have bought a firm. The firm they bought was large enough to justify their existence and allowed their access to be more rapid than if they had set up on their own.

7.4.6 Retail financial services: insurance companies

The insurance company also views advantages from takeover as it provides an established sales network through which to sell their products. However, there are also options in the insurance sector to operate through market intermediaries, and thus, particularly at an early stage of expansion and exploration, committing financial resources to the market is not essential.

7.5   UK and Foreign Competitor Foreign Market Servicing Compared

Again, it is difficult to identify many differences between foreign market servicing options followed by UK firms and their international competitors. Factors characterizing the industries clearly determine availability of certain options and, generally, also the preferred choice for achieving the optimal mode of market servicing. The only apparent differences appear to exist in scientific instruments and retail financial services. In these sectors there appears to be a greater propensity to invest in foreign markets. In the scientific instrument industry, although firms clearly demonstrated their preference for establishing sales/ marketing subsidiaries, the realization of this strategy is, in many cases, severely constrained by the need to generate short-term profits. In addition, in the retail financial services sector, although the benefits of takeover were discussed by several firms, the high capital risk of such an option was feared unjustifiable given that the capital could have earned greater returns elsewhere. This reiterates the problem facing UK firms in their strategic planning as a result of the demands imposed on them by the City to continually show positive profitable performance. Although some managers interviewed suggested that this was merely an excuse made by firms whose performance was not satisfactory, there does appear to be a greater tendency for British firms to plan on shorter time horizons than their international counterparts. Whether or not this is an actual result of the demands placed on firms by the stock market is debatable. What is clear, however, is that many managers believe that they are constrained by the British stock market and this influences the pervading business culture in the UK, making planning short-term and dictating that profits should drive organizations rather than growth and expansion.

7.6   Expected Impact of the Single European Market Act

British legislators and managers have been accused of not doing enough in preparation for 1992. By comparing the comments of British managers to the Single European Market Act with those of European, Japanese and American competitors, some suggestions of whether or not Britain is lagging behind in its approach to 1992 can be made.

7.6.1 Pharmaceuticals

Like their British counterparts, European pharmaceutical firms wel-
come the proposed changes to drug registration and licensing across
Europe. By standardizing the licensing procedure, firms will be able to
make considerable cost savings through reducing the administrative
burden. The French pharmaceutical manufacturer see this as potentially
allowing them to close their manufacturing operations in small countries such as Portugal and Greece – and to export to these countries
from larger markets (Spain and Italy) in an attempt to maximize scale
economies. It is possible, then, that this directive will stimulate increased
company efficiency wherein companies will rationalize their production
into larger scale, centralized plants. This idea was not reiterated by the
German manufacturer, who rather believes that the Single Market will
continue to stimulate mergers and takeovers and promote rationalization within the industry. This will be catalyzed by the breaking down of
price barriers which, as a result of the different pricing structures which
currently operate in various European markets, will benefit some and
disadvantage others. Those firms which have operated in markets where
government-controlled prices have not been high, will, potentially, be
more prepared for tighter price competition after 1992. Alternatively,
those firms which have been cushioned from tight margins by their
governments, may find the lower prices hard to achieve competitively
and thus may become vulnerable to takeover. Thus, a degree of large
firm dominance is expected, further promoted by economies of scope.
However, this will not preclude small firms from being active – the
German manufacturer believing that niche firms will always have a place
in the pharmaceutical industry. Thus the expected future pattern is one
of industry polarization.

Neither firm believes that 1992 will stimulate an increased volume of
business as the size of Europe has already been realized in the pharmaceutical sector. Consequently, those firms which are concerned
with increasing their market share will be restricted to takeovers and
mergers to increase their ranking in Europe.

The Japanese Ministry of Health and Welfare has, in the 1980s had
two incompatible roles in the Japanese pharmaceutical market: to contain costs and to promote the growth of the industry. In achieving the
first they have followed a rigourous period of price controls on pharmaceuticals, severely restricting the margins to be earned by their domestic
firms and thus limiting funds for growth and expansion. The Japanese
firms are showing great interest in 1992 and the potential of the Single
European Market and they are interested to know whether or not the
Japanese government can respond to the challenges. They hope that

support will be given to allow them to make a serious attempt to penetrate Europe.

7.6.2 Scientific instruments

The Single European Market is not expected to have a great impact on the business of the French and two German firms. The fragmented nature of the industry, in which firms operate in specific product areas, which individual markets cannot support, has meant that many scientific instrument producers have operated on a pan-European, or indeed global, scale for some time. Generally, firms will continue to follow the policies they have already established. Increasing their sales and marketing commitment to markets which are currently served by intermediaries, in the case of the French firm and one German manufacturer, in order to benefit from the advantages of market proximity (particularly in terms of information gathering and service), and continued development of good relations with intermediaries in the case of the other German manufacturer, will continue to dominate. However, the French firm does fear that 1992 is persuading foreign competitors, particularly the American and Japanese, to enter the market. The result is price competition, which is spoiling the market for everyone, including the new entrants. However, as margins are squeezed it is the Japanese and American firms who are expected to suffer more as a result of their lack of knowledge of European markets. One of the German firms fears that Japan and America will become more protectionist, and in an effort to protect their position, large competitors will buy-up the small players, as gaining expertise through acquisition is far easier than developing it internally. In order to respond effectively to this kind of challenge, it is believed that European companies should move closer together as there are specific areas where they could combine their expertise and make themselves stronger. Generally, they fear that individual European companies do not compare well with large American and Japanese companies and thus joint programmes (although not necessarily involving joint ownership) may be the only lever available to them.

The American firm on the other hand sees the lowering of physical barriers as opening up opportunities for establishing centralized warehouse facilities in Europe from which rapid deliveries can be made. The firm has experienced problems in getting its distributors to hold adequate stock and by setting up a warehousing facility it could ensure adequate stock and also reduce its overall freight costs through economies in large-scale stockholding.

7.6.3 Industry champions

There is a fear that 1992 will make the Americans and Japanese more protectionist and more likely to activate a round of mergers and acquisitions as they attempt to get bigger to counteract the new competitive threat from Europe. Generally, increasing concentration of the industry is thought likely and ultimately it is expected that four to five players will remain in the industry. There is consequently a race to get bigger, stronger and more financially stable. For some, this is taking the form of mergers, although they are expecting an increased number of strategic alliances. However, as far as Europe is concerned, a lot depends on future merger policy. Currently, as a result of monopoly policies, firms are prevented from growing any bigger. However, American firms are not constrained in this way and therefore 1992 may ultimately disadvantage European oligopolistic players.

7.6.4 Retail financial services: banks

Generally, 1992 is not expected to have a great impact on the banks as opportunities for expansion of retail financial services are limited. Although Europeanization is not ruled out, firms are currently still in the process of getting an impression of the global scenario. But, quite clearly, along with looking for global opportunities (and possibly the potential for offering products across borders) protecting their domestic markets from possible foreign competition (particularly from American and Japanese firms) is taking priority.

What is potentially more important to the future of the banks is the liberalization of financial markets on a domestic scale. This has already begun in many markets and is prompting a period of mergers, takeovers and alliances, as firms are attempting to extend their product ranges and benefit from accessing the distribution networks of organizations offering synergistic products and services. Consequently a degree of rationalization is expected in the industry and many small players are expected to be absorbed in the major groups.

7.6.5 Retail financial services: housing finance providers

The German Bausparkasse stresses the point that despite the removal of physical, technical and fiscal barriers, the nature of housing finance markets will continue to differ between the 12 member states. The German system will continue to be unique and therefore the threat of penetration of the German market by overseas companies is considered to be small. They don't imagine that a foreign firm will attempt to set up a network of branches or a sales force, although liaison with foreign firms and cross shareholdings are possible. Like the banks, they view deregulation of financial markets as promoting greater change. While other Bausparkasse have linked with banks, because of the cross-selling opportunities this offers and the growing fear of several firms that if they don't cross sell they will lose customers to their competitors, this firm has decided to remain independent. They are confident that customers will continue to buy their housing finance from separate suppliers.

Alternatively, the French firm is taking a very proactive stance in the light of 1992. They are looking to become a Europe-wide company – hopefully with subsidiaries in the major European markets. Although they recognize that operating abroad will always be a problem, even with an integrated Europe, because of different cultures and nationalistic tendencies, and problems of funding in international currencies with respect to mortgage laws, they see the opportunities for extending their market coverage as clearly outweighing the problems. They also expect that many firms will follow a course of increased Europeanization, which will involve a lot of mergers, takeovers and joint ventures.

7.6.6 Retail financial services: insurance companies

The insurance company sees there being a degree of increased potential offered by the Single European Market Act because firms will be permitted to sell all kinds of insurance across borders without the need of a subsidiary. This, while opening up advantages abroad, will also raise the intensity of competition at home. Consequently, 1992 will involve weighing up the pros and cons of both offensive and defensive strategies. However, the firm sees more security in future expansion in new niches in which there is no head-to-head competition, as opposed to geographic expansion which involves entering unknown markets.

7.7   UK and International Attitudes to 1992 Compared

It is evident from this review of attitudes towards 1992 of the managers of non-UK firms that 1992 is not perceived as offering the wide degree of opportunities proposed by the European Commission and the various promotional publications associated with the Single Market. An apparent degree of scepticism exists about the new opportunities which the Single European Market Act is likely to promote. Pharmaceutical, scientific-instrument and industry champion sectors are already highly internationalized and European potential has, for the most part, been realized. Potentially more important than the generation of greater opportunities within Europe and the stimulation of European competition, is the encroachment of Japanese and American competitors on the European market as they attempt to secure a position within the 'fortress' which is being created, and their increased efforts to protect their domestic markets from increased competition from the, supposedly, more powerful European competition.

7.8 Conclusions

It should be noted that any conclusions drawn here rest on a very small number of cases. However, this is counterbalanced by the fact that the firms surveyed here are facing (as far as reasonably possible) the same international competitive environment as our UK sample. They are all identified directly as competitors by at least one UK firm. Consequently, differences which arise are due to national perception, not industry factors.

Perhaps the most striking conclusion is actually the similarity of views of this group of firms with those of the UK firms. This is particularly striking in view of some of the criticisms levelled at UK firms. Overall, the concept of competitiveness seems to be similar, if not identical, in many respects, to that held by the UK companies and although there are nuances in interpretation, a broadly similar conception of performance, potential and management process appears to be universal.

More surprising is the lack of marked differences in attitude to the Single European Market Act 1992 and its consequences. Attitudes to 1992 vary by *industry*, not significantly by *nationality* of ownership. An illustration of this finding occurs in the retail financial sector. British firms have consistently been criticized for their defensive attitude to the Single Market. In particular, their lack of positive aggressive strategies has been highlighted. Our examination of their French and German competitors shows exactly the same attitudes and stance. Our conclusion is that the appropriateness of a firm's competitive position can only be understood in relation to its industrial environment and in comparison to some other feasible strategy – as illustrated by that of a close competitor. Seen in this light, the caution castigated by some observers may be a rational (and virtually universal) position. A further aspect of 1992 is its differential perception by outsiders versus insiders. Whilst British, French and German companies are pondering whether 1992 really does represent an extension of the 'home' market, the Japanese and US firms in our sample are contemplating whether it means 'Fortress

Europe'. Both the Japanese pharmaceutical manufacturers and the US scientific instrument maker were keen to establish a stronger presence in Europe in order to avoid the disadvantages of trying to deal with the new Europe at arm's length. There is one important difference, however, which seems to divide the UK from other insiders and that is attitudes to rationalizing pan-European operations into a smaller number of larger units. This seems to underlie the attitudes of Continental European competitors. Perhaps the influence of the English channel prevents such an overall European view from permeating UK firms.

On the question of an overall coherent foreign market servicing strategy, again there do not appear to be radical differences in approach. It is tempting to take the view that 'it ain't what you do, its the way that you do it'. It may not be the precise form of market servicing strategy which influences the competitive success of a particular firm in a particular market but the way that the form of doing business is linked to the other elements of success, such as the right product at the right time in the right place. For all our firms, UK and foreign, the market servicing strategy is one important part of competitive success. What is disturbing from the UK point of view is the relative lack of attention to the needs of foreign markets and a more blinkered approach, often bordering on ethnocentrism, to foreign-market opportunities.

This leads to a point which can be made unequivocally. There does appear to be a difference in the time frame of planning between British firms and their foreign competitors. British firms seem to examine their international operations over a shorter time span than their competitors. There is a tendency to concentrate on short-term returns rather than long-term growth. Whether this is an internally imposed constraint or whether it can be blamed on that currently fashionable scapegoat, 'short termism', in the City financial institutions is a moot point. It is more than possible that the total funds available to British firms from the external capital market are more constrained than for their major competitors. Certainly, German and Japanese companies have access to capital on more favourable terms than do UK firms. (However, for the large international firms in our sample, these sources of funds are also in the main available.) So there may be an overall lack of 'patient money' for British firms, which may constrain their international expansion. It is also possible that the capital market exhibits a bias against foreign expansion versus domestic. This seems unlikely for large firms; it may be a minor constraint for smaller ones. What our investigation does show in a non-trivial number of cases is that UK firms exhibit a bias against international expansion in the allocation of funds from their internal capital markets. In other words, foreign projects appear less likely to obtain funding and backing then domestic ones. One excellent illustration of this is a medium-sized scientific instrument manufacturer which was driving its international division manager to distraction because his proposals for moving from agents to sales subsidiaries in key foreign markets were constantly turned down by the main board. To make the point even more starkly, this strategy was provoked by the decisions of his major German competitor (one of our sample of competitors) which was taking market share precisely because it had moved to a network of sales subsidiaries. He believed no projects in the firm could show such excellent projections of returns, yet he could not raise internal funding (and was not permitted to try to raise separate external funding).

This discussion leads on to a further important point. Many British managers see themselves as constrained by nationalistic attitudes at top management (often Board) level. The lack of understanding of foreign-market conditions and the necessity of adaptation to them is a serious constraint in several UK companies. In general, foreign projects are regarded as more risky and less manageable than appears to be the case in the foreign competitors. There is often considerable frustration amongst managers responsible for international operations (or particular foreign markets) at the lack of understanding of local conditions. This finding was particularly strong in three Japanese affiliates of our UK sample, who were separately interviewed.

Consequently, although general attitudes to competitiveness and market servicing and to 1992 are superficially similar, there do seem to be some peculiarly British constraints on achieving improved international competitiveness. These come through not in relation to particular foreign market servicing decisions, but in some constraints on international strategy (often attitudinal), which are reflected in foreign market servicing decisions.

8

Industry Study 1: The Global Pharmaceutical Industry

8.1 Introduction

The term 'pharmaceuticals' covers a wide spectrum of healthcare products ranging from drugs used in the clinical treatment of heart, respiratory and nervous-system disorders to items used to treat more minor ailments such as headaches, coughs and colds. 'Ethical' pharmaceuticals refers to the former category of drugs and forms the focus for this study.

Within the ethical pharmaceuticals sector, firms can be divided into two distinct groups: global firms specializing in research-intensive 'patented' drugs with a wide distribution network for their products, reflecting the significance of economies of scale and the vast sums of money required to undertake risky research and development; and firms who concentrate on 'off-patent' drugs, principally in their own national markets.

National governments' drug approval and procurement practices have had a pervasive influence on the industry, tending to produce fragmented national markets and differential pricing levels. The customary policy of governments, the main purchasers of ethical pharmaceuticals, to place the bulk of their orders with indigenous producers, has encouraged international companies to invest in local manufacturing plant or license local suppliers, rather than service these markets through exports. In consequence, international trade in drug products *overall* is on the low side (around 20 per cent of total world sales) but for some countries, including the UK, exports make an important contribution to foreign exchange earnings.

Competition in the industry is focused primarily on the search for new drugs. New products, protected by patent rights for 20 years can bring a substantial profit return if accepted on to governments' 'approved' drug lists. For the leading companies research and development intensity is high (R&D expenditures typically average 10–15 per cent of company turnover), with companies operating under a constant imperative to bring out a succession of new products to augment/replace ones whose patent protection has expired or which have been made obsolete by technical advances.

8.2 Structure of the Pharmaceutical Industry

8.2.1 Demand for pharmaceutical products

The demand for pharmaceutical products is fundamentally related to the incidence of ill health in the community at large and is affected by the comprehensiveness and sophistication of a country's health-care infrastructure, as well as various socio-economic factors such as per capita income, living standards, (including nutritional and hygiene levels), demographic trends (especially the proportion of the elderly in the total population) and the availability and price of drugs.

The pharmaceutical industry in most countries operates within a health-care system which is not funded directly by patients but by the state and/or private insurance companies. Within this framework 'authorized' medical practitioners (doctors, dentists, etc.) act as arbiters on behalf of patients, with drugs being prescribed as part of an in-house (hospital, etc.) course of treatment, or obtainable only on prescription 'over the counter' (OTC) from drug retailers such as pharmacists and clinics. Some ethical drugs, however, are obtainable 'over the counter' without prescription, as are those proprietary medicants (aspirin, cough syrups, etc.) used to treat common ailments.

The demand for ethical pharmaceutical products has grown rapidly since the launch of the celebrated antibiotic, penicillin, in the 1940s. In the 1970s, demand expanded at some 15 per cent per annum, but in the 1980s the growth of expenditure on drugs slowed down. This was due mainly to a retrenchment in government spending on health care and stricter controls over drug prices (see below). Nevertheless, world-wide sales of ethical pharmaceuticals topped over £80 billion in 1989.

Table 8.1 shows the relative size of the six leading national markets for pharmaceutical products: the USA, Japan, West Germany, France, Italy and the UK. Although their combined share of world pharmaceutical consumption has declined in the face of expansion elsewhere, these six still account for upwards of 74 per cent of world sales. The USA continues to remain the single most important market but the Japanese market has been the fastest growing, increasing its share of world sales to around 20 per cent of the total in 1989.

Table 8.1 Leading countries' share of world pharmaceutical consumption, 1960-89

Country	1960[1] (%)	1989[2] (%)
USA	45	29
Japan	7	20
W. Germany	17	8
France	7	7
Italy	5	7
UK	5	3
	(86)	(74)
Other	14	26

Source: [1] NEDO, Pharmaceuticals, EDC, *A New Focus on Pharmaceuticals*, 1986, HMSO.
   [2] Glaxo Holdings Plc, *Annual Report and Accounts 1990*.

8.2.2 Suppliers

One of the most important influences on the structure of the pharmaceutical industry is the increasing significance of economies of scale in production, marketing, and research and development. These favour the large companies and provide obstacles to new entrants. Economies of scale apply not only to reductions in unit costs but also in a broader way allowing companies to lessen the high risks associated with research and development and marketing in the research-based sector of the industry.

Global sales of pharmaceutical products are dominated by large multinational companies, mainly American and West European. Japanese companies primarily sell in their own market and have yet to make a major impact as multinational operators. Table 8.2 shows the top 25 companies by market share in 1988. The picture has somewhat changed recently following a spate of mergers and other alliances centred on the key US market.

Although multinational companies occupy an important position in the industry at large, the degree of seller concentration in the pharmaceutical industry is much lower than in many other industries, where the advantages of scale are similarly important. Merck, the leading company in 1989, accounted for only 4 per cent of total world sales and the top ten concerns combined accounted for some 26 per cent of the total. The pharmaceutical industry is characterized in most countries by an active fringe of smaller and medium-sized companies operating in niche segments as well as the 'off-patent' generic sectors (see below). In

Table 8.2 Ranking by market share, 1988

Company	Share (%)
Merck (US)	4.1
Ciba-Geigy (Switzerland)	2.9
Hoechst (WG)	2.8
Glaxo (UK)	2.6
Takeda (Japan)	2.4
American Home Products (US)	2.4
Pfizer (US)	2.3
Sandoz (Switzerland)	2.3
Eli Lilly (US)	2.3
Bristol-Myers (US)[1]	2.2
Smith Kline Beckman (US)[2]	2.1
Johnson and Johnson (US)	1.8
Rhone-Poulenc (France)	1.8
ICI (UK)	1.8
Boehringer (WG)	1.7
Sankyo (Japan)	1.6
American Cynamid (US)	1.4
Beecham (UK)[2]	1.4
Wellcome (UK)	1.2
Shionogi (Japan)	1.1
Dow (US)[3]	1.1
Fujisawa (Japan)	1.1
Sanofi (France)	1.1
Warner-Lambert (US)	1.0
Yamanouchi (Japan)	1.0

1989 [1] Bristol Myers merged with Squibb (US)
[2] Smith Kline Beckman merged with Beecham
[3] Dow merged with Marion Labs (US)
Source: BZW Research, 1989.

the UK for example, there were over 230 pharmaceutical producers in 1989. In some cases these companies are independent (Evans Medical, for example), while others are the subsidiaries of international companies (Cox UK, for example, is owned by the German concern Hoechst).

A particular feature of the research-based sector of the industry is the fact that even major companies tend to be dependent upon only a few products for a high percentage of their sales (see table 8.3). In these circumstances a company's market ranking is liable to be volatile unless an effective new-product development can be sustained over the longer-term. Geographical exposure too can affect a company's sales potential. Companies with a high European Community profile stand to suffer

Table 8.3 Top drugs of selected companies

Company	Top drug	1988 estimate top drug sales as % of group
Merck	Vasotec	12
Glaxo	Zantac	54
Hoechst	Claforan	15
Ciba–Geigy	Voltaren	20
Sandoz	Sandimmun	10
American Home	Ativan	9
Pfizer	Feldene	25

Source: Phillips and Drew, 1989

should there be a post-1992 averaging down of Community drug prices (see below).

8.2.3 Buyers

A significant feature of the industry in most countries is the concentration of buying power in the hands of the state through its provision of publicly-financed health-care facilities. In the UK, for example, the National Health Service purchased some £2 billion of drugs in 1989, accounting for around 90 per cent of total UK ethical drug sales. Such state controlled bureaucracies have in the past been criticized for being too price insensitive in their desire to obtain the most effective drugs or too acquiescent in their dealings with the drug companies (see the Monopolies Commission's (1973) condemnation of the overpricing of the tranquillizers, Librium and Valium, by the Swiss multinational Hoffman–Roche). More recently, governments' desire to moderate their spending on drugs has been reflected in the application of more stringent price controls and their support for 'generics' (see below).

Monopsonistic buying power has also affected the structure of the industry in one other important way. Given that patented ethical drugs are high value added products, this, combined with low unit production and distribution costs would indicate a centralization of production activity and a preference for exporting as a foreign market servicing strategy. However, while some countries are significant exporting centres for multinationals, most notably Switzerland, the US, Germany and the UK, foreign trade in pharmaceuticals remains on the low side accounting for around 20 per cent of total world consumption. In most countries, government procurement policies favour sourcing from indigenous

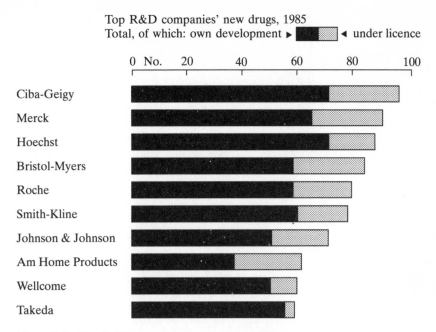

Figure 8.1 Top R&D companies' new drugs, 1985
Source: BZW, cited in *The Economist*, 7 February 1987.

suppliers and this has led foreign companies to establish local manufacturing subsidiaries and to a lesser extent the licensing of local producers. Historically, licensing arrangements have played an important part in the worldwide development of the industry. The initial spread of antibiotics in Europe in the late 1940s and 1950s was built on various licensing deals including Glaxo's rights to pencillan from Merck. Licensing continues to be a feature of the industry; for example, ICI has acquired the European rights to 'Apatet' (1985) from Yamonuchi (Japan) and 'Zestril' (1987) from Merck. Figure 8.1 indicates the relative importance of licensing for a number of the leading companies.

However, the shortening of effective patent lives is increasingly favouring self-manufacture by global producers as the most profitable way of exploiting major new drug innovations.

In the UK, the government operates a profit control system for drugs companies (see below) which explicitly favours locally based suppliers – generally speaking, the higher the volume of sales originating in the UK the higher the percentage return on capital that the company concerned is permitted to make. Companies with a large capital investment in the UK in terms of production and research facilities are also permitted higher prices. The system takes into account drug-development costs

Table 8.4 Top-ten selling drugs worldwide, 1988

World position		Brand name	Company	Therapeutic category
1	(1)*	Zantac	Glaxo	anti-ulcer
2	(2)	Tagamet	Smith Kline	anti-ulcer
3	(3)	Tenormin	ICI	betablocker
4	(4)	Capoten	Bristol Myers	ACE inhibitor
5	(5)	Vasotec	Merck	ACE inhibitor
6	(6)	Adalat	Bayer	calcium antagonist
7	(8)	Voltaren	Ciba-Geigy	NSAI
8	(9)	Feldene	Pfizer	NSAI
9	(10)	Ceclor	Eli Lilly	antibiotic
10	(7)	Naprosyn	Syntex	NSAI

* 1987 positions.
Source: Robert Fleming Securities, 1990

by allowing companies to spend set amounts on research before profit levels are worked out. In this way, as in many other countries, the UK positively discriminates in favour of local producers. While practices vary from country to country, it may well be that there is some 'covert' bias in procurement towards national producers as against foreign-owned subsidiaries, but this is not readily discernable. In the UK, foreign-owned subsidiaries supplied between 40–50 per cent of NHS purchases over the period 1960–88.

From a broader perspective, buy-local policies have tended to result in plant proliferation and over-capacity in the industry world-wide. The European Community's 1992 harmonization initiative will undoubtedly produce some rationalization and restructuring of the European market, although the European Commission (surprisingly) estimates a less than 1 per cent saving in production costs.

8.2.4 Competition

Competition in the industry is based primarily on the invention and marketing of patented drugs. Table 8.4 lists the ten top selling drugs in 1988. Intra-sector competition (for example, Glaxo's Zantac versus Smith Kline's Tagamet in the anti-ulcer sector) focuses mainly on the relative therapeutic properties of the drugs concerned, with companies seeking to stimulate prescription sales by obtaining practitioners' endorsement of their products. 'Aggressive' price competition in the patented drug sector is negligible, but in some countries low price 'off-patent' generics have become a powerful competitive force.

8.2.5 Distribution

Physical distribution systems in most countries follow a similar pattern. Large buyers of ethical pharmaceuticals (hospitals, etc.) are usually supplied direct by the manufacturers. Other prescription and 'over-the-counter' products are supplied through wholesaler and retailer networks, including specialist drug retailers (chemists and pharmacies) and supermarkets. In the UK, there are five major wholesaling groups (Barclays, McCarthys, Sangers, Unichem and Vestric) and several integrated wholesaling–retailing chains such as Boots and Woolworth's 'Super Drug'.

Occasionally, new manufacturers have encountered difficulties in obtaining effective distribution for their products. For example, DDSA, a small UK company which had taken out a licence to produce Chlordiazepoxide in competition with Roche's 'Librium' complained to the Monopolies Commission (1973) that Roche had 'discouraged' wholesalers from handling its version. For the most part, however, distributors are prepared to handle new drugs subject to normal trade terms and customer demand.

8.2.6 Restructuring

In the past the leading companies in the industry have grown largely by organic expansion rather than take-over and merger. This growth has been sustained by the development and marketing of new drugs on a world-wide basis, sold through overseas subsidiaries and to a lesser extent by exporting and licensing. Take-over activity remained relatively low key down to the late 1980s, although some companies had moved into the fast-growing generic sector for both defensive and offensive motives. For example, American Home Products took a controlling interest in Quantum Pharmics in 1986 while Baxter–Travenol acquired Ascot, a generics distributor. Other producers have taken a less sanguine view of competing in the low-price generics sector, with Glaxo, for example, divesting its Evans Medical arm. Other alliances have included the acquisition of Key Pharmaceuticals by Schering–Plough in the US, the take-over of the UK concern Searle by the US chemical giant Monsanto and Eastman Kodak's entry into the drugs business through the acquisition of the US-based Sterling Drugs.

A number of significant developments occured in 1989. In March 1989, Merck established a joint-venture company with Johnson and Johnson to promote its products in the OTC sector, and subsequently acquired ICI's OTC business in the US. A major restructuring of the

American prescription market occurred in April–July with three substantial mergers: Smith Kline Beckman and Beecham, Bristol Myers and Squibb, and Dow and Marion Labs. The year 1989 also saw further inroads into the US market by a number of Japanese companies, Fujisawa, in particular, with its takeover of Lypho-Med. (having previously bought a 22 per cent stake in 1985). However, there have been no significant pan-European mergers in the build-up to 1992, although, as in the US, some Japanese companies have taken steps to increase their presence in the EC. Fujisawa and Sankyo have acquired majority stakes in the German companies, Kling Pharma and Luitpold-Werk, respectively, while Chunghai has acquired a stake in British Biotechnology (UK) and Dainippon has established a joint venture company with Rhone-Poulenc (FR).

8.3   Competitive Factors Influencing Market Structure

The declining rate of growth in pharmaceutical demand has attenuated a number of competitive pressures facing the major drug companies. These include the high cost and risk involved in developing new products and getting them on governments' 'approved' drug lists, tighter government regulation of drug prices and procurement policies, the erosion of patent protection, together with heightened competition from 'parallel imports' and 'off-patent' generics.

8.3.1   New product development and governments' 'approved' drug lists

The discovery and development of new pharmaceutical products is a speculative and costly exercise with no guarantee of an eventual commercial pay-off. A large number of the major breakthroughs in drug research owe more to individual inventive flair than the amount of money spent. Sir James Black, for example, played a leading role in the development of 'betablockers' such as 'Inderal', while at ICI, and anti-ulcer drugs ('Targamet' in particular) while at Smith Kline. Nevertheless, companies require substantial financial resources to pilot such discoveries to the market place. On average, the leading companies spend between 10–15 per cent of their sales turnover on research and development activity. In the US alone spending on R&D exceeded four billion dollars in real terms in 1988.

Moreover, before they can be sold commercially, new drugs must first satisfy stringent government requirements relating to safety and efficacy before being registered on an 'approved' drug list. In most countries new drugs are subjected to various screening and testing procedures which takes, on average, ten years to complete. Approximately seven of these years are spent in development work, consisting of, after the initial patenting of the chemical formulation, two years preliminary test-tube and animal studies, two years of small-group clinical trials in human patients followed by three years large clinical trials. The remaining three years is occupied by government vetting procedures. Over the years, concern with the possible harmful side-effects of drugs has grown, particularly after the tragic thalidomide case in 1960, and governments have applied more exacting standards. In consequence, only a small number of new drugs find their way on to the market, and industry estimates suggest that major new drug developments can cost upwards of £100 million.

The picture world-wide is further complicated by the fact that each national market has its own separate approval and registration procedures so that the length of lead-in times for new drugs can differ markedly from country to country, while in some cases, because of differences in standards, a drug acceptable in one country may be rejected by another country. One of the objectives of the European Community '1992' initiative as it applies to drug applications is the introduction of a uniform approval system, which should bring administration savings as well as speeding up the introduction of new drugs.

8.3.2 Price Regulation

In some countries, most notably the US and Germany, drug prices are largely market-driven but in many countries prices are regulated by the government either directly by various forms of price controls (as in, for example, Japan, Denmark, Portugal, Italy, Spain, Greece, France and Belgium), or indirectly, as in the UK and Ireland, by profit ceilings. Varying national practices together with differences between countries in cost levels and inflation rates have encouraged multinational companies to price discriminate between markets according to 'what the traffic will bear' leading to significant inter-country differences in price levels as table 8.5 shows.

In principle, governments as the main purchasers of ethical drugs have an interest in keeping drug prices down as low as possible, but at the same time must be mindful of allowing companies a sufficient return on their investments so as to provide resources/incentives for further research and development spending. Getting the 'balance' right is difficult and companies frequently complain the system is too inflexible and profit returns inadequate. In the UK, drug prices are indirectly

Table 8.5   Comparative price index for EC pharmaceuticals, 1986

Spain	100
Portugal	107
Italy	113
France	119
Belgium/Luxembourg	132
UK	201
Holland	230
West Germany	251

Source: Bureau of European Consumer Unions

controlled under the government's Pharmaceutical Price Regulation Scheme, which sets 'allowable' rates of return on capital employed for *each* drug company. A company can set its own prices, but must not exceed its profit ceiling. Individual details are not disclosed, but the industry's published target rate of return was reduced in 1983 by the government from 25 per cent to 17 per cent. In Japan, the government has lowered drug prices by 60 per cent since 1981, while 'price freezes' have been operated recently in France and West Germany. The European Community 1992 proposals to remove country-specific authorization of drugs and other obstacles to free trade are expected to bring about a big expansion of intra trade and with it a general averaging down of drug prices by as much as 10–20 per cent.

8.3.3   Erosion of patent protection

One consequence of governments' approval requirements has been a shortening of the *effective* patent life of a new drug. Nominally it is 20 years (17 years in the USA) but allowing for the time taken from patenting a drug to its appearance on the market, the effective patent life is almost halved. Thus, there is greater pressure on companies to recoup development costs and achieve an adequate return on investment by charging high prices for new drugs, but in many countries, as noted above, price controls make this difficult. Accordingly, the industry has proposed that patents should run from a later date in drug development to restore some of the intended patent.

It is also important, given the time span of patents, that new drugs gain as wide a market as possible, hence the need for international marketing. The innovating company must satisfy the regulatory requirements in each foreign country and generally file for patent protection in each. However, in Europe, under the European Patent Convention, a patent taken out in one European country is then valid in the other 21 participating countries which has assisted in removing time-consuming and costly separate patent applications. One problem facing the industry, however, is that there are a number of countries where patent laws are weak or non-existent and this has led to a flourishing trade in copying patented drugs. A notable example of this until recently was Italy where 'pirate' producers exported drugs to other non-patent protected markets in Africa, Latin America, Eastern Europe and Asia.

8.3.4 Parallel importing

Parallel importing is the practice of dealers buying a particular drug in a relatively low-priced market (for example, France) and selling them in a higher-priced market such as the UK, undercutting the patentee company's local prices. As seen by pharmaceutical producers, the disadvantage with parallel importing is that the bulk of a drug's profit goes to the importers and pharmacists and not to the patentee company. Moreover, safety standards may suffer as the repackaging of drugs can obliterate expiry date and dosing instructions. However, parallel importing is common to many other internationally traded goods and by 'averaging prices down' (as envisaged by the European Community 1992 initiative, for example) the practice can prove beneficial to consumers, particularly in the over-the-counter sector.

8.3.5 Generic competition

When the patent on a drug product expires, it may be manufactured by other companies in direct competition to the original innovation. New producers often market the drug under its 'generic' name which is the official name of the compound as opposed to its 'brand name' which is the proprietorial trademark owned by the innovating company.

Once a drug goes 'off patent' competition tends to shift towards a greater emphasis on efficient mass production and lower prices. Off-patent imitations are mainly supplied by the smaller and medium-sized companies outside the big league of research-based companies. With their lower overheads, particularly the absence of expensive research and development commitments, they are able to bring out cheaper versions of the product. Price competition in this sector of the prescription and over-the-counter market is accordingly very strong. In the relatively unregulated US and West German markets, generics have been a potent source of competition to established brands capturing around 10 per cent and 15 per cent of total US and West German drug

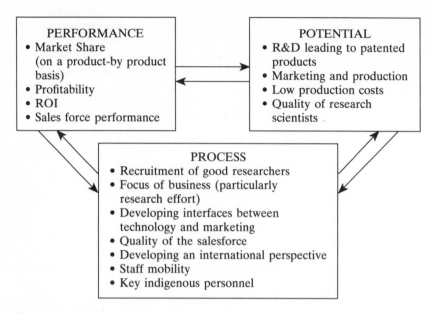

Figure 8.2   The competitive process in the pharmaceutical industry

sales respectively. Elsewhere, both in Europe and Japan, generics have been making headway, actively encouraged by those governments seeking to keep their health-care budgets in check.

8.4   The Competitive Process

Figure 8.2 summarizes the measures of competitiveness used by the firms in our sample.

8.4.1   The patented ethical pharmaceutical sector

The principal forces driving competition in this sector can be simply stated: quality of research personnel, the upward spiralling costs of research and development, the need to sustain long-term profitability for reinvestment in research initiatives, and the buyer power of governments.

Research and development forms the lifeblood of the patented pharmaceutical industry. Continual introduction of new medicines to replace those which have been taken up by generic manufacturers after patent expiry, provides the key to long-term sustained competitiveness. Research personnel are consequently an important competitive asset, and attracting and retaining top research scientists is critical to long-term success. In this respect, competitive advantage is, to a degree, attached to individuals, and only by harnassing their expertise to the organization can firms internalize such critical assets. By creating a highly stimulating environment for research in which key researchers attract other top industry scientists, firms are able to retain a competitive advantage in their R&D. However, even with a strong research team in place, there is no guarantee that research initiatives will lead to commercial product development, and the inherent risks of funding large research products cannot be overstated. In an attempt to minimize risks, the promotion of strong interfaces between departments, most notably marketing and R&D, is designed to initiate research projects with a clear market application. Products which gain approval by drug authorities are thus intended to have a wide global market application, and returns can be made to compensate for heavy R&D spending. The development of departmental interfaces is often achieved through staff mobility. Encouraging scientists and research personnel to spend time in each other's departments facilitates the transfer of information and ensures that research initiatives follow changing market demands.

The salesforce provides the frontline between the marketing department and the buyers, and thus its role in monitoring the needs of key buyers – not only government procurement departments but also doctors and dentists who specify drugs on prescription – in turn is important in determining long-term initiatives and directions of future research. International staff mobility also adds to the breadth of knowledge on which the determination of research initiatives is based. By extending the horizons of search for new research projects beyond the national market, a greater number of opportunities may emerge from markets where a different profile of disease and ailments may exist.

The monopolistic nature of buyers also adds weight to the importance of establishing a quality salesforce. Developing and sustaining good relationships with key buyers is essential to generating the width of market coverage necessary to recoup the costs of R&D on a global scale. As failure to secure a contract with a state-owned health authority cannot be easily compensated for by finding alternative buyers, employing staff who understand the buying process in individual countries, usually indigenous staff with knowledge of the market and the industry, can be crucial to success.

The overriding importance of sustaining long-term profitability and a wide network of customers from which returns can be made are clearly reflected in the measures of performance used by firms in our sample. An inability to sustain profits has a detrimental impact on market ranking through the knock-on effect profitability has on securing resources for future research projects. This is, in turn, related to the extent of global coverage and world market share. However, due to the often highly focused nature of many organizations, market share is measured on a product-by-product basis, global market share being regarded as a meaningless indicator as firms only operate in a handful of specialized markets.

8.4.2 The generic sector

In the generic, off-patent, ethical sector, a slightly different set of factors comes into play. Low-cost manufacturing supplants R&D as the key factor for success. Through the absence of heavy R&D investment, firms are able to offer imitations of branded goods at a significantly lower price and are thus able to win-over markets from the major multinational producers after their patents have expired. As price drives competition in this sector, continual cost-cutting initiatives are followed in order to sustain long-term price competitiveness. It should be mentioned, however, that, although generic manufacturers are not faced with the costs of primary research, development of products to meet the changing needs of customers remains an important element of competitive potential. The salesforce also plays a key role in this sector. Sales representatives are not only concerned with securing contracts with key buyers, but are also faced with the task of persuading 'specifiers' (doctors and dentists) to alter their prescriptions from stating a particular brand name, to merely specifying the generic product name. This process is being facilitated by some governments so that their expenditure on pharmaceuticals can be kept to a minimum, a considerable lowering of prices being brought about by active competition in the generics sector.

Although many generic producers are concerned with assessing their market share and profitability in their domestic markets (which generally account for the major proportion of their sales) in foreign markets they are more concerned with salesforce effort as a means of assessing performance.

8.5   Global Strategic Approach

8.5.1   Pharmaceutical MNE's

The companies listed in table 8.2 (with the exception of the Japanese concern, Takeda) have all developed an extensive international presence which has been an important factor in sustaining their leading positions in the industry over the longer-term. Specifically, the establishment of global production and distribution networks has enabled such firms to gain a wide-spread and rapid market penetration for their new products and hence make the necessary returns to finance on-going R&D initiatives leading to the next generation of new products.

The impact of the various competitive forces (particularly the importance of new innovation contribution and establishing a global network through FDI to gain access to local government procurement contracts) on the nature of firms' activities can be demonstrated by assessing the activities of some of the UK's leading multinational pharmaceutical companies. The leading UK supplier in 1987, and the world's number two company, was Glaxo (having raised its ranking from 12th in 1984) with a UK market share of around 11.5 per cent. This position in the industry owes much to the anti-ulcer drug 'Zantac' as well as broad spectrum antibiotics. ICI is the UK's second largest company. The basis of the company's success in the 1960s and 1970s was 'Inderal', the first in the beta blocker range of cardiovascular drugs and this has continued with 'Tenormin' the world's third largest selling drug. Beecham offers direct competition to Glaxo in broad spectrum antibiotics and is a leading supplier of OTC products. The company was a pioneer in the 1950s in commercializing penicillin ('Penbritin') and its more recent major products 'Amoxil', 'Augmentin' and 'Tiementin' have continued the tradition. Wellcome has made a particular specialism of anti-viral drugs and has had particular success with its herpes drug 'Zovirax'. The company stands poised for a substantial up-grading in its market position with the introduction in 1987 of 'Retrovir', the first AIDS drug to gain widespread approval. Fisons is world leader in respiratory drugs and has been particularly successful with its asthma drug 'Intal'. 'Tilade', launched in 1987, extends the company's range in this area.

Glaxo, ICI, Wellcome, Beecham and Fisons all have major overseas interests and, although their home and export sales are relatively small, their direct sales in overseas markets give them a strong position on a global basis (see table 8.6). The intensity of worldwide competition means that individual market shares tend to be relatively low.

Each of the leading UK companies has widespread foreign manufacturing and marketing facilities. Glaxo, for example, carries out local manufacturing in 30 countries, local marketing in some 50 countries (around 150 countries including sales agencies) and research in the UK, Italy and the United States. Beecham manufactures in 18 countries, sells in 130 countries and has research centres in the UK, France, West Germany and the United States.

In recent years, the leading companies have taken steps to strengthen

Table 8.6 Regional distribution of sales turnover

Region	Glaxo*	ICI**	Beecham***	Wellcome**	Fisons***
UK	12	12	23	10	19
Europe	33	26	32	21	19
Americas	45	41	34	47	45
Rest of World	10	21	11	22	16
Total Sales £M	2,854	1,334	1,083	1,083	327

* 1990 accounts
** 1989 accounts
*** 1988 accounts (Beecham last available: merged with Smith Kline, 1989)
Source: Company Annual Report and Accounts

their international positions, particularly in the two largest world markets, the United States and Japan. This has been achieved through a wide range of foreign market servicing policies including greenfield ventures (for example Glaxo's new operation in Zebulon, North Carolina, built after their acquisition of a small American producer; Wellcome's establishment of a new manufacturing plant in Southern France and ICI's establishment of a second sales and marketing subsidiary in America) joint ventures (such as Beecham's marketing arrangement with Upjohn in the United States to jointly market its new product 'Eminese' and Fisons 50:50 joint venture with Fujisawa in Japan) and acquisitions (for example, Fisons acquisitions of Orbit Chemicals in Australia, Intersinct in Italy and Laboratorios Casen in Spain).

8.5.2 Japanese producers

The UK illustrations are fairly typical of the major global ethical pharmaceutical companies. However, some comment should be made about the major Japanese producers who are, by contrast, fairly parochial in their business operations. Domestically, the Japanese industry is highly fragmented with around 1300 producers. The largest producers in the market, as table 8.7 shows, have relatively small market shares. Takeda was the leading Japanese supplier in 1986 with a market share of around 5.5 per cent, closely followed by Shionogi with 5.3 per cent. The top ten Japanese companies have a combined market share of around 35 per cent, the remainder of the market being supplied by smaller local concerns, foreign-owned subsidiaries of American and West European companies and imports.

Table 8.7 Market shares of the top-ten Japanese pharmaceutical companies, 1986

Company	Market share (%)
Takeda	5.5
Shionogi	5.3
Fujisawa	4.7
Sankyo	4.1
Eisai	3.5
Green Cross	2.6
Yamamouchi	2.5
Meiji Seika	2.5
Daiichi	2.5
Chugai	2.3
Total	35.5

Source: James Capel

Export revenues as a percentage of companies' total revenues were small for all of the leading companies. One of the major reasons contributing to Japanese under representation in international markets has been the lucrative profits which firms have been able to earn in their domestic markets. Until the 1980s Japanese drug prices were some of the highest in the world propelled by a rapidly rising demand for pharmaceuticals and a high state funding programme (drugs accounting for around 40 per cent of Japan's state health care bill compared to around 10 per cent in the UK). Thus, the Japanese market itself presented a 'sellers' market and reduced the imperative to seek overseas sales. A number of more technical factors have played their part. Japanese expertise in drugs research has lagged behind that of the Americans and Europeans. Building on technology transfer from abroad the Japanese have established an enviable record in physics and engineering, but emphasis on biology and chemistry has been accorded a relatively low priority. As a result many Japanese drug products have limited transferability to international markets because they are insufficiently sophisticated compared to the products of the leading American and European multinationals. A lack of marketing know-how and experience in selling drugs in world markets, together with a reluctance on the part of foreign governments to accept Japanese drug test data, have also worked against the interests of the industry.

However, things are changing. The Japanese government has cut drug prices and has cultivated a more 'open' economic policy, encouraging imports as well as inward investment by foreign companies to provide stiffer competition to complacent indigenous producers. The government has also attempted to upgrade and modernize the industry's research capabilities, targeting what many observers consider to be the key drug technology of the future, biotechnology, for special attention. In 1981, the Ministry of International Trade and Industry set up a biotechnology research programme providing funds of Y26 million for private sector initiatives. In addition, various companies outside the established pharmaceutical sector such as Mitsubishi Chemical Industries, one of Japan's biggest producers of basic chemicals, have been encouraged to undertake work in biotechnology. However, the amount spent on R&D is still much lower, on average, than that spent by the leading American and European companies.

Nevertheless, it can be confidently predicted that the recent spate of increased international activity by Japanese-based pharmaceutical firms will continue as organizations seek to generate increased levels of profit for future R&D investment. Recently, Japanese companies have demonstrated their intent to gain greater international penetration and the acquisition of local marketing know-how through joint ventures (for example, Fujisawa–Smith Kline, Takeda–Abbott, Yamanouchi–Eli Lilly, Fujisawa–Fisons KK) is a sign of their commitment to dedicated expansion programmes. This has been augmented, as highlighted above, by a number of acquisitions in the USA and the EC.

8.5.3 Generic producers

By contrast, generic, non-patented pharmaceutical producers are more nationally oriented in their dealings, principally producing for their own domestic markets. International business tends to be export dominated. Heavy price competition in the sector has closed investment options to many firms who are forced to consider the least cost routes to international markets. Consequently, firms mostly sell via foreign agents or establish distribution rights to foreign pharmaceutical companies manufacturing complementary, but not identical products. Furthermore, by centralizing production, firms can benefit from scale economies in production which allows them to compensate for additional transportation costs to foreign markets.

8.6   Managing the Process

As foreign market servicing decisions play a critical role in managing the competitive process on an international scale, decisions about the best way to enter and service foreign markets has an important bearing on firms' ability to exploit their competitive advantages in foreign markets and sustain long-term competitive performance.

8.6.1 Foreign investment

It has been noted that the nature of the buyer market for pharmaceuticals often necessitates the setting up of foreign subsidiaries by global ethical pharmaceutical producers. In order to gain access to government procurement contracts, which are frequently biased towards local manufacturers, some form of foreign presence is often the only way in which firms can penetrate international markets. Where markets are large, or where governments provide incentives for local manufacture, there is much justification for firms decentralizing their production operations and locating manufacturing in the host market. Production abroad, however, can place a strain on the economic efficiency of organizations, decentralized structures resulting in lost scale economies and duplication of effort. Furthermore, quality control can be difficult to manage on an international scale and can prove costly where engineers are required to monitor activities across a highly geographically dispersed production base. This can lead to a splitting up of production activities into two distinct functions: the manufacture of 'active ingredients' and assembly manufacture which principally involves measuring, weighing and packaging. By locating upstream production activities in the domestic market there are consequent benefits to be earned from generating scale economies and monitoring the quality of output. In turn, there are benefits in locating downstream activities in the host market in terms of gaining a local profile and thus accessing government procurement contracts.

Sales and marketing investment is a critical strand in global ethical pharmaceutical firms' rapid penetration of international markets, whether it be associated with production investment, or, in markets which are too small to sustain a local manufacturing plant, a stand-alone operation. In order to compensate for the restricted 'effective' patent lives of new pharmaceutical products, it is essential for firms to maximize their returns as quickly as possible through extensive global networks and dedicated sales/marketing activities. Only in this way can firms generate the necessary returns to cover their extensive research and development costs and generate profits for investment in future research and development initiatives.

Although over-capacity in the market, brought about by government 'buy-local' policies which persuade firms to invest abroad, would suggest takeover as a more favourable foreign entry option, much market entry is greenfield. Even where acquisitions are made, major plant investment, or the establishment of further greenfield plants frequently follows the initial move. This results from the stringent production clearance initiatives of many host governments wherein adapting old production runs of the acquired firm is not feasible to accommodate a new, and often very different, product.

8.6.2 Exporting

Exporting via sales/marketing offices, as has been discussed, is an approach used by patented ethical pharmaceutical producers in small markets which cannot sustain local market production investment. Exporting via market based intermediaries, on the other hand, tends to be more associated with the activities of generic producers. The motives for their using this form of market servicing are principally two-fold: firstly, exporting provides a way of extending the customer base for the firm and employing excess capacity in domestic production; secondly, exporting via intermediaries is the lowest cost route to international markets and thus supports generic firms' price competitiveness. The relatively low incidence of international activity of firms in this sector reflects the problem of competing effectively with overseas generic manufacturers, given the additional transportation costs and consequent erosion of profit margins. Given the adverse effect of transportation costs to the firms' profitability in overseas markets, local production would be beneficial to international dealings in the generics sector. However, two specific barriers to achieving this exist: obtaining a critical mass in domestic production, which would allow the firm to consider production expansion; the small scale of organizations, which results in their having limited resources, both financial and managerial, for making foreign investments.

Although sales/marketing-supported exporting is generally favoured by the large multinational companies, exporting via intermediaries cannot be ruled out as an option. Where patented products are clearly differentiated from their competition and are actively sought out by buyers, or where markets are too politically or economically unstable to consider local investment, firms export on an arm's length basis.

8.6.3 Licensing

Licensing is clearly an option available to patented pharmaceutical manufacturers given their technological advantages which can be included in a licensing package to an overseas manufacturer. However, the fact that licensing fails to secure the full economic rent available to manufacturers deters firms from following this course. In order to recoup the costs of R&D and secure profits for future technological investment, it is essential that organizations exploit their patented products for maximum returns. This does not, however, preclude their licensing their drugs to overseas manufacturers in exceptional circumstances. Licensing may be used where it is not possible to enter the market through any other form of market servicing, or where a drug is discovered which the innovating firm cannot manufacture themselves due to limited capacity or lack of ability and resources to screen and register it in foreign markets. Overall, however, protecting proprietary technology is an important issue for patented pharmaceutical manufacturers in their developing market servicing strategies. Again, driven by the high costs of R&D and restricted 'effective' patent lives, managers plan their strategies around a clear goal of maximizing profits.

Alternatively, generic producers lack the technological advantages necessary to initiate licensing contracts. Once a product has gone 'off-patent', the technology is available to all players in the market.

8.6.4   Joint ventures

The growing international development of Japanese pharmaceutical manufacturers through joint-venture agreements, particularly with leading American producers, may be partly explained by their desire to gain pharmaceutical technology and marketing skills. However, there are other factors which are increasingly motivating firms to consider possible joint ventures with foreign partners. Firstly, as the cost of research and development continues to escalate, there would seem to be advantages for firms to pool both their financial and entrepreneurial management resources to create new technologies. By sharing the costs and risks, cooperating rather than competing, firms can develop new technologies at a much lower cost. Secondly, the ability to enter into partnerships to market and sell products abroad further reduces the cost base of the company by removing the need to establish foreign manufacturing plants or sales and marketing subsidiaries. Although the profits accruing to joint ventures obviously have to be shared, as the high costs of R&D and developing a global network are also shared, firms can maintain their market positions without incurring the same level of risk. In the branded pharmaceutical sector, where research products may never come to fruition, and ideas may never be commercialized, the reduction of risk may have an important bearing on a firm's decision to enter a joint venture. Furthermore, the pooling of entrepreneurial talent may have synergistic effects, top industry researchers being able to cross fertilize technological know how, which can prove to be the stimulus for major pharmaceutical breakthroughs.

8.7 The Future

The pharmaceutical industry is highly dynamic, with new products continually coming on stream and new drugs constantly being sought to combat disease. As a result, there is no guarantee for branded pharmaceutical producers that the markets they operate in today will be the growth markets of the future. Therefore, targeting research initiatives according to the needs of the market today, and potentially the perceived needs of the future is the only course for survival. As a result of the need to target efforts and concentrate resources on particular sectors, the number of leading global players will remain quite high (relative to other global industries) with a number of speciality niche producers and generic producers manufacturing low cost pharmaceuticals, supported by government initiatives to reduce health care budgets.

The initiatives related to the Single European Market Act, whilst not increasing the level of European activity in branded pharmaceuticals (most firms having secured a presence in most markets in order to extend their global networks), will impact on the activities of pharmaceutical manufacturers. Firstly, the aim is to standardize the registration procedure for drugs sold by European manufacturers which will eliminate the time delay and costs of gaining clearance in each EC Member State, a move which is long awaited by European manufacturers. Whether this is achieved through establishing a common ground for registration of products or through mutual recognition of home country registration and clearance, it will reduce the costs of operating across Europe. Secondly, and potentially damaging to UK branded pharmaceutical manufacturers, standardization of price controls across Europe may result in firms losing out in markets where governments had previously set favourable prices for indigenous producers. As the UK is one such market, firms with a high exposure in the UK will suffer. Thirdly, opening up of government procurement contracts means that the incentive to produce abroad will be less, and rationalization of production, in order to reap economies of scale in larger, more efficient production plants, may result. Whether or not this will also include a retrenchment of sales and marketing activities is debateable. Ostensibly, this directive means governments will look outside their indigenous markets for suppliers of pharmaceuticals. In reality, however, nationalistic tendencies may still prevail and active promotion and marketing may still be essential to selling to major health authorities.

A further development, likely to have a very important impact on the pharmaceutical industry is the move towards extending the 'effective' patent lives of pharmaceutical products. It has been recognized, and according to many pharmaceutical manufacturers not before time, that, due to the extensive period necessary for testing and registration, it is difficult for firms to recoup the costs of ever upward spiralling research and development. Consequently, there is talk by the patent authorities that patent lives will be measured from the first marketing of pharmaceutical products, and not the initial time of registration. This will obviously greatly benefit patented pharmaceutical producers. However, for generic pharmaceutical producers, when products come off-patent, it is possible that market demand will have tailed off, new, more sophisticated products having been introduced to take their place, which could result, in the long-term in a degree of rationalization in the generics market.

Finally, as has already been noted, an increase in the number of joint ventures may be expected to increase as firms seek to pool their resources to reduce the ever increasing costs of research and development and international market penetration. As many Japanese firms are actively involved in extending their positions globally through such policies, increased competition from the Pacific Basin may become an important feature of the pharmaceutical industry in the future.

9

Industry Study 2: The Scientific Instrument Industry

9.1 Introduction

The scientific instrument industry is principally an intermediate good industry providing a diverse range of products for research, healthcare, defence and industrial process control and automation. Internationally, the industry is highly fragmented comprising a small number of multi-national companies and a large number of small and intermediate players. Whereas the small firms tend to operate in specialized niches, the larger companies often produce scientific instruments alongside other capital goods (notably laboratory chemicals and diagnostic kits). The majority of firms are based in the developed west – the USA, France, Germany, Italy, the UK, Holland, Sweden and Switzerland. These countries also comprise the major user markets for scientific instruments because of their high technology levels, the importance of their research and development sectors and their sophisticated industrial production systems.

In 1989, global sales of scientific instruments totalled $40 billion despite a continuing slow-down in demand in some key sectors – notably the procurement of instruments by government-financed healthcare agencies.

9.2 Products and Customers

The broad range of products manufactured by the industry can be categorized into three basic groups (1) electrical instruments and control systems (including electronic timers, counters, recorders and testing equipment and electronic process control equipment) (2) measuring, checking and precision instruments and apparatus (for instance, ultrasonic equipment and counting and velocity measuring equipment) and

(3) optical precision instruments (examples including microscopes and lasers). Cutting across these groupings are two product sectors distinguished by their level of technological sophistication: low- to medium-technology products which include old or out-dated patents and high technology products incorporating patented technologies often with sophisticated microprocessor control and computer interfacing.

In general, a high proportion of the industry's products are 'international' in nature in that they can be offered without major modification in the key markets, Japan, the USA and Western Europe.

There are five main customer groups served by the industry:

1 Other industrial sectors
2 Government (including defence)
3 Academia
4 Healthcare
5 Research laboratories.

Although some firms supply all sectors many firms, especially the smaller ones, specialize in specific markets. Specialization does, however, carry a high degree of risk. Publicly financed sectors of the market (specifically, universities, hospitals, medical research, schools, research councils and the defence industry) are subject to falling demand in the face of economic downturn. Niche-market firms may, therefore, be overly dependent on sectors characterized by fluctuating demand. Industrial customers include the chemical and pharmaceutical industries, the food industry, the engineering industry and contract-research firms. These customers have provided the scientific instrument industry with a growth impetus in recent years, but here, also, there are signs of retrenchment in some sectors, pharmaceuticals in particular.

All customer groups may be regarded as erudite and knowledgeable, consisting of scientists, technicians and engineers. Companies are thus required to pay a high degree of attention to the technical needs of their customers. Thus, certain aspects of the marketing mix are especially important. In terms of the product, quality and performance are critical to customer confidence, plus the added back-up of equipment servicing which the suppliers of high-technology products have to offer via a network of service engineers. Promotion is also important, in the form of advertising in trade magazines or specialist scientific and engineering journals, and by personal selling and demonstrations. In recent years, price, has become a more important factor, especially to those customers reliant on public funding. This has also had the effect of changing the nature of purchasing practices from outright purchase to the use of other arrangements such as leasing agreements.

Products are distributed to customers via two main types of distribution channel: direct sales from manufacturer to end-users (both domestic and foreign) and sales via local and overseas distributors, agents and dealers.

9.3 The International Market

The international scientific instrument industry is highly fragmented with a number of major international companies coexisting alongside smaller niche companies. International data across the whole scientific instruments sector is poor and the most comprehensive international data available is that compiled by the A11 Report service. However, this data is restricted in its coverage, principally to scientific instruments used in laboratories. However, it yields some interesting insights into the structure of the industry. Table 9.1 highlights the top firms in the industry with sales revenues exceeding $100m. In 1989, the top 20 analytical instrument companies accounted for around $5 billion in revenue out of a world-wide sector total of some $8 billion. Of this group, seven are US owned, four are Japanese and nine are based in Europe. Thus, although the industry is fragmented, the top 20 firms account for well over half the world total. This suggests a large number of firms with very small revenues operating in highly specialized niches. Table 9.2 shows the numbers of firms categorized in the $40–100 million category and the $10–40m grouping. Overall, in 1989, there were 228 companies world-wide with revenues greater than $1 million – with a greater proportion of European firms emerging in the smaller revenue categories.

In 1986, the top ten scientific instrument producers in the world were made up of four American (Perkin–Elmer, Hewlett–Packard, Waters–Millipore and Varian), three Japanese (JEOL, Shimadzu and Hitachi), one British (Fisons), one Dutch (Philips) and one Swedish company (Pharmacia/LKB). Clearly, then, there are three dominant source markets, America, Europe and Japan.

9.3.1 The US market

US firms have always dominated the industry. As far back as the 1960s US-owned firms enjoyed a higher rate of technical innovation than their European counterparts. This resulted from a number of factors:

1 The large scale of the US market allowed firms to benefit from economies of scale in production and the spreading of R&D costs across larger production runs

Table 9.1 Global analytical instruments industry: companies with sales revenues above US $100 million, 1989

Sales category ($ million)	Company
500–550	Perkin–Elmer (US)
450–500	Hewlett–Packard (US)
400–450	Shimadzu (J)
	Fisons (UK)
350–400	Beckman (US)
300–350	—
250–300	Hitachi (J)
	JEOL (J)
	Pharmacia/LKB (SW)
	Philips/Analytical (NL)
	Waters/Millipore (US)
200–250	Varian (US)
150–200	Bruker (WG)
	Cambridge Instr. (UK)
	Ciba-Geigy/Mettler
	Spectra-Physics Autolab
	Linear Instr. & Ingold (SZ)
	Figaku (J)
100–150	Finnigan (US)
	Kontron (IT)
	LECO/Spectruma (US)
	Sartorius (WG)

Source: Analytical Instruments Industry Report

2 A very large government procurement market (public funds influencing directly, or indirectly 40 per cent of the market as opposed to 25 per cent in Europe)
3 Intense competition in the USA forced firms to pursue a policy of continual product innovation
4 A high degree of liaison between instrument companies and component manufacturers helped to stimulate successful innovation programmes
5 Experience in new-product development led to improved lead times in the creation of new products in the USA.

Such advantages in product technology not only benefited American firms in their domestic market, but also gave them considerable

Table 9.2 Global analytical instrument industry: sales revenue range US $1–100 million, 1989

Sales category	Country	Number of firms
$40–100 million	US	20
	Japan	4
	European Community	
	France	(2)
	UK	(1)
	West Germany	(4)
	TOTAL	7
	Other European	
	Sweden	(1)
	Switzerland	(2)
	TOTAL	3
	Others	
	RSA	(1)
	TOTAL	1
$10–40 million	US	30
	Japan	6
	European Community	
	Denmark	(2)
	France	(2)
	Italy	(1)
	Netherlands	(2)
	Spain	(1)
	UK	(7)
	West Germany	(6)
	TOTAL	21
	Other European	
	Sweden	(1)
	Switzerland	(2)
	TOTAL	3
	Others	
	Canada	(2)
	RSA	(2)
	TOTAL	4
$1–10 million	US	48
	Japan	4
	European Community	
	Belgium	(1)
	Denmark	(1)
	France	(6)
	Netherlands	(3)
	Spain	(3)

Continued

Table 9.2 (*Cont.*)

Sales category	Country	Number of firms
	UK	(22)
	West Germany	(9)
	TOTAL	45
	Other European	
	Switzerland	(2)
	TOTAL	2
	Others	
	Australia	5
	Canada	2
	Israel	2
	New Zealand	1
	TOTAL	10

Source: Analytical Instrument Industry Report

competitive advantages on an international scale. These they exploited through the establishment of wholly-owned production facilities in Europe and joint ventures in Japan. Furthermore, firms increasingly pursued strategies involving the international division of labour at the level of the firm. New instruments were developed and manufactured by the subsidiaries and then distributed on a world-wide basis. A marketing orientation was also adopted by these firms at an earlier stage – and through the careful selection of new products and markets yielding high potential and exploitation of scale economies, the leading firms have carved a powerful position in the industry.

9.3.2 Europe

In Europe, lower levels of government procurement and small, fragmented markets resulted in a very different industry profile characterized by short production runs and custom-made equipment. Through the 1970s, Germany led the field – accounting for approximately 40 per cent of European output with the UK contributing approximately one third. International activity, until recently at least, involved the establishment of subsidiaries in various parts of the world, but rarely in the US.

European firms, however, recognizing their limited scope *vis-à-vis* their major American rivals, have become actively involved in a spate of mergers and acquisitions, joint ventures and restructuring moves. For example, Fisons, the UK-based group, through a round of acquisitions

Table 9.3 Fisons' acquisitions

Year	Firm	Nationality	Nature of business
1972	MSE	British	Manufacturer of high performance centrifuges
1976	Haake	German	Manufacturer of viscometers and material testing equipment
1984	Curtin Matheson Scientific	American	Leading distributor in the US clinical laboratory market
1985	Carlo Erba Strumentazione	Italian	Specialists in chromatography, elemental analysis, surface characterization and amino-acid analysis
1986	Applied Research Laboratories	Swiss	Producers of X-ray flourescence and emission spectrometers
1989	VG Instruments	British	Various

has moved into the $400m category of international firms and the world's fourth largest scientific instrument company. Table 9.3 highlights the nature of the acquisitions which have resulted in their attaining this position.

Other restructuring initiatives by UK firms include, VG Instruments (then controlled by British American Tobacco) takeover in 1987 of the American Kevex Corporation, which allowed it to consolidate its position as a major supplier of X-ray analytical equipment. Cambridge Instruments, which had likewise built up a prominent position in the US optical instrument sector through its acquisition of Reichart Industries and Baurch and Lomb, further extended its world-wide interests in this area by merging with the Swiss based company, Wild Leitz Holdings in 1989. Also in 1989, Oxford Instruments acquired Link from the US Carlton Communications giving it world leadership in the X-ray analytical equipment sector. In addition, Pharmacia, the Swedish manufacturer, acquired LKB, another Swedish firm, putting the combined analytical product revenues at over $250 million.

This period of restructuring has consequently allowed European firms, after a slow start, to catch up with their American counterparts in the race to develop a substantial international presence.

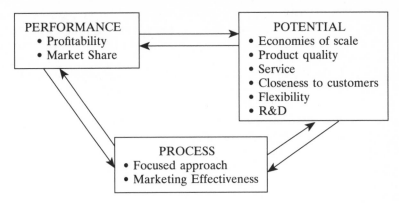

Figure 9.1 Measures of competitiveness highlighted by scientific instrument manufacturers

9.3.3 Japan

In the 1960s the Japanese market experienced a period of rapid expansion both in terms of domestic demand and growing exports. As an intermediate good industry, the scientific instrument sector clearly benefited from growth and international expansion by Japanese manufacturers and the resultant economic upsurge which boosted public spending. This forced Japanese instrument manufacturers to adopt a policy of rapid product innovation. This has been sustained over the intervening period, and resulted in the Japanese attaining a strong position in specific sectors, particularly opto-electronic devices.

9.4 The Competitive Process

The following diagram reveals the main measures of competitiveness highlighted by interviewed firms.

The overriding success of American firms in the international arena clearly demonstrates the importance of new-product development and scale economies in the competitive process of scientific instrument manufacturers. The highly competitive, fragmented markets characteristic of the industry have forced firms to place a high degree of emphasis on continual product innovation in order to sustain technological competitive advantages. This has necessitated committing resources to R&D effort and pursuing strategies to minimize costs and thus maximize profits to generate the resources required for increasingly expensive R&D

initiatives. Cost cutting programmes have been further promoted in recent years by falling demand in key sectors. Two important customers for scientific instruments are the government health authorities and the defence industry, which, in many countries, are subject to tight budgetary controls. As their purchase decisions become increasingly constrained by price considerations, competition between supplier firms is orientated towards cost, especially in the medium-technology area of the industry where switching costs incurred in changing suppliers are low. Tight expenditure controls also affect government research establishments, universities and polytechnics, with equipment replacement and upgrading becoming less frequent. In addition, the apparent decline in the customer base in certain industry sectors will introduce cost pressures in due course.

Price competition is particularly critical in the older technology, non-patented sectors, with the pressure to sustain volume sales depressing prices and profit margins. Furthermore, although the higher-technology sectors critically centre on innovation, differentiation and service back-up, price pressures are becoming increasingly important as customers become more price conscious. The nature of customers for scientific instrument – technologically aware and erudite – makes product quality and the provision of service key factors for fostering good manufacture–client liaison. Customer interaction is also important to scientific instrument manufacturers in another way: it provides a source of new product ideas and areas of development. As synergy between instrument manufacturers and their customers is an important issue, developing systems which facilitate interaction with clients is an important part of the competitive process (as will be discussed later).

Of equal importance to developing systems to promote customer liaison is the establishment of processes to harness the ideas and directives provided by clients. This involves concentrating on marketing strategies whereby efforts are focused by firms according to those products and markets most likely to yield the best returns. This raises a further issue; many firms (particularly small firms) concentrate their activities on specific markets or products. By concentrating scarce resources they can potentially maximize the opportunities to be derived from specific niches. Although there is little demand for product adaptation on an international scale, differing technical demands, even within the same customer groups, can affect a need for production flexibility. It is, perhaps, the exploitation of flexible systems which allows small firms to compete so successfully with their larger rivals who concentrate on mass production and the pursuit of scale economies and market share. Catering to the specific needs of customers raises the value-added of products and serves to enhance profitability.

Many of these competitive factors raise barriers to entry in the industry

– particularly product differentiation which involves 'state-of-the-art' technologies, service back-up (which requires establishing international networks for the provision of service), capital requirements (for instance, for research and development and the establishment/management of distribution networks), scale economies, and cost disadvantages independent of size (for example, patents and proprietary technologies).

9.5   Managing the Process

The above assessment of the competitive process reveals that there are differences in strategic approach between the large and small players in the industry. In fact, a number of strategic groups can be identified which, as a result of different competitive forces, raise implications for modes of foreign market servicing to facilitate managing for competitive success.

9.5.1   International broad-range suppliers

This category includes the industry leaders Perkin–Elmer, Shimadzu, Hitachi and Philips. These companies are characterized by a wide range of advanced-technology product offerings giving them competitive advantages over smaller, less-sophisticated rivals. Technological leadership holds three important strategic implications. Firstly, there is a tendency to internalize functions, which precludes licensing being the preferred strategy. Through company controlled domestic and foreign production, control can be maintained over proprietary technology. Secondly, heavy investment in R&D, necessary to sustain a position of technological leadership, prompts firms to establish extensive global operations in order to maximize the customer base from which the costs of R&D can be recouped and profits for future R&D generated. Finally, high levels of technological sophistication demand high levels of service back-up, necessitating the establishment of sales and marketing offices in those markets which are too small to justify production investment, or fostering good relations with intermediaries who can provide customer service on their behalf.

Shimadzu, for example, provides a range of spectrophotometers, clinical analysers, gas and liquid chromatographs, data processors, electronic balances and scanners and has its main production and marketing bases in Japan, America and Germany. They are represented by intermediary companies who sell and service their diverse array of products in 14 other European countries. Firms such as Shimadzu are consequently able to offer 'packages' of equipment to meet most customer needs, often with preferential financial arrangements linked to the scale of purchase and service back-up required. Product differentiation and economies of scope therefore feature highly in the competitive process.

To sum up, target markets are world-wide, with foreign market servicing being undertaken by direct investment in production subsidiaries in the key markets – particularly the USA, Japan and the European Community – and other markets being served by a mix of FDI and exporting (often with sales/marketing subsidiary support). It is also worth noting that subsidiaries have been set up in the EC in a variety of ways, including greenfield investment (for example, Perkin–Elmer in the UK), acquisition (for example, Philips takeover of Pye Unicam UK) and joint venture (for example, Merck–Hitachi) in Germany.

9.5.2 Technology umbrella organizations

Technology umbrella companies supply a diverse array of high technology products to a broad group of markets. Thus, they are similarly product-technology led, with the underlying difference that acquisition drives the attainment of new technologies rather than research and development. The firms acquired generally produce products which diverge from existing company group technologies. Growth is thus mediated via conglomerate diversification. Leading firms in this category include Ciba–Geigy and Fisons, who have developed internationally through the acquisition of scientific-instrument manufacturers in many countries.

Acquired companies generally serve particular product and geographical markets and although they are fairly autonomous, they often distribute and service the products of other group members. This permits the exploitation of acquired technologies on a global scale, which fuels further acquisitive directives. Servicing other geographical markets is through exporting which, again, may be supported by sales/marketing subsidiaries to provide the desired levels of service.

9.5.3 Concentration on end-user markets

Here, the strategic focus is on narrow markets but wide geographic coverage. Thus, the overriding aim is market penetration on a global scale. The relative small size of firms prevents foreign direct investment being pursued in all but a handful of select markets. Thus, for these firms, production and research and development is conducted domestically.

Leading international companies in this category include Beckman (covering life science laboratories) and LECO (covering metallography and spectography laboratories). Beckman, for example, has three centres of operation: production and research and development in the USA, production and sales and marketing for Northern Europe in the UK (in Glenrothes in Scotland) and sales and marketing for central European markets in Switzerland. From these centres they develop and produce a diverse, yet complementary range of products such as spectrophotometers, high performance liquid chromatgraphs (hplc), ultra centrifuges, scintillation counters, pipetting/dispensing work stations, laboratory management systems and ancillary supplies and consumables – specifically for life science laboratories. In addition, the company provides ongoing applications assistance, technical assistance and training to customers.

This latter point reveals how firms in this sector seek to preserve their market share by fostering good relations with their clients and through close interaction benefit from the inherent synergies of such interrelationships. Of critical importance, then, is the development of systems to facilitate the direct interfacing between manufacturer and customer. This raises the significance of sales/marketing activities amongst firms in this strategic group.

9.5.4   Concentration on certain techniques

This category includes companies offering specialist technology products, sometimes internationally, but often in limited geographical markets. For example, in the UK, JEOL and Cambridge Instruments specialize in electron optics, Finnigan specializes in mass spectrometry and Varian in magnetic resonance instruments. Strategically, these firms are narrow-line producers, seeking to establish competitive advantage by product differentiation. Foreign expansion focuses on exporting, principally as a result of the limited resources of these small firms who cannot justify capital investments in production. Certain firms, operating in highly specialized niches, are compelled to export domestic manufactures in order to attain a critical mass in production. Exporting is usually conducted through small sales/marketing subsidiaries or agents which represent the least capital intensive options facing the firm. Alternatively, licensing may be viewed as an alternative option, particularly for some markets (for example, Japan) presumably because of its relatively low commitment of resources. However, the returns are often low, and the risk of dissipating the firm's specific advantage in technology can be high.

9.5.5 Low- to medium-technology products

Whereas the previous groups principally refer to the higher technology end of the industry, this group includes producers of older technology products which have low profit margins and are easily copied by competitors. Many UK firms fall into this category (for example, Philip Harris, Jencons, Techne, May and Baker). The competitive advantage generally pursued is that of cost focus, sometimes in limited geographical areas to minimize transportation costs. Home country competition is usually intense, often with products sourced via offshore production. Foreign expansion is limited as the low added-value nature of products makes exporting too costly in terms of transportation costs, and intense domestic competition makes markets hard to enter except via takeover, which is too costly (both in capital and risk terms) to justify.

9.6   Future Developments

Levels of government spending will continue to have a pervasive effect on many sectors in the industry. This will be felt in terms of government R&D spending, defence initiatives, and funding of public sector services, notably healthcare and education. All are linked to the economic welfare of nations although defence expenditure will, most likely, continue to display a downward trend as world initiatives promote peace. Also affecting government spending in the near future will be the Single European Market Act. One of the key directives being promoted is the opening up of government procurement contracts which, in theory, will make bidding for contracts more competitive. This suggests that further downward pressure will be imposed on market prices as firms aim to put in the most price-competitive bids for major contracts. This will further emphasize, low-cost initiatives in the competitive process of scientific instrument firms.

1992, and initiatives to stimulate competition may increasingly dictate that foreign expansion be achieved via takeover as domestic markets are too saturated to permit greenfield investment options. This will promote a degree of rationalization in an industry which is characteristically highly fragmented and in which a shake-out is almost inevitable.

10

Industry Study 3:
The Paint Industry

10.1 Introduction

The paint industry comprises a relatively wide array of products: paints, varnishes, lacquers and allied products, along with a multiplicity of decorative and protective substances including stains, preservatives, enamels, pigments, thinners, strippers and removers. Accordingly, the industry is characterized by a diverse set of customers and applications. These fall into four main groups: decorative, general industrial applications, automotive and marine. This study is concerned with the decorative paint sector, which includes branded and own-label goods sold direct to end users and paints sold to the professional decorating trade. Sales of decorative paint total approximately 50 per cent of industry sales (see table 10.1) and it is thus an important sector for many of the world's leading manufacturers.

Within the decorative sector, the split between decorative retail and decorative trade is approximately 50:50 by volume, although decorative retail accounts for slightly more business (55 per cent) by value (see table 10.2).

Own label sales account for approximately 50 per cent of retail sales, and as packaging and presentation continue to improve the threat to premium brands increases.

10.1.1 Production

The raw materials for paint production (resin, pigments, solvents, extenders, fillers and additives) are sourced by the chemical industry, which converts basic raw materials into products for paint manufacturing.

Table 10.1   Product distribution of sales

Sector	%
Decorative	50
General Industrial	37
Automotive	10
Marine	3

Source: Industry Estimates

Table 10.2   Sectoral breakdown, 1988

	Volume M litres	% Volume	Average price £/litre	Value £M	% Value
Decorative retail	158	50.97	1.57	248	54.87
Decorative trade	152	49.03	1.34	204	45.13

Source: Jordan Information System Paint Industry Review 1989

The suppliers are predominantly large international chemical companies who supply directly to the paint manufacturer or through local agents. Due to their significant purchasing power and resources, they are better placed in the industry to conduct basic research. Thus, the technical role of the paint manufacturer is more concerned with development than research. The importance of chemical and petrochemical raw materials in paint manufacture is reflected in the prominent position occupied in the industry by chemical companies such as ICI, DuPont and Hoechst.

10.1.2   Distribution

In many countries (and notably the UK) the retail end of the market is dominated by big multiple DIY chains. In other countries, however, retail distribution is more fragmented, paint being sold through specialist outlets. In other markets, manufacturers (for example Sherwin–Williams in the US) hold prominent positions as paint retailers.

Table 10.3 shows the breakdown of distribution in the UK.

The figure demonstrates the difference between the retail and trade sectors. In the latter case, greater emphasis is placed on direct contact with end users, (local authorities, government departments, industrial

Table 10.3 Channels of distribution in the UK

	Via wholesalers (%)	*Direct (%)*
Decorative Retail	100 (Factors 20) (Retailers 80)	Nil
Decorative Trade	47	53

and commercial companies), although wholesale intermediaries still play an important role in the distribution channel – particularly building and decorators' merchants.

10.1.3 Advertising and promotion

Paint is heavily advertised by the leading manufacturers in the industry in the mass-media and at point-of-sale. This is partly due to the highly competitive nature of the branded sector, but also stems from the growing importance of the own-label sector. Most leading manufacturers supply both branded and own-label markets in order to maximize their market share and customer base.

10.2 Industry History

The driving force behind change in the paint industry emanates from the extent to which paint technology has developed over the years. As manufacturers of the chemicals required to make paint, and paint producers themselves, have researched and developed paints for numerous different applications, paint has become less of a commodity and more of a value-embodied substance. In response, many manufacturers have concerned themselves with concentrating their resources on satisfying the needs of specific segments, both domestic and global. This has necessitated structural change in the industry, companies buying into areas of strength and divesting segments of their business where added-value cannot readily be achieved.

In 1988, global sales of paint totalled around £20 billion. Paint volume has been increasing by around 5 per cent per annum since 1980, but in many mature markets, notably Japan and the UK, there has been little growth in value terms (in constant prices). The demand for paint, however, has grown rapidly in many newly industrializing countries, particularly those in Asia–Pacific with the expansion of manufacturing and improved living standards.

In many mature markets, the limited growth in value may be partly attributed to structural changes taking place in the retail sector. The growth of DIY superstore centres has squeezed many of the small specialist paint and wallpaper shops and builders merchants out of the market. As the bargaining power of the superstores has increased, margins have been squeezed for the manufacturers, who are continually being forced to offer price discounts, and raise prices at a disproportionate rate to their spiralling research and development and promotion costs. Freedom to raise prices has been further restricted by over-capacity in the industry and competition from own-label lines prevalent in the product ranges of the DIY multiples.

The increasing costs of research and development and growing domestic competitive pressure has resulted in two major industry developments. Firstly, the industry has become more concentrated as many small firms have been squeezed out of the market or bought out by the larger producers keen to reduce competition and build market share. In the US, the five largest firms account for around 55 per cent of the market, and in Japan the five leading firms supply some 70 per cent of total sales. In Australia, three companies account for 80 per cent of the market, while in the UK the decorative paint sector is dominated by two manufacturers, ICI (33 per cent) and Nobel (26 per cent). The markets of Europe are less concentrated (50 per cent of West Germany's sales accounted for by 15 firms, 55 per cent of France's by 20 firms and 80 per cent of Italy's by 20 firms) although there is an increasing trend towards concentration, not only on a national scale, but internationally as well. In 1980, the ten largest paintmakers in the world accounted for around 18 per cent of the global market, but by 1988 this figure had increased to some 30 per cent. Table 10.4 lists the top ten paint producers in 1988. Secondly, in order to recoup the growing costs of research and development and to maintain a growth impetus in decorative paints, leading manufacturers have looked to expand internationally to compensate for limited potential in their stagnant mature domestic markets.

The growth in global concentration has principally been achieved through acquisition. In particular, the top five companies (ICI, PPG, BASF, Akzo and International) have made a concerted attempt to secure a comprehensive global presence and geographic spread of markets served. (Table 10.5 presents the major acquisitions which have taken place in the 1980s in the paint industry as a whole.) The other companies listed are predominantly regional concerns with a limited number of overseas subsidiaries and low volume of international trade. Although they are at a disadvantage in terms of their lack of market coverage, their regional concentration together with licensing of other paint makers' products enables them to compete effectively at this level. Paint

Table 10.4 Ten largest paint producers, 1988

Company	Volume (M litres)	% World market share
(1) ICI (UK)	780	6.5
(2) PPG (US)	460	3.8
(3) BASF (Germany)	460	3.8
(4) Sherwin Williams (US)	360	3.0
(5) Akzo (Netherlands)	350	2.9
(6) Nippon (Japan)	257	2.1
(7) International (UK)	235	2.0
(8) Kansai (Japan)	231	1.9
(9) DuPont (US)	228	1.9
(10) Valspar (US)	200	1.7

Source: BASF, ICI, Nippon, International, Kansai and Industry Estimates

manufacturers were slow to internationalize their business activities mainly as a result of the relatively recent move from commodity-type products to value-added branded goods. The low value commodity nature of paint, and its volume bulk, meant that it was not economically viable to export it abroad. This meant that only those firms with resources to invest abroad or acquire foreign manufacturers were able to contemplate international expansion. Recent competitive pressures in indigenous markets have resulted in firms actively pursuing this option. Furthermore, the increase in added value has made it possible to export paint profitably, although the long-term effects of strong indigenous manufacturing in foreign markets means that they are difficult to penetrate. When coupled with over-capacity in many developed markets, takeover continues to be the most preferred method of market entry by many manufacturers. However, the experience of acquisitive paint manufacturers has not always been favourable in the decorative retail and trade markets. Although acquiring competitors appear an assured way of improving profitability, customer loyalty to particular brands can make rationalization difficult to achieve and economies in production, marketing and promotion elusive.

Table 10.5 also serves to highly the predominance of international expansion in industrial, motor and speciality sectors. Decorative paints is the least internationalized division, remaining principally indigenous in nature. This is partly due to the importance of developing strong ties with local intermediaries, difficult to achieve when operating at arms length, with high tariff and tax rates in many markets, and the lack of value growth in the market as a whole.

Table 10.5 Restructuring the world paint industry

Company	Acquisition	Year	Sector
Akzo	Wynadotte (US)	1983	Motors
(Netherlands)	Levis (Belgium)	1984	Decorate/motors/industrial
	Bostik (US)	1985	Aircraft
	Blundell–Permoglaze (UK)	1985	Decorative
	Lanchem (US)	1985	Resins
	Sandtex (UK)	1986	Decorative
	Procolor (Spain)	1986	Decorative/industrial
	Brink Molyn (Netherlands)	1986	Decorative
	Ypiranga (Brazil)	1987	Decorative/industrial
BASF	Valentine (UK)	1984	Vehicle refinishing
(Germany)	Immont (US)	1985	Motor/refinishing/can coatings
	Mobil Coatings (Netherlands)	1985	Motor/industrial/ can coatings
	Lusol (Argentina)	1988	Motors/industrial
DuPont	Ford Moter Paints (US)	1986	Motors
(US)	SFDUCO (France) – part	1988	Motors
	IDAC (Joint venture with ICI)	1988	Motors
Hoechst	Renault Paint (France)	1986	Motors
(Germany)	Ault & Wiborg (UK) – part	1986	Motors/refinishing/ industrial
	Divested – part W. Germany	1984	Decorative
	Berger (UK*) Divested to William Holdings (*Australia)	1987	Decorative
ICI	Holdens (UK)	1982	Can coatings
(UK)	Valentine (France)	1984	Decorative/refinishing
	Ault & Wiborg (UK) – part	1985	Can coatings
	HGW Paints (Ireland)	1985	Decorative/refinishing industrial
	Knopp (W. Germany)	1986	Powder coatings
	Glidden (US)	1986	Decorative/can coatings/powder
	Bonaval (W. Germany)	1986	refinishing
	Attiva (Italy)	1988	Can coatings
	DuPont (Spain)	1988	Powder
	Berger (Australasia) from Williams Holdings	1988	Decorative/industrial
	IDAC (joint venture with DuPont)	1988	Motors

Continued

Table 10.5 (*Cont.*)

Company	Acquisition	Year	Sector
PPG	Cipisa (Spain)	1982	Motors
(US)	IVI (Italy)	1984	Motors/refinishing/ industrial
	Wulfing (W. Germany)	1984	Motors
	International (UK) – part	1985	Motors
International	Silap (France)	1982	Powder
(UK)	Litoverti (Brazil)	1982	Can coatings
	Oxyplast (Australia)	1985	Powder
	Porter Paint (US)	1987	Decorative/yacht
	Extensor (Sweden)	1987	Marine
	Taubman (Australia)* increased equity holding to 100 %	1987	Decorative/industrial
	La Minerva (Italy)	1988	Powder
	Suministros (Spain)	1988	Powder
	Epiglass (New Zealand)	1988	Yacht/marine
Williams	Crown Paints (UK)	1987	Decorative/industrial
Holdings (UK)	Berger (UK & Australia)	1987	Decorative
	Divested – Berger (Australia) to ICI Crown Berger Paints – Divested UK business to Nobel Industries (Sweden)	1987 1990	

Source: Company reports

10.3   The Competitive Process

Figure 10.1 summarizes the measures of competitiveness used by the firms in our sample.

Analysing this framework in the light of the structure of the industry provides a foundation for highlighting forces driving competition. The growing sophistication of paint and the need to add value is clearly reflected in the emphasis placed on research and development and marketing advantages which can be exploited through marketing and promotional activities, pursuing a strategy of developing a positive identity with customers and integrating knowledge from various production units. This in turn provides organizations with satisfactory profitability, market share and brand leadership. Overcapacity in the industry has resulted in manufacturers pursuing a strategy of cost

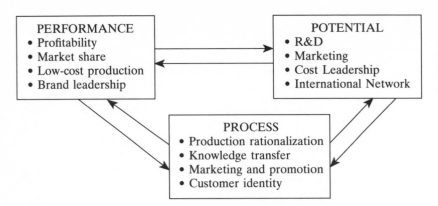

Figure 10.1   The competitive process in the decorative paint sector

leadership, rationalizing production in order to minimize costs and raise profitability. These elements of the competitive process also stem from the changes taking place in the retail sector, wherein increased buying power of multiple DIY chains is forcing firms to reduce their costs wherever possible in order to protect profit margins. Related to this is the growing importance of the own-label sector, which not only allows firms to tie-in distribution to retailers' networks in an effort to sustain profitable market share, but also provides the opportunity to pass on inherent savings from the lack of advertising in the price charged to consumers, reinforcing market share and profitability over time. In order to secure such contracts, firms recognize that maintaining their identity with major retail customers is critical to long-term success.

The growing importance of developing a global network, whilst not applicable to all firms in the sample, is definitely reflected in the measures of competitiveness used by a leading international manufacturer. In order to recoup their heavy research and development investments, designed to sustain their position at the technological forefront of the industry, they believe it is necessary to have an international network. In turn, the established network provides them with a wide pool of resources on which to draw in their research, development, innovation and merchandizing. By moving staff around the international organization, they are making a concerted attempt to integrate fully the skills of the highly dispersed organization, the quality of the resultant products and services allowing them to sustain their reputation and profitable market share. Furthermore, rationalization of production on an international scale allows them to compensate for over-capacity in individual markets, and benefit from scale economies in production, advertising and branding.

It is interesting to note that there is little difference between the identified measures of competitiveness in the retail and trade sectors. Thus, although the changing nature of DIY retailing is not an important factor in the decorative trade, the other identified forces driving competition, namely the growing sophistication of paint and influence of R&D investment, resulting in innovation and differentiation, and overcapacity in the industry causing firms to cut costs and rationalize production, are equally applicable across both sectors.

10.4 Strategic Audit

10.4.1 International producers

There is a relatively small number of firms in the global paint industry who have pursued international expansion in the area of decorative paints. *ICI (UK)*   ICI manufactures paint in 29 countries, has licenses in 14 others and marketing agencies or sales subsidiaries in a further 50 countries. Approximately half of its paint sales are decorative brands (most notably the Dulux brand). The rest of its sales are concentrated in high technology industrial sectors, although the company has a growing interest in the automotive sector. ICI was the fourth largest paintmaker in the world in 1980 but became industry leader in 1986 with its acquisition of the US concern, Glidden (then ranked eighth in the market). This gave ICI a prominent position in the North American market. ICI historically strong in the decorative paint sector in Europe has recently consolidated its position in that area and broadened its product range with acquisitions in France, West Germany, Italy and Spain. The rapidly expanding Asia–Pacific region has also been a focus of ICI's expansion plans. In 1988, it acquired the Berger decorative paint interests of Williams Holdings (acquired by that company the previous year from Hoechst) in Australia, securing its position as market leader (40 per cent market share) against International Paints (22 per cent) and the local concern Waltyl (17 per cent). The rapid industrialization of Thailand, Malaysia, Singapore and Indonesia, lacking a strong local paints industry, has prompted ICI to establish a number of greenfield plants in these countries.
BASF (Germany)   BASF is the second largest global paint manufacturer. It focuses primarily on the industrial and automotive sectors.
PPG (USA)   Pittsburg Plate Glass is the joint-second largest paintmaker in the world. PPG's main strength is in the automotive sector, but it is also represented strongly in the industrial paint sector, and to a lesser extent decorative paints.

International (UK) International's original paint business was centred on marine paints where it still remains clear industry leader with around 40 per cent of the world market. It has, however, used its world-wide experience to move into other sectors, including decorative paints. Recently, it has significantly reduced its dependence on Europe and further developed its non-marine interests with the acquisition of Porter Paint of the US (which has a sizeable decorative paints operation in North America) and Taubmans of Australia. Taubmans is one of the largest manufacturers of industrial paints in Australia and is second to ICI in the decorative paint sector. Also, in the Asia–Pacific region the company has established operations in Korea, Hong Kong and Malaysia and is building two greenfield plants in Taiwan and Thailand to service the industrial and decorative paint sectors.

Akzo (Netherlands) Akzo is the leading supplier of decorative paints in the European market, having consolidated its position recently with the acquisition of two UK decorative paint producers, Sandtex and Blundell–Permoglaze, together with Levis of Belgium and the Spanish concern, Procolor. Although Akzo has reduced its dependency on Europe in the 1980s in the industrial paint sector, its decorative business still remains firmly centred on the European markets.

Overall, there are three important features of global decorative paint manufacturers which gives them a leading edge over their regionally based competitors. Firstly, the fact that the organizations concerned are divisions of large multinational groups means that they have deep-pocket advantages which allow them to pursue a series of acquisitions and effectively buy international market share in particular sectors. Furthermore, international experience in other industrial sectors reduces the risk of securing market entry through acquisition as the paint divisions can draw on the international experience of other business departments. Secondly, the existence of a global customer base allows international manufacturers to recoup more rapidly the costs of R&D, and in turn commit more resources to future innovation and new product development. Thirdly, the opportunity to rationalize production and promotion on an international scale allows global manufacturers to minimize their costs and sustain levels of profitability.

10.4.2 Major regional producers

A second tier of companies exists in the industry which comprises those firms who, although they have some overseas subsidiaries, operate mainly in specific regions in specialist product areas.

US producers Sherwin Williams, ranked as the fourth largest paint-maker in the world, is a major force in the US decorative and industrial paint sectors with manufacturing and distribution operations in 48 states. In the decorative paint sector Sherwin–Williams has a number of main brands which it promotes nationally and which is reinforced by its ownership of around 2000 paint and wall-covering stores. Sherwin–Williams has a relatively small volume of international business, mainly through overseas sales subsidiaries based in Canada, Brazil, Mexico and the West Indies and the granting of licensing rights to affiliates in some 25 other countries.

Japanese producers   Unlike the European and American markets where decorative paints account for one half of total paint sales, in Japan they account for only 20 per cent. The strength of the Japanese paint industry has come from its industrial customers, the appliance and car manufacturers in particular, and shipbuilders. Two paintmakers, Nippon Paint and Kansai dominate the Japanese market and have grown to join the world's top-ten biggest paintmakers on the strength of their domestic sales.

Japanese paintmakers have internationalized their activities in response to the migration of many of their industrial clients. This has taken the form of cross-licensing agreements with other leading international manufacturers – although this is still restricted to the industrial and automotive sectors.

European producers   European second-tier manufacturers have, for the most part, disappeared from the decorative paints sector in recent years, preferring to concentrate on industrial and automotive sectors. Hoechst, the world's third largest paint producer in 1980, decided to pull out of the decorative paints sector, divesting its German decorative paints interest in 1984, and selling its UK-based Berger business to Williams Holdings in 1987. More recently, Williams Holdings has divested all of its UK paint interests (to Nobel of Sweden) in response to sustained competitive pressure from ICI. This divestment also included all the Crown interests acquired from Reed International in 1987.

Another major European company, Beckers of Sweden has also opted for a niche approach. Beckers has sold-off its decorative paint operations including its Valspar (US) licenses (the US license being sold to Macpherson) and now specializes in industrial coatings where it holds the number-one position in Europe.

The instability of this second-tier in the decorative paints markets of Europe stems from the lack of global coverage, which restricts the customer base from which R&D costs can be recouped, and the lack of economies in production and promotion. The decision to specialize in areas of strength (notably industrial and automotive applications) allows firms to concentrate resources on more profitable market sectors. In this way, they can maintain their competitive impetus in specific sectors and secure long-term potential and consequently profitable market share.

Their major strengths rest on the strength of their regional networks and local brands, which serves to provide entry barriers to foreign firms contemplating market entry. However, due to the strength of their indigenous networks and barriers to greenfield entry, these firms are potential takeover targets for the large international players seeking to enhance their global market share.

In the US, forward integration by regional manufacturers like Sherwin Williams ensures long-term market share and enhances profitability at the retail end of the distribution system. Such profits enhance the resources available for innovation and new product development and consequently make the second-tier sector more stable, and less likely to divest their decorative paint activities. Alternatively, the relative small size of the Japanese decorative sector, and the dominance of indigenous producers makes it an unattractive market for investment and thus their decorative paint sector is protected to some degree from outside pressures.

10.4.3 The smaller specialist producers

Those small manufacturers who have not been squeezed out of the industry have survived by concentrating their activities in specific market niches. By concentrating resources on specific sectors they have managed to protect their market share. In the decorative sector in the UK this has principally been achieved by firms specializing in 'own label' products for major DIY retailing groups. In this area of business, there are two principal advantages. Firstly, tying distribution to a leading retailer ensures long-term market share. Secondly, as firms do not need to commit a high proportion of their resources to major advertising and promotional campaigns, they are buffered from the competitive pressures of the branded sector. Own-label products are, however, also supplied by larger industry players, limiting the size of the market for which the small manufacturers can bid.

10.5 Managing the Process

Within the bounds of the competitive process, foreign market servicing plays a critical role in facilitating firms' management of competitive potential in order to achieve international competitive performance. The firms in our interviewed sample, and indeed firms in the industry as a whole (as identified from secondary sources) show various different approaches to international expansion. These approaches will be discussed in the light of the nature of the industry and the forces driving competition in the decorative paints business.

10.5.1 Acquisition

As has already been discussed, acquisition and divestments are important features of the decorative paints industry. Major international players have extended their business globally by acquiring foreign paint manufacturers and have rationalized production on an international scale by divesting production and business units not conducive to economic performance. The major motivations behind this approach are two-fold. Firstly, due to over-capacity in many of the mature developed markets, there is little scope for greenfield entry, which only serves to add further capacity to already over-burdened markets. Secondly, acquisition allows firms to buy into already established distribution networks including wholesalers, retailers and DIY merchants and access personnel with good customer contacts in the decorative trade sector. This latter point is growing in importance in markets where major DIY multiples are emerging as the major retail outlets for decorative paint. In these markets, it is essential for manufacturers to gain access to such dominant retail chains in order to secure market share.

Many acquisitions involve major restructuring of the organizations acquired. Closure of production units, investment in new plant and equipment, and sometimes major readjustments in product lines (for example from industrial to decorative) are often deemed necessary to achieve a critical mass in production and generate economies of scale in the targeted business discipline. This allows firms to take advantage of the most up-to-date technology in an industry where efficient production is critical to minimizing production costs and sustaining profits, and where pressure from environmental lobbyists means that out-dated plants and technological processes can no longer satisfy the stringent requirements being set.

Acquisitions are not restricted to international manufacturers. Middle-tier players and even some of the smaller niche players are not averse to acquiring competitors. Here, however, the major motivation is to reinforce their strength on a regional basis by eliminating the competition. This kind of industry concentration raises the barriers to entry for foreign investors, adding to the threat of takeover by large international firms keen to penetrate the market.

An important factor for firms acquiring foreign producers is the access to strong indigenous sales and marketing units, which means that the foreign producer can be close to its customers. Although some of the major global players are actively pursuing a strategy of global branding for the sake of earning economies in advertising and promotion, different building materials in different countries demands a wide variation in paint formulation. Thus, gathering market information is essential to the localised activities of R&D departments and the development of products capable of satisfying local needs.

10.5.2 Greenfield entry

Although greenfield entry is generally not viable in the mature developed markets of the world, many firms have opted for this strategy in newly industrializing countries, lacking their own indigenous paint industry, and showing high levels of growth.

In the developed markets, however, some firms, whilst ruling out production investment, are setting up sales and marketing subsidiaries to support their export trade. This reinforces the notion that successful market penetration depends on developing products on a country-by-country basis to satisfy the needs of local consumers – adapting products to suit the different building materials prevalent in each market. It also suggests that developing contacts with key buyers is difficult to achieve at arms length, a problem which can be most effectively overcome by locating personnel in the country. Distribution and warehouse facilities are a further area where investment can benefit foreign manufacturers operating at a distance from the market. By establishing local facilities, foreign manufacturers are better able to convince buyers of their ability to deliver on-time. As profit margins on many paint products (for example, glosses and emulsions) are relatively small, and firms consequently seek the most economical methods of transportation which tend to be the slowest modes available (road, rail and water), buyers may doubt the ability of foreign manufacturers to supply an adequate service. Although firms can, and often do use the services of foreign intermediaries, available storage space can be limited, and local intermediaries may be reluctant to hold stocks of a full range of the firms' products, including a full range of colours. This can disadvantage foreign firms *vis à vis* their indigenous competitors and can make it difficult to secure contracts with key buyers, so critical to generating market share.

10.5.3 Exporting

Due to the low profit margins to be earned on decorative paints and their volume bulk, exporting is generally restricted to markets which are relatively close to the manufacturing unit. Major exceptions to this tend to be those markets lacking their own decorative paints sector and showing high levels of growth (for example, the Middle East in recent years) where buyers are prepared to pay a premium, lacking the alternative of a local supplier.

International paint manufacturers tend to export to those countries where acquisition opportunities do not arise. For second-tier companies and niche players, the aim is to extend their customer base beyond their own highly competitive indigenous markets. As a result of the problems of operating at arms length such activities are frequently supported by local sales and marketing operations and/or warehouse and distribution facilities. In markets characterized by strong indigenous competition, market entry depends on establishing contracts with key buyers (major retail networks) or in the case of the decorative trade, key specifiers. Alternatively, the manufacturers need to offer foreign buyers some compensating advantage. Certain own-label manufacturers in the UK, able to pass on the cost savings made through not advertising, are beginning to see opportunities in Continental Europe, where the own-label market is less developed, for competing on price.

10.5.4 Licensing

Licensing is a relatively effective way for firms, lacking an international network, to exploit their innovations and product developments on an international scale. Although licensing in the decorative paints sector is less prevalent than in other business areas, particularly high-technology industrial applications, it is, and continues to be a viable option, particularly for smaller firms wishing to raise funds for future research and development projects. Some firms, however, show a reluctance to license their technology, seeing it as an important source of competitive advantage which it is advantageous to protect at all costs.

10.6   Future Prospects

Whilst management of the competitive process, and decisions on foreign market servicing are dependent on the structure and nature of the industry, the strategies being pursued by firms, in turn, dictate the future shape of the market. Although external forces, particularly the Single European Market, will impact on the strategies followed by firms, it is the way in which companies react to these changes that will ultimately determine the pace and nature of change.

Innovation and new-product development is likely to continue as firms make efforts to remain competitive. Consequently, the process of internationalization can also be expected to continue in order that the ever-rising costs of research and development can be borne by manufacturers. This will continue to put pressure on the smaller manufacturers who, lacking access to international networks will be limited in the extent to which they can actively compete on technology. Although niche operators are likely to survive as a result of their heavy concentration of resources, firms in the second-tier may find survival hard unless they follow the cue of the second-tier players who have already seen the advantages of specialization. It is likely, therefore, that increased concentration will continue its momentum.

In the face of continued over-capacity, production rationalization and cost-cutting strategies will continue to be important. In Europe, this process will be facilitated by the Single European Market Act, which will allow firms to rationalize production on a larger scale as transport across country boundaries is made easier, and economies of scale in large regional production sites becomes a viable proposition. However, it is likely that firms will maintain or establish sales and marketing facilities and/or warehousing and distribution facilities in the separate markets due to the importance of securing contracts with major retailers.

11

Industry Study 4:
Industry Champions

11.1 Introduction

'Industry Champions' are firms who have achieved a position of dominance in their domestic markets and who compete within global markets which are oligopolistic in nature. Lack of domestic competition and a focus which is not only global, but also concerned with achieving a balance in global coverage, characterizes their strategic planning and thus distinguishes them as a separate case. Although the two industries from which our industry champions are drawn – flat glass and industrial gases – are very different, similarity in market structures affords a high degree of commonality in planning foreign market servicing strategies to achieve competitiveness.

11.2   The Global Flat-Glass Industry

The global flat-glass industry is characterized by high levels of market concentration reflecting the large capital costs of building new plant (around £70 million) and the importance of economies of scale.

11.2.1 Product, processes and user markets

Flat glass is of two main types: 'raw' or generic flat glass is produced in strips to a variety of specifications (length sizes and thicknesses, clear and translucent) depending on end usage. Safety glass consists of glass which is 'toughened' (specially heat treated) or 'laminated' (interlayered with a plastic film) to provide greater strength and shatter resistance.

Formerly glass was produced by the 'sheet' and 'plate' processes, but these have now been largely superseded by the 'float' glass process. The particular advantages of the float-glass method over the other two processes is that not only is it less costly to produce glass because of savings in the 'forming' stage of manufacture but also the glass produced is of a superior quality (more uniform surfaces and thicknesses, and blemish-free finishes).

Flat glass is used predominately in the building and construction industries for glazing into house, factory and office windows, doors and roofs. Other applications include mirror manufacture, picture framing, photographic plates and lenses and clock faces. In the period since 1945, with the expansion of the motor-vehicle industry, a large demand for safety glass has developed for glazing into windscreens and rear and side windows.

Historically, the demand for glass from the building and construction industries was cyclical in nature, resulting in profit instability, and this has encouraged flat-glass producers both to seek export markets for their products and new user applications, as well as diversifying their business interests. The problem of cyclical downturn and consequent overcapacity in the industry was compounded in the mid 1970s and again in the early 1980s by the onset of world-wide recessionary conditions. Recently, however, there has been a strong increase in orders which has brought about a closer balance between industry supply and demand (see figure 11.1) and with it firmer prices and profits.

The production of flat glass in most national markets is highly concentrated. Economies of scale are of such significance that even the larger markets such as the United States can viably support only a handful of indigenous producers, while the smaller economies tend to be characterized by quasi-monopoly supply conditions. Established indigenous producers, however, have been exposed to foreign competition to varying degrees – from exports, foreign investments and licensing agreements.

11.2.2   Distribution

The custom of the industry is to sell flat glass only to 'recognized' trade buyers, including (1) merchants and distributors of flat glass (2) fabricators and processors who turn 'raw' flat glass into toughened and safety glass, mirrors, etc. (3) glazing contractors. Other buyers are required either to purchase through recognized dealers or to satisfy their requirements from import sources.

Economies of scale on the whole dictate large scale production in centralized sites with physical distribution being undertaken to regionally-

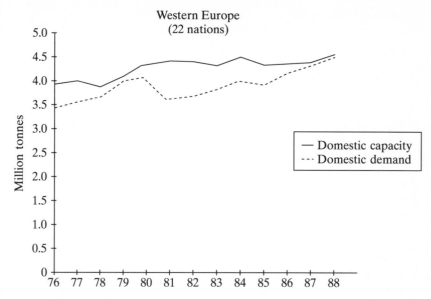

Figure 11.1 Supply and demand of flat-glass
Source: County Securities.

dispersed customers through a network of independent and producer-owned warehousing facilities, or in the case of large users, direct drops. In some instances, this centralized production can be combined with proximity to customers so as to capitalize on producer–buyer synergies. For example, LOF in the United States has three plants located within a 150-mile radius of its largest customer's (General Motors) nine assembly plants in the Great Lakes region, while it has a plant located in the main centre of mirror manufacturing (North Carolina) to service the requirements of that industry. Flat glass it not an easy commodity to transport and high levels of breakage and its bulky nature further impinge on manufacturers' decisions to produce local to the market.

11.2.3 The leading flat-glass producers and the world markets

In 1988, world production capacity of flat glass was estimated at just over 11 million tonnes and industry sales $11 billion, with West Europe and North America each accounting for around 37–8 per cent of these totals (see table 11.1).

Six companies make up the global oligopoly. The UK-based Pilkington

Table 11.1 World-wide float capacity by region, 1988

Region	Existing plants		
	No. of Tanks	*Saleable capacity tonnes per year*	*%*
N America	36	4 194 000	38
W Europe/Scan.	28	4 153 000	37
Japan	10	1 186 000	11
SE Asia/China	6	666 000	6
Latin America	3	394 000	3
Australia	1	115 000	1
South Africa	1	115 000	1
E Europe (Official)	3	308 000	3
Middle East	–	–	–
Totals	88	11 131 000	100

Source: Pilkington

with around 21 per cent of total world capacity is industry leader, followed by Pittsburgh Plate Glass, St Gobain, Asahi, Ford Motors and Guardian (see table 11.2).

Other large producers who operate mainly in their own national markets include AFG Industries (US), Nippon Sheet Steel and Central Glass (Japan), and SIV (Italy). The *de facto* influence of Pilkington on the worldwide scene, however, is much greater than its 'raw' market share would indicate when account is taken of its many licensing deals with other leading international and national suppliers. In 1959, it developed a revolutionary 'float glass' process which it sought to exploit on a world-wide scale by licensing the technology to indigenous producers.

The European market   In Western Europe, the French concern, St Gobain (formerly state-owned, but a public company since 1986) is the leading producer, followed by Pilkington, Pittsburgh and Asahi (see table 11.3). The structure of the industry in Western Europe was dramatically reshaped in the early 1980s when the French conglomerate BSN divested its flat-glass division and the US concern Guardian entered the European market. BSN had been the industry leader until, in 1980, the general unprofitability of its flat-glass operations during the 1970s, together with the company's desire to focus on its core food and drink businesses, precipitated the sale of most of its flat-glass operations. Pilkington acquired a controlling (62 per cent) stake in BSN's German subsidiary, Flachglas, for £141 million later raising the share to

Table 11.2 World-wide float capacity by manufacturer/group, 1988

Group manufacturer	Home-Base	No. of tanks	Saleable capacity tonnes per year	%
Pilkington (incl. LOF)	UK	15.5	2 324 500	21
PPG	US	16	1 992 000	18
St Gobain	France	10	1 514 000	14
Asahi	Japan	9	1 185 000	11
Ford	US	8	807 000	7
Guardian	US	6	640 000	6
AFG	US	5	558 000	5
Nippon	Japan	4	442 000	4
Central	Japan	3	292 000	2
Hankuk Glass	South Korea	2	256 000	2
Vid. Plano de Mex	Mexico	2	239 000	2
SIV	Italy	1.5	197 500	2
Turkey Sise	Turkey	1	156 000	1
Llodio	Spain	1	120 000	1
Taiwan Float Glass	Taiwan	1	100 000	1
Other (E. Europe)		3	308 000	3
Totals		88	11 131 000	100

Source: Pilkington

Table 11.3 Western Europe: main markets and leading producers, 1988

Country	Country % of W. European Sales	Leading Indigenous Producers
West Germany	21	Pilkington, St Gobain
Belgium	13	St Gobain, Asahi
France	13	St Gobain, Pittsburgh
Italy	13	Pittsburgh, St Gobain, SIV
UK	12	Pilkington
Spain	9	St Gobain, Guardian
Scandinavia	6	Pilkington
Netherlands	3	Asahi
Portugal	1	Covina
Luxembourg	1	Guardian
Other	8	Local companies plus subsidiaries of the above

Source: Country Securities

Table 11.4   United States: leading suppliers, 1988

Company	Estimated market share – % general flat glass products	Auto-glass (original equipment)
Pittsburgh Plate Glass	31	25
AFG Industries	11	–
Guardian	11	5
Ford Motor	10	23
Libbey–Owens–Ford	7	37
Imports	30	1
Chrysler	–	9

Source: Country Securities

77 per cent, making it the largest German producer with around 35 per cent of the market. Pittsburgh, who had established a European presence by taking over the Italian concern, Vetreria di Vernanti, acquired BSN's French flat-glass interests shortly after. The third segment of BSN's flat-glass operations, its Belgian and Netherlands subsidiaries, were acquired by the Japanese company Asahi which, like Pittsburgh, became a significant supplier in the European market for the first time.

These takeovers intensified competitive pressures in Europe at a time of low demand for flat-glass products, particularly from the building and construction industries, and this was further exacerbated by the appearance of Guardian. Guardian built a new float-glass plant in Luxembourg in 1981 and acquired the Spanish producer Llodio, in an aggressive attempt to establish a strong customer base in Europe. They targeted West Germany in particular with a marked impact – their exports to Germany capturing 60 per cent market share with Flachglas' share falling from 35 to 20 per cent and Vegla's (St Gobain) from 30 to a similar one fifth stake. Flachglas, however, as a result of its move out of the commodity end of the market into higher value-added sectors, was able to maintain relatively high levels of profitability despite its fall in market share.

The American market   The United States market is the largest single market in the world for flat glass with total sales in 1987 of some $3.6 billion, of which $2.1 billion constituted general flat-glass products and the remainder 'original equipment' and 'replacement' safety glass sales to the motor vehicle industry. In the general sector, Pittsburgh is the dominant indigenous producer with a market share of almost one-third (see table 11.4), followed by AFG Industries, Guardian, Ford Motors and Libbey–Owen–Ford (LOF).

LOF is the leading producer of auto glass, with Pittsburgh and Ford Motors also prominent suppliers. LOF supplies around 65 per cent of General Motor's (the leading US car producer) auto-glass requirements, with Pittsburgh supplying the remainder. Ford Motors supplies all its parent company auto-glass requirements, while Chrysler buys in flat glass produced by the others and processes it in-house into safety glass.

In 1982, Pilkington, whose previous involvement in the market was a small export trade, purchased a 30 per cent holding (from Gulf and Western) in Libbey–Owens–Ford, a conglomerate company, of which LOF flat glass was but one division. In 1986, Libbey–Owen–Ford decided to divest its flat-glass operations and Pilkington acquired the whole division in exchange for its 30 per cent stake in the parent company. The acquisition brought Pilkington LOF's six float plants and gave it the right to retain the original corporate name, Libbey–Owens–Ford – an important 'brand loyalty' consideration for a relatively unknown supplier. The acquisition of LOF, however, was by no means straightforward for the US anti-trust authorities made it conditional on Pilkington divesting its Canadian flat-glass plants. At that time Pilkington was the dominant producer in Canada operating two float-glass plants, the country's only other plant being owned by Pittsburgh. Pilkington had entered the Canadian market in 1967 and its operations were run by a wholly-owned subsidiary company. In 1981, however, Pilkington sold a 51 per cent stake in its subsidiary to Ford Motors in order to gain access to the US vehicle market. Following the US Federal Trade Commissions' objection to a combined Pilkington–Ford–LOF tie-up, Pilkington sold its Canadian operations to Ford.

In 1989, Pilkington sold 20 per cent of LOF to the Japanese concern Nippon Sheet Glass (NSG). NSG is a licensee of Pilkington's float-glass process in Japan and is involved with Pilkington in joint ventures in Mexico, the US, South Korea and Taiwan. Currently, Pilkington is the sole supplier of windscreens to Nissan cars in the UK and the US joint venture supplies windscreens to Toyota in the States. The new move is seen as a means for both companies to strengthen their positions as more Japanese car producers locate production in overseas markets, particularly in the US and the European Community.

Additionally, since acquiring LOF, Pilkington has repositioned the company away from its over-dependency on the US auto-glass sector towards mainstream and higher value added general flat-glass products. *The Japanese market and the rest of the world* The Japanese market, the second largest individual national market after the US is dominated by a handful of indigenous producers led by Asahi, Nippon Sheet Glass and Central Glass. All of these companies are, or were, Pilkington licencees for the float glass technology. Elsewhere in the world economy, the smaller national markets tend to be supplied by a mix of indigenous producers and subsidiaries of the leading international companies. Again, Pilkington is a prominent force in these areas through its licensing agreements and subsidiary/associate companies in Australia, New Zealand, South Africa, Mexico, Argentina, India, Taiwan, etc.

11.3 The Global Industrial Gases Industry

Industrial gases sales have risen rapidly in the 1980s following a period of depressed demand in the 1970s. Total global sales in 1989 amounted to some $13 billion. Sales of gases to traditional user industries such as steel and chemicals have declined in relative importance with the development of new applications in growth areas such as the food processing, beverages, fibre optics, oil and electronic industries.

The industrial gases industry is also characterized by high levels of market concentration and barriers to entry. The global scene is dominated by seven suppliers who have maintained their leading positions in the industry by exploiting economies of scale and through plant and product innovation. Although the larger suppliers have penetrated each other's 'established' markets, in many areas local monopolies still prevail, buttressed by high distribution costs and contractual ties with users.

11.3.1 Industrial gas products and user markets

The industrial gases industry comprises a range of gases derived from the atmosphere and from chemical processes.

Atmospheric Gases Atmospheric gases constitute the core of the industry. Oxygen is a highly reactive oxidizing gas used to improve the efficiency of combustion processes and chemical reactions. As such, it is used in a number of applications involving heat in the metal, glass, ceramic and mineral industries, while in the chemical industry, it is used in the synthesis of materials such as ethylene oxide and vinyl chloride.

The expansion in oxygen use began to decline in the 1970s as the demand for steel and the products of other metal-working industries fell following the onset of general economic recession. This was compounded by the increasing movement of world steel production towards the newly-industrializing countries of Asia and Latin America with their preference for in-house oxygen capacity. Volume growth rates for oxygen in the 1980s averaged only 1–2 per cent per annum.

Nitrogen has long been used in the steel, metallurgical and petrochemical industries. It has greater versatility than oxygen and this has led to an expansion of its usage in new growth areas such as the frozen foods, electronics and oil industries. Nitrogen has recorded a volume growth rate in the order of 5–12 per cent per annum in the 1980s. Argon, an enhanced form of nitrogen, is used primarily for producing low-carbon steels.

The production of these atmospheric gases involves various air-separation processes, the refrigeration of air to a liquid form and separation by distillation. This is a highly capital intensive operation and there are significant economies of scale from operating large plants. Through technological innovation and regular investments in new plant and developments, the leading manufacturers have been able to maintain their positions as low-cost producers.

Gases derived as by-products   The development of gases derived as by-products from chemical processes has given the industry greater flexibility. Carbon dioxide, for example, is used to carbonate beverages and as a refrigant and chilling agent in the food industry. Carbon dioxide, however, is interchangeable with nitrogen in many of its uses and this has tended to lead to geographically localized markets with the prices of the two gases, which depends mainly on the proximity of the source, dictating the boundaries. In Britain, for example, unlike the USA and Continental Europe, there is greater use of nitrogen in the food industry reflecting the more cost-effective source of nitrogen.

Hydrogen is mainly used as a reducing agent in the chemical, pharmaceutical, metallurgical and food industries, and has found new applications in fibre optics, ceramics and electronics. A large part of this sector is supplied by the in-house capacity of oil-refiners and chemical companies, but industrial gas companies have become increasingly involved through the development of a 'merchant market' (see below) for the liquid and pressurised forms of the gas. All the major industrial gas suppliers are involved in this sector to a greater or lesser degree (L'Air Liquide, in particular, has developed a world-wide presence), but here they face competition from other companies such as Distillers/Guinness in the UK.

Speciality gases   These gases are generally high-value, low-volume products covering a wide range of items, including gaseous chlorine, sulphur dioxide, ethylene oxide, xenon, krypton and neon. The electronics industry has been the area of fastest growth in special gases.

11.3.2   Distribution

Industrial gases are difficult and expensive to transport and this has tended to produce local monopolies. Foreign direct investment by the main international companies, together with more 'portable' technologies, has increased competition in the industry, but the logistics of gas distribution and established contractual practices mitigate against widespread competitive encroachment. For example, in the case of 'on-site' tonnage deliveries (see below) transport costs account for up to 40 per cent of product selling price, which makes it uneconomical to deliver gas beyond a 200-mile radius.

There are three main distribution channels for industrial gases:

'On-site' or tonnage. In the case of high volume users of oxygen and nitrogen gases, such as steel and chemical concerns, it is most economical for gas to be supplied by pipelines to 'on-site' customized air-separation plants. Because of the size of investment involved in pipeline networks and related plant, 10–15-year supply contracts are commonplace which provide for an agreed return on the capital invested by the gas supplier. These contracts require the customers to agree to a 'take or pay' clause and to pay for increases in energy costs, which protects the suppliers' revenues from downturn in customers' activities and insulates them from the direct effects of energy inflation. In return, the gas company carries the risk of changes in the cost of financing its capital investment and undertakes to pass on lower energy costs by reducing gas prices.

Merchant. The merchant market is the main source of supply of industrial gases for lower volume users. Supplies are obtained either from plants specifically catering for this sector, or the surplus offtake from tonnage plants, distributed in the main by road tankers to the customers' storage tanks. Supply contracts are usually for three to five years. Competition, which occurs largely on the boundaries of a merchant plant's economic radius of supply, tends to be more intense than in the tonnage market, reflecting the shorter duration of contracts and the greater variability of demand both in terms of existing volumes and new customers.

Cylinders. The smallest amounts of gas are supplied to customers in cylinders, with customers contracting to take supplies on a rental basis. The bulk of low-volume specialist gases are supplied in this way.

All three methods of distribution are widely used in most countries, the exception being Japan. In Japan, on-site installations are typically joint-ventures between the user and the gas company. The user pipes the gas off at cost and the gas company distributes the excess through the merchant market.

11.3.3 The leading industrial gas suppliers and the world market

The global industrial gases industry is highly concentrated, with seven international companies accounting for around 78 per cent of industry

Table 11.5 The world industrial gases industry, 1988

Company	Home base	Market share %
L'Air Liquide	France	21
BOC	UK	16
Union Carbide	USA	14
Air Products	USA	11
AGA	Sweden	6
Messer Griesheim	Germany	6
Linde	Germany	4
Others		22

Source: Hoare Govett; County Nat West

sales. L'Air Liquide of France is the world-wide industry leader with a market share of 21 per cent (see table 11.5) followed by BOC, Union Carbide, Air Products, AGA, Messer Griesheim and Linde. Two other large suppliers, Nippon Sanso of Japan and CBI of the US, mainly operate in their respective home markets.

In recent years, international competition has increased as the leading companies have moved into each other's traditional spheres of influence. The exploitation of new applications for gas products has been one important competitive stimulus. Another has been the introduction of new manufacturing techniques for atmospheric gases, in particular that of 'pressure swing absorption', which has both reduced production costs and increased plant 'portability' (the new systems can be housed in a shed the size of a domestic greenhouse). Finally, companies have become more aware of the opportunities accorded to global operators to take advantage of world-wide technical developments and market growth.

Foreign expansion has involved mainly direct investment in acquisitions, joint-ventures and greenfield plants. There is a small export trade in speciality gases but otherwise transportation logistics dictate a local market presence.

In 1989, world industrial gases sales (including related equipment) totalled some $13 billion. The Americas accounted for around 40 per cent of the world market, Europe for nearly one-third and Japan for 15 per cent. Table 11.6 gives the geographical spread of the leading industrial gases companies, while the extent of their involvement in particular national markets is discussed in more detail below.

The American market The United States is the world's largest market and one of the most advanced in terms of gas usage, reflecting the size of the US economy and its sophisticated industrial base.

Table 11.6 Geographical analysis of industrial gases sales, 1988

	% by region	% of company sales by region						
		L'Air Liquide	BOC	Union Carbide	Air Products	Messer Griesheim	AGA	Linde
Americas	40	22	28	84	81	*	33	*
Europe	30	64	21	12	16	93	64	94
Japan	15	*	*	*	*	–	–	–
Other	15	14	48	*	*	*	*	*

* Under 5 %
Source: Hoare Govett

Table 11.7 Industrial gases sales in North and Latin America, 1988 estimated market shares$^{\pm}$ (%)

	% by region	Union Carbide	L'Air Liquide	Air Products	BOC	CBI	AGA
USA	81	29	21	20	14	6	2
Canada	7	35	41	7	*	*	
Mexico	3	*		*		*	25
Brazil	5	70	10	5		*	7
Rest of Latin America	4		12		*	10	40
	100						

+ Other US Messer Griesheim* Linde*
+ Other Mexico Industrias Franco (50 %)
+ Other Brazil Linde*
* under 5 % market share
Source: Hoare Govett

Some 60 per cent of the US market is accounted for by indigenous companies. Union Carbide is the market leader (see table 11.7) with a market share of around 29 per cent, followed by Air Products with a market share of one-fifth and CBI with 6 per cent. Both Union Carbide and Air Products have reorientated their operations towards the higher growth products, hydrogen and speciality gases, and are prominent suppliers to the processed foods, electronics and oil industries.

European companies have become a more important force in the American market in the past 20 years. BOC entered the market in 1978 with the acquisition of Airco, then the third largest supplier. BOC's current market share is around 14 per cent. L'Air Liquide's US interests are more long-standing through its wholly owned subsidiary, Liquide Air Corporation. Liquid Air has traditionally operated in the merchant gas sector and it was the lack of growth in this market in recent years that prompted the company, in 1986, to acquire the Big Three concern in order to establish a strong presence in the tonnage market. As a result of the acquisition of Big Three, the fifth largest US supplier, Liquide Air, has increased its market share to some 21 per cent. Smaller market shares are held by AGA which entered the US market in 1978 through the acquisition of Burdox, and the German concerns Messer Griesheim and Linde.

In Canada, L'Air Liquide and Union Carbide account for 76 per cent of the market with smaller shares being held by Air Products, BOC and CBI. Air Products has recently added to its interests in this area with the take-over of Inter City Gas in 1985.

America is, however, one of the slowest growing of the leading world markets and consequently the returns to be made by foreign manufacturers are limited. The result is that firms entering the American market look for takeover opportunities as opposed to setting up greenfield operations. This has caused much consternation with the American government, who are opposed to foreign firms buying competitors, as opposed to generating new competition. In the past, foreign takeover bids have been contested in an attempt to protect indigenous manufacturers.

The European market Unlike the US market where there are a few large regional companies, the national boundaries of Europe have helped indigenous companies to maintain leading positions in their 'home' markets. In particular, Germany, the largest market in Europe followed by France and the UK, which together account for around two-thirds of the total European market, are all dominated by indigenous companies (see table 11.8). In the West German market, Messer Griesheim and Linde hold market shares of 46 per cent and 28 per cent, respectively. L'Air Liquide dominates the French market with a 70 per cent market share, while BOC is similarly placed in the UK and AGA in Sweden. The smaller markets of Europe, too, tend to be dominated by L'Air Liquide and AGA. L'Air Liquide, in particular, is the leading supplier in Italy, Austria, Spain, Portugal, Belgium and Luxembourg, where it has market shares variously in excess of 50 per cent. AGA is the major supplier in the Netherlands, Finland and Norway (through the acquisition of Norgas in 1984) and is second to Hede Nielsen in Denmark. AGA has smaller operations in Germany and France. Messer Griesheim and Linde are represented by a 50–50 joint-venture company, Likos, in

Table 11.8 Industrial gases sales in the European market, 1988 estimated market shares (%)

	% by region	L'Air Liquide	BOC	Air Products	Messer Griesheim	Linde	AGA	Union Carbide	Other
West Germany	24	7	*	5	46	28	8	*	
Franch	21	70		6	*	*	*	*	
UK	18		75	20					
Italy	8	50						12+	+
Netherlands	6	55		20	*	*	43		
Spain	5	15		+		*	*		
Sweden	5						70		
Rest of Scandanavia	5	*					60		
Other	8	++			*	*	*	*	+
	100								

++ market leader (50 % +) in Austria, Portugal, Belgium, Luxenbourg
+ Italy Joint-venture with En-Chem
  Netherlands–Hoek–Loos (30 %)
  Spain–Carburos Metalicos (40 %) – Air Products 20 % stake
  Rest of Scandinavia–Hede Nielsen (Denmark – 50 %)
* under 5 % market share
Source: Hoare Govett

France, the Netherlands and Belgium, but their market shares are relatively small. Messer Griesheim also has a toehold in the Spanish market through a joint-venture with Hoechst (Messer's major shareholder with a 66 per cent equity stake in the company, and joint co-venture partner in Venezuela and Japan), while Linde is also represented in the Spanish and Austrian markets.

The major American companies have yet to establish themselves as leading suppliers in most of the European markets. At the present time, the UK, the Netherlands, Spain and Italy constitute their main areas of operation. Air Products entered the UK market in 1961 as a greenfield supplier and has built-up a market share of 20 per cent. It also has around 20 per cent of the Dutch market and smaller operations in France, Germany, Belgium and Luxembourg. In 1982, it acquired a 20 per cent stake in Carburos Metalico, the leading supplier in Spain. Union Carbide is less well established in Europe, but has sizeable interests in Spain and Italy, the latter through a joint-venture with a local company En-Chem. Elsewhere, its operations in France, Germany and Belgium are small scale.

Cross-frontier competition in the European market has intensified recently, particularly as a result of the termination of a joint-venture agreement between L'Air Liquide and AGA, and the 1992 'single market' initiatives of the European Community. The joint-venture between L'Air Liquide and AGA was established in 1971 and provided for territorial rights in West Germany, the Netherlands, Belgium and Luxembourg, with AGA running the two companies' operations in West Germany and the Netherlands, and L'Air Liquide similarly in Belgium and Luxembourg. These arrangements, however, were terminated at the beginning of 1987 as a result of L'Air Liquide's determination to go it alone in the large West German market and the objections of the West German Cartel Office to the joint-venture. AGA took control of the Netherlands and three-quarters of the West German operations, with L'Air Liquide taking control of the remainder as well as the Belgium and Luxembourg businesses. Immediately prior to the *formal* ending of their alliance, however, both companies had taken steps (in 1986) to strengthen their positions in the expanding carbon-dioxide sector of the West German market, L'Air Liquide acquiring Agefko and AGA acquiring Maatsshappij Romenhoeller. The take-over of the latter concern, the leading supplier of carbon dioxide in the Netherlands has further consolidated AGA's position in that country as well as securing its re-entry to the Belgium market. Additionally, the two companies have moved to build-up their operations in each others' 'home' market. L'Air Liquide now holds a 15 per cent share of the Swedish market, while, in 1987, AGA expanded its French interests with the take-over of Duffour et Igon.

Table 11.9   Industrial gases sales in the rest of the world, 1988 estimated market shares (%)

	% by region	BOC	L'Air Liquide	Air Products	Union Carbide	Linde	Messer Griesheim
Japan	50	+	+	+	+		*
Australia	12	70	10	*	*	*	
South Africa	9	60	*	*		*	
Taiwan	3	70++					
South Korea	3		*	*	*		
Other	23	+++	+++	*	*		
	100						

* under 5 % market share

+ Japan	Estimated market share	Foreign ownership
Nippon Sanso	32	None
Teisan	12	L'Air Liquide 64.1 % equity
Daido Sanso	11	Air Products 10 % equity, 15 % convertible bond
Osaka Sanso	10	BOC 25.3 % equity, 24.3 % convertible bond
Iwatani	(Distributor)	Union Carbide 25 % joint-venture holding

++ 50 % equity stake in Lien Hwa Industrial Gases
+++ BOC and L'Air Liquide 50 % + market shares in various countries
Source: Hoare Govett

Of all the European-based companies, BOC is the least represented in this area. Historically, BOC has developed overseas in former British Empire countries, where it holds leading positions, and latterly in North America. Apart from the export of speciality gases to West Germany (where it now holds a 25 per cent market share of the electronics sector) and a dominant position in the Irish market, BOC has neglected the wider European market. However, with an eye on '1992', the company has signed a 15-year contract to supply tonnage gases to Dow Chemicals in the Netherlands and has built a new plant alongside Dow's complex at Terneuzan. This plant will also be used to develop markets in the Benelux countries, West Germany and France.

The rest of the world   The Japanese market is the second largest single area after the US (see table 11.9), and has been long dominated by indigenous companies. In recent years, however, a number of leading foreign companies have entered the market. The locally-controlled Nippon Sanso is the largest supplier with a market share of around 32 per cent. Foreign companies, however, have acquired strategic stakes in the next three leading producers. L'Air Liquide holds 64 per cent of the

equity in Teisan, while BOC, in 1982, obtained a 49 per cent equity/
bond holding in Osaka Sanso. Both companies have set up new plants
recently and are committed to a long-run presence in the market. Air
Products has a 25 per cent equity/bond stake in Daido Sanso, used
mainly at the present time to keep abreast of technological developments, while a fourth international company, Union Carbide has a 25
per cent holding in a joint-venture with Iwatani, a leading industrial
gases distributor. Messer Griesheim also has a small operation in the
country. The recent economic slow-down in Japan has adversely affected
the industrial-gas business. The shift away from heavy-industry to hi-
technology market sectors means that a reassessment of market opportunities in nitrogen and speciality gases is the necessary way forward.

Australia is the second largest market after Japan in the 'rest of the
world'. BOC holds a dominant 70 per cent share of this market through
its (60 per cent-owned) subsidiary, Commonwealth Industrial Gases,
which also coordinates BOC's involvement in various other smaller
Pacific countries. The company's only significant rival in Australia is
L'Air Liquide with a 10 per cent market share, although Linde and Air
Products are also developing their interests. BOC holds leading positions
in a number of other Far East countries, stemming from its Empire-
orientation, including New Zealand, Hong Kong, Malaysia, Singapore,
India and Bangladesh. In 1986, BOC purchased a 50 per cent stake in
Lien Hwa Industrial Gases, the leading supplier in Taiwan with 70 per
cent of the market, and has recently concluded a joint-venture deal with
a Chinese concern. Other international companies involved in the area
include L'Air Liquide, Air Products and Union Carbide.

The African market is dominated by South Africa where BOC is the
market leader through its 60 per cent stake in Afrox. L'Air Liquide, Air
Products and Linde have smaller operations in this area. BOC is also
the leading supplier in a number of other African countries, including
Kenya, Nigeria, Uganda, Zimbabwe and Zambia, again reflecting its
Empire heritage. Likewise, L'Air Liquide is the leading supplier in a
number of French controlled North African countries.

11.4   The Competitive Process

Figure 11.2 presents the measures of competitiveness used by the two
industry champions.

The identified measures reflect the forces driving competition in the
two industries – which show a high degree of commonality in their
structure and character. Large-firm dominance, arising out of aggressive
cost-cutting policies of leading organizations, has produced global

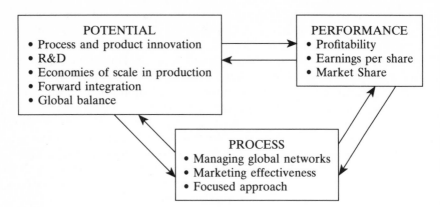

Figure 11.2   Measures of competitiveness

oligopolies in which firm size and a broad geographic coverage have become pre-requisites of competitive success. Internationalization has proceeded to such an extent that attaining a global balance in activities has become a key strategic factor, particularly between the three major developed economic regions – The Americas, Europe and the Pacific Basin – and between the developed and developing world. A good balance allows firms to minimize risks and maximize global potential.

11.4.1   Industrial gases

The commodity nature of industrial gas products has had a pervasive influence on the industry. As product differentiation is not an available option, competition has centred on cost management, specifically exploitation of scale economies and investment in process technology innovation to develop the most efficient production techniques. Additionally, product standardization raises the importance of developing good ties with customers.

This has led to degree of forward integration wherein pipelines have been established to serve directly leading customers. These pipelines serve as surrogates for the traditional wholesaler channels of distribution, where customer ties are fostered through long-term contractual supply arrangements which protect long-term market share.

More recently, falling demand for core products – oxygen and nitrogen – as a result of the decline in metallurgical sectors, prompted a shift in competitive focus. A production and sales orientation has now given way to research and development and marketing, as firms are attempting to discover new products and user applications. This new phase of product and market development is now viewed as essential to future competitive success in the industrial gas sector, enhancing profitability as a result of higher value added products and rejuvenating a business portfolio characterized by mature and declining products. New developments are, however, clearly focused, being centred on existing technologies and customer groups, with a degree of reluctance to diversify beyond existing competencies. The areas of development stem from changing consumer needs and new emerging markets – identified through dedicated marketing efforts. This is facilitated by global networks which extends the market and customer coverage from which new ideas may be generated. Effective management of the global organization, particularly the quality of communication and interfaces between functional departments clearly promotes this process.

11.4.2 Flat glass

The flat-glass sector has, for many years, been dominated by process technology. This is reflected by the powerful world position of Pilkington (the UK multinational) which developed the float-glass process used by all multinationals for the production of high quality flat glass. Other multinationals have also, through investment in new production techniques, developed efficient production methods to enable them to reduce costs and preserve profit margins.

Flat glass, like industrial gases, is highly standardized, which promotes low-cost production as a key to competitive success. However, there is some scope for differentiation and through research efforts firms have brought glass more into the forefront as a building material rather than an ancillary window product. Such higher value-added products have enhanced profitability and stimulated product innovation. Generally, however, close customer relationships feature highly in order to sustain long-term market share by retaining customers. Unlike the gas sector, these relationships are not contractual, but depend largely on the manufacturer's proximity to the customer. As glass is bulky and costly to transport, many manufacturers have located production close to their leading customers, permitting low cost and rapid delivery. This has particularly been a feature in the relationships developed between the glass manufacturers and car producers as was highlighted earlier.

11.5 Managing the Process: FDI and Licensing

The foreign market servicing decisions of firms provide the framework in which the competitive process is managed and therefore is an integral part of firms' strategies for competitive success. In the case of flat glass and industrial gases the bulky nature of the product constrains strategic choice to some form of local market production – either foreign direct investment or licensing.

11.5.1 Flat glass

The choice between foreign direct investment and licensing can, perhaps, be best illustrated by examining the decision made by Pilkingtons in the late 1950s following the development of the revolutionary float-glass process. In terms of the world-wide exploitation of the process, the firm was confronted with two strategic options (1) it could license established overseas manufacturers to produce and sell float glass, or (2) it could itself invest in new float-glass capacity abroad. In the event, the FDI option was initially rejected on both financial and strategic grounds. At this time, Pilkington was still a private unquoted family business (it did not get a public Stock Exchange quotation until 1970) and had strained its financial resources to the tune of some £4 million in developing the float-glass process. There was thus a serious question mark surrounding its ability to raise the capital to establish new plant even on a joint-venture basis. Also to be considered was the likely reaction of local producers to the entry of Pilkington into their established markets bringing with it the threat of cut-throat competition and the likelihood that the invention would be 'pirated', raising attendant 'policing' costs. The option of licensing, therefore, appeared to be far more appealing, whilst at the same time leaving Pilkington room for FDI initiatives at some later time as its finances improved. This, then, was the broad strategy pursued by Pilkington with a heavy emphasis initially on licensing producers in the older industrialized markets and subsequently producers in the newly industrializing countries, augmented as time went on by an FDI presence with Pilkington building new greenfield plants in Canada, Australia, South Africa, New Zealand, Scandanavia, etc., and acquiring Flachglas and LOF.

This example raises two key issues: firstly, investments in the glass industry are 'lumpy', that is, they are large scale and demand a critical mass to justify such a large capital outlay. This perpetuates the oligopolistic nature of the global market and suggests that, in the short-term, establishing a presence in the market and generating a critical mass may potentially be achieved through licensing. The scale of required investments also makes joint ventures a likely proposition. Secondly, licensing of technology, whilst diluting the competitive advantage of the firm, helps to sustain the competitive buoyancy of the world market. This is not to say, however, that Pilkingtons attained little advantage from their innovative technology.

Licensing income has provided the resources for increased R&D effort, which has resulted in new product and process innovations, enhancing overall group profitability. The licenses have also provided valuable learning experience in foreign markets providing an ideal foundation for future capital investment and fostering relations with indigenous firms who may, potentially, become joint venture partners.

11.5.2 Industrial gases

Foreign direct investment dominates strategies in this sector and there is much greater reluctance to dissipate competitive advantages through licensing contracts – particularly in the new product areas being developed. Whereas Pilkington's float glass process was highly innovative, the advantages gained from new process technologies in the industrial-gas industry are relatively marginal, minimizing the threat of aggressive competitive reaction. Similarly, however, production investments are large scale and necessarily require a critical mass being attained. Again, this perpetuates the global oligopoly and also suggests that joint ventures may be necessary where capital outlay is too great. An argument for joint ventures is further strengthened given the reluctance to license and may, potentially, offer a lower-risk means of entry into markets which are unknown.

Exporting Although exporting is not viable in the core 'commodity' sectors of both industries, in the higher value-added, niche markets products can withstand the costs of transportation. As firms expand business in the area of new innovations, increased exports may be expected, although ultimately, as products mature and market size expands, foreign production may be more cost effective.

11.6 Future Prospects

11.6.1 Industrial gases

It has already been suggested that new entrants and growing small businesses may be expected in the industrial gas sector given the scope for new innovations. Changing world demand patterns – for example, the now rapid decline in CFC gases – are giving rise to new opportunities (in this case for an ozone-friendly substitute). It is debatable, however, whether these small firms will, in any way, erode the entrenched oligopoly currently characterizing the industry. Given the rapid rates of technological diffusion in most industrial sectors, the option of gradual strategic expansion is growing less viable, which limits the possibility of small firms growing into large multinationals. Alternatively, exploitation of new technologies can be achieved through joint-venture agreements with leading multinational industrial gas firms in order to access rapidly the developed international networks. This clearly benefits the small firm in the short-term allowing it to exploit its new technology on a global scale. However, it puts the firm at risk from takeover by the multinational seeking to internalize the benefits derived from the innovation.

This suggests a power-struggle between two organizations with distinct competitive advantages. On the one hand is a firm with a technological advantage, on the other an organization boasting multinational dimensions particularly extensive financial resources and geographic networks. Ultimately, it would appear that the deep-pocket advantages of the multinationals should mean they pursue joint-ventures with smaller firms as an active policy of extending their technological base.

11.6.2 Flat glass

A recent move by St Gobain, the leading French producer, suggests a way in which competition in the flat glass sector may develop. Despite many years of actively avoiding encroachment into the UK market for fear of the competitive reaction from Pilkingtons, they recently acquired a major UK distributor, securing for themselves an extensive distribution base and customer network. As firms other than the leading multinationals have been squeezed out of the market, international expansion by takeover has been limited. Forward integration, therefore, remains one of the main ways in which firms may enter markets in which the leading player holds a quasi-monopoly position. If this is, indeed, the way in which competition proceeds, it will have two distinct effects. Firstly, it will break down the quasi-monopolies held by firms in their domestic markets and stimulate competition on a nation-by-nation basis. Secondly, forward integration will further raise barriers to entry and perpetuate the oligopolistic nature of the world market. Those firms who will derive the most from such a development will be those who, through forward integration overseas, are able to erode the position of the indigenous producer and strengthen their position within the oligopoly. The major danger, of course, is that cut-throat competition of this nature will spoil the industry for all players!

12

Industry Study 5: The European Retail Banking Sector

12.1 Introduction

Deregulation throughout Europe is changing the face of European banking. Traditionally passive, reactionary, saving, lending and current account bastions, banks are now facing up to fierce competition challenges from not only their leading banking rivals, but also other financial-service providers whose markets now merge with their own. Expanding into new business sectors, notably the housing finance and insurance markets, has provided greater scope in their product portfolios. It has also shown banks to be strong aggressors prompting far from passive competitor reaction. Emerging from a period of over-regulation, the European market exhibits a high degree of over-capacity and as firms seek to overcome this difficulty, mergers and acquisitions are inevitable. In this potentially hostile environment, only the strong will survive. This is refocusing attention on profitability rather than size and the potential for efficiency that may be derived from new technologies.

12.2 The Changing Banking Environment

Until fairly recently, the European banking market yielded low levels of competition. Product sectors were protected by legislation, and profitability was assured by the continual generation of new customers. This was possible in an environment where the population was expanding and in which increasing affluence was raising the propensity of individuals for using banking institutions to handle their money. A series of developments has, however, disturbed this comfortable position of European banks. Firstly, stagnating levels of population growth have depressed

Table 12.1 Projected EC population

Population 000s	1995	(%)	2000	(%)	2010	(%)	2020	(%)
Belgium	9915	3.0	9880	2.9	9687	2.9	9387	2.9
Denmark	5619	1.5	5176	1.5	5073	1.5	4776	1.5
W. Germany	61 359	18.6	61 160	18.4	58 585	17.7	54 704	16.9
Greece	9973	3.0	10 115	3.0	10 300	3.1	11 149	3.4
Spain	40 094	12.2	40 746	12.3	41 193	12.4	40 699	12.5
France	57 060	17.3	57 880	17.4	58 763	17.8	58 664	18.1
Ireland	3500	1.1	3471	1.0	3412	1.0	3347	1.0
Italy	57 585	17.5	57 610	17.3	56 408	17.1	53 484	16.5
Luxembourg	374	0.1	375	0.1	375	0.1	369	0.1
Netherlands	15 329	4.7	15 716	4.7	16 101	4.9	16 160	5.0
Portugal	10 819	3.3	11 140	3.3	11 473	3.5	11 814	3.6
UK	58 144	17.6	58 858	17.7	59 391	17.9	59 838	18.4
Europe total	329 321		332 127		330 761		324 381	

Source: European Commission

the opportunity to generate new customers. Secondly, domestic capacity has further affected opportunities for new customer generation. Finally, deregulation has opened up markets to new competition from non-bank financial firms. Such developments, almost generally applicable across Europe, have occurred at different times and affected markets to different degrees. Consequently, firms based in individual Member States approach 1992 at different stages of development. Nevertheless, the competitive challenges being determined by the changing environment affect all players. Worthy of comment is the projected population decline across Europe as table 12.1 demonstrates.

Overall, six countries are expected to grow their population (Greece, Spain, France, Netherlands, Portugal and the UK) and six are expected to decline (Belgium, Denmark, Germany, Ireland, Italy and Luxembourg). However, the combined decrease in population of approximately 10.7 million is not made up by growth in the other countries. What this suggests is a growing interest in expanding markets – particularly the likes of Spain and Portugal in which increasing affluence is extending the number of bank users – from banks based in the more developed saturated markets. More important, perhaps, is the changing age structure of the European population as demonstrated in table 12.2. This has important implications for the European banks. Increasing aging of the European population is raising fears about the ability of Member States to make adequate pension provisions for their indigenous population. Governments are therefore actively promoting personal pensions providing enormous potential for European insurers. In the UK, for example,

Table 12.2 Changing age structure of EC population

Population 000s	*1991*	*(%)*	*2000*	*(%)*	*2010*	*(%)*
0–14	58 964	17.9	59 011	17.8	54 170	16.3
15–44	142 878	43.3	139 971	42.1	129 288	39.1
45–64	77 089	23.4	80 092	24.1	89 686	27.1
65+	50 390	15.3	53 053	15.9	57 617	17.4

Source: European Commission

Table 12.3 Per-centage growth of real GDP by member states, 1984–90

	1984	*1985*	*1986*	*1987*	*1988*	*1989*	*1990*
Belgium	2.2	0.8	2.1	2.1	4.0	4.2	3.3
Denmark	4.4	4.3	3.1	−0.7	−0.2	1.6	2.0
West Germany	3.3	1.9	2.3	1.8	3.4	2.5	2.3
Greece	2.8	3.1	1.2	−0.4	3.5	2.5	2.3
Spain	1.8	2.3	3.3	5.5	5.0	4.7	4.0
France	1.3	1.9	2.3	1.9	3.4	3.3	3.2
Ireland	2.0	−0.1	−1.3	4.7	3.7	5.1	4.6
Italy	3.0	2.6	2.5	3.0	3.9	3.5	3.0
Luxembourg	6.2	3.7	4.7	2.7	5.2	3.7	3.0
Netherlands	3.1	2.6	2.0	1.4	2.7	3.8	3.0
Portugal	−1.6	3.3	4.3	4.7	4.1	4.7	4.6
UK	2.2	3.5	3.2	4.6	3.7	2.2	2.1
EC	2.5	2.4	2.5	2.7	3.6	3.6	3.2

Source: European Commission

following the Social Security Act of 1986 a market of 11 million customer's emerged.

During the period of an individual's lifetime, the demand for various financial service products changes according to their propensity to borrow (take up assets), save and consume. The changing age structure means a changing emphasis on various parts of the consumer behaviour life cycle. The decline in the 0–14 and 15–44 age ranges in all markets (with the single exception of Portugal) is likely to affect demand for products associated with net borrowing and asset accumulation. Although in the short to medium term markets are likely to show some momentum, particularly where population and economic growth (see table 12.3) are expected to be favourable (particularly Spain, France and Portugal) in the longer-term, the effects of the ageing EC population will raise the importance of products based on net savings and asset management.

Demographic trends have and will continue to have a pervasive influence on the sector, as will deregulation, which is continuing apace throughout the community. By opening up traditional banking sectors to more rigorous competition from foreign and domestic financial institutions, EC governments have stimulated increased efficiency and product development with positive ramifications for European customers. Price competition and product differentiation, once absent from banking competition, have become a key focus for competitiveness in the EC. Consumers therefore face a wider choice of more competitively priced products. This new wave of competition has also changed the management focus of banks – money management now is critically combined with effective marketing and product development altering the nature of skills being demanded by financial institutions.

Many industry commentators expect the Single European Market Act to have an important bearing on the future of the European retail financial service market. Specifically, mutual recognition and harmonization of controls which have served to capitalize European expansion, promote size as a prerequisite for success (and thus prompt a spate of mergers and acquisitions) and alter the relative effectiveness of banks based in different Member States. 1992 has turned many institutions' strategic focus towards the implications of a wider Europe both in terms of new markets in which opportunities can be exploited and a bigger arena from which competition may emerge. With this wider market in mind, size is perceived as offering vital advantages in terms of financial and managerial resources; acquisition an important strategy for reaching the critical size perceived as necessary to compete in Europe in the future.

12.3   Products

Changes in the market environment for banks has determined a change in the nature of products and the product portfolio. As has already been suggested, deregulation and the accompanied competitive pressures are raising the importance of competition based both on price and differentiation. In terms of prices table 12.4 identifies cost/price positions for a range of products.

The UK, Dutch and Belgian markets, the most deregulated in Europe reveal the effects of deregulation on cost/price indices, and although low positions do not apply across all three products in each case, it may be argued that free competition promotes efficiency and provides scope for competing effectively on price. Consequently banks based in the

Table 12.4   Relative cost price* positions for banking products

	Belgium	*Spain*	*France*	*West Germany*	*Ireland*	*Netherlands*	*UK*
Consumer Credit	−41	39	105	136	NA	31	121
Credit Cards	74	26	−30	60	89	43	16
Mortgages	31	118	78	57	−4	−6	−20

* per cent discrepancies from price of average of lowest four producers.
Source: Price Waterhouse

least regulated markets are likely to be the best placed to compete in other Member States. Having grown through diversification, product development and innovation, and sustained relatively high levels of profitability in so-doing, UK institutions, for example, have developed skills in marketing and the development and introduction of new products. Not-withstanding the fact that new products are easy to replicate and cannot in themselves be considered a source of competitive advantage, the skills developed to allow firms to create new products should stand them in good stead, at least in the short-term, to develop products for new markets and adapt to the changing legislation. Given the different level of penetration of different products in the twelve Member States, there is scope for banks to expand into markets less well serviced in specific product areas. For example, whereas in the UK credit cards are a familiar and well-used form of payment, with around 1100 cards per thousand head of the working population, in Germany the corresponding figure is 75 per thousand. In Spain the next largest European market, the figure is 550 per thousand, half the UK figure. Considering these figures and the fact that in America there are 2000 cards per 1000 head of the working population, and in the UK in 1987 less than 8 per cent of the £250 billion consumer spending was accounted for by methods other than cheques or cash, there appears to be a great room for expansion. However, the different rates of penetration have emanated not solely from the competitive environment but also demand factors, specifically local preferences exercised by individuals in their use of disposable income. It has been argued for example that the German market offers false promises for credit-card firms given their aversion to credit and preference for saving rather than spending and borrowing.

Changing demographics also raises important issues regarding the products offered by banks. As the ageing population places more emphasis on products based on net savings and asset management rather than net borrowing and asset accumulation, banks need to adapt their product portfolios accordingly. They are beginning to consider, particularly, pensions, life assurance and PEPs. This has important ramifications for the banks, some of which are currently reacting to this challenge by entering the life assurance market or forging links with insurance companies. Germany's largest bank, Deutsche, has started up its own life-insurance business in direct competition with the also German based Allianz, Europe's biggest insurer.

This means intensified competition, with Allianz entering into an alliance with Dresdner Bank (Germany's second largest banking institution) to sell its insurance through Dresdner's branches. Deutsche Bank obviously viewed the risks of such aggressive competitive reaction as palatable given the fact that around 20 per cent (and rising) of Germany's DM2.4 million of household savings now goes into insurance, compared to 48 per cent (and falling) in bank deposits. Alternatively, in the UK, LLoyds has taken a controlling stake in Abbey Life which has one of the most successful salesforces in England.

Demographic change is not the only factor influencing the decision to expand the product portfolio. Over-capacity means that it is difficult to generate new customers as this entails attracting them away from competitors. Alternatively, firms may generate additional income from existing customers by offering them a wider range of products in much the same way as do retailers in goods markets. The trend towards 'Allfinanz' is not, however, a necessary progression and some commentators argue vehemently that concentration on core strengths and specialization are essential to long-term survival. The two approaches need not, however, be regarded as mutually exclusive and there is a growing school of thought which suggests that the choice facing banks is either to invest in developing their own top-quality products or buy them in from other producers and sell them through their distribution networks. In the light of experience, in the manufacturing sector in which product diversification, popular in the 1970s and 1980s proved unsuccessful, banks may prefer to buy in the skills required to manage other groups of products.

With increasing European deregulation, price competition, product development and innovation and the pooling of resources between specialized producers will all put pressure on bank efficiency and profitability. One of the major 'tools' for achieving these goals is technology, particularly in the form of computers. Traditionally, the greater proportion of banks costs comprised processing – 'paper-pushing'. With the introduction of computer processing, this no longer necessarily the case and staff traditionally employed in processing could be released to perform selling tasks. Equally, whilst 90 per cent of branch space was required for processing, more space is now available for the customer bringing retail banking more in line with traditional retail activities. Consequently, through the 1980s the role of bank staff and the face of retail banking have changed dramatically. Nevertheless, labour remains the biggest element in bank costs, and many staff are still involved in relatively routine tasks of processing. Redundancy, which has been witnessed among the British clearing banks, is likely to prove an important feature of the efficiency drive.

Technology also permits firms to exploit scale economies which suggests advantages for large firms. If this is achieved through acquisition, then banks will be required to develop skills in integrating systems to unlock the opportunities for scale economies.

12.4 European Markets

The twelve Member States of Europe exhibit very different characteristics, partly as a result of the impact of legislation and levels of economic development and partly due to different cultures and thus the propensity of consumers to face-up certain products. These differences have tended to effect a predominantly national focus, but with attention being turned towards Europe in the lead up to 1992, the differences may raise areas of opportunity rather than barriers to expansion.

12.4.1 The UK market

The liberalized environment in the UK has produced a highly competitive market in which banks are permitted to offer a full range of banking services. The market is dominated by the four leading Clearing Banks, Barclays, Nat West, Midland and Lloyds. Barclays and Nat West are of sufficient scale to compete Europe-wide and resist the threat of takeover. On the other hand, Midland and Lloyds are potentially vulnerable to takeover, particular as the Bank of England has become less restrictive. The UK clearers have already established a presence in Europe to pursue the niche operations in which they are interested. A move to develop an extensive retail presence greenfield is unlikely, as it would prove costly and entail banks operating on thinner margins than their competitors. Acquisition would also be costly and would involve good-will right-offs at a time when the UK banks have improved their capital ratios to an acceptable level. Small scale acquisitions are most likely to act as bridgeheads for the provision of niche products, including mortgages and insurance products that banks have recently developed for their own domestic market. They are also showing interest in the scope for growth in private banking and provision of unit trusts and stock-broking services to high net worth customers across Europe.

12.4.2 The German market

The German market is dominated by the big three banks, Deutsche, Dresdner and Commerzbank – all of which are universal banks providing a full range of banking services. Despite this, however, the market has been tightly regulated and the limited extent of competition has failed to promote aggressive price competition and product differentiation. More recently, the Bundesbank has become less rigourous in its controls and this has opened the market up to increased competition. Deutsche bank, Germany's largest, has made a positive commitment to become a pan-European player making acquisitions in Italy, Spain and France. Commerzbank has focused on strategic cross-holdings in European partners and is equally active in consolidating its European presence. By contrast, Dresdner bank has been less active and has chosen to concentrate on expanding domestically into wider retail financial services in Germany. Whilst these top tier banks are of a scale to become important European players and exempt from serious takeover threat, there is a large second tier and regional banking sector in Germany offering potential to foreign firms wishing to acquire a presence in Germany.

12.4.3 The French market

Development of the French market has been constrained by tight regulation restricting bank capital, promoting cartelized interest rates and credit-ceiling arrangements, resulting in a relative sparsity of financial instruments. Recent liberalization and financial deregulation has proceeded apace, however, to preserve Paris's position as a leading European financial centre, in the light of Europe-wide deregulation. CCF, Societé Generale, Paribas and Suez have all been privatized, releasing them from the burdens of under-capitalization which prevailed under government control. Such important changes in the domestic market have focused French banks' attentions away from European expansion to some extent. However, a number of joint ventures and acquisitions have been established, for example, Societé Generale has formed a line with the Skipton Building Society in the UK to fund mortgage lending through Skipton's retail network. Credit Lyonnais has bought Chase Manhattan's banking operations in the Netherlands and is now ranked fourth in the market.

12.4.4 The Spanish market

Like the French market, the Spanish financial regime has recently gone through a period of deregulation. Until recently, the closed system protected from foreign competition, was characterized by low levels of innovation. Deregulation has brought major changes in the market – in particular, it has intensified competition in pricing following the liberalization of interest rates and promoted market segmentation as differentiation has become a focus for banking strategy. A degree of continued agreements between the large banks regarding interest rates is, however, preserving margins and, as Spanish banks have relatively high cost structures, the market is proving very attractive to foreign competitors. Recognition of this threat has resulted in two major mergers: Vizxaya/ Bilbao and Banesto/Central. Potentially, there are two advantages of such mergers: firstly, to sustain entry barriers – eroded through deregulation; and secondly to realize the scale and scope economies and management efficiencies in large-scale institutions. However, on the second issue, problems of integration have restricted the ability of mergers to produce the desired economies and, as this has failed to promote greater efficiency, it has, in turn, limited the power of combined size acting as a barrier to entry. Alternatively, Santander and Hispano have made agreements with foreign banks in other European countries in an attempt to generate scale in a pan-European context and protect themselves from hostile takeovers. The government has been supportive in these mergers, promoting Spanish banks on a European scale and avoiding inward acquisition.

12.4.5 The Italian market

This highly-regulated market is characterized by a handful of national players and a large number of very small government-owned banks. Realization of the ineffectiveness of this system has prompted the authorities to extend the branch coverage of some of the small banks and initiate mergers between others. This phase of concentration is likely to continue, particularly among the regional banks, aware of the need to be of a particular size to compete with investing foreign banks and other financial institutions showing a keen interest in this very underdeveloped market. Italian banks have taken a proactive stance to this domestic encroachment and have embarked on a series of joint ventures and acquisitions. For example, Banco San Paulo's has acquired a majority stake in France's Banque Verne, Banca Commerciale Italiana has established a joint venture with Pambas of France and Camplo has acquired Campagnie Internationale de Banque, a small French bank.

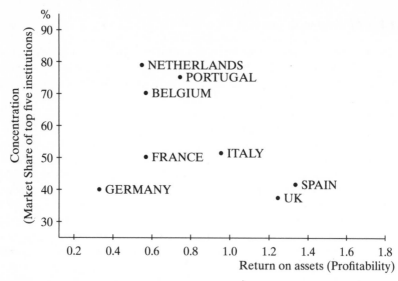

Figure 12.1   Concentration vs profitability
Source: Beddows & Co.

12.5   The European Market in perspective

The ineffectiveness of parts of the Italian banking system in which there are a large number of very small regional banks which lack the scale to be serious European players, begs the question – if it is ineffective, is it also inefficient? Figure 12.1 sets out rates of concentration (market share of top five institutions) and profitability (return on assets) for various EC countries in 1988. There is a very wide disparity in concentration rates from the Netherlands, where the top five institutions have over 80 per cent of the market, to the UK, where the leading five institutions account for less than 40 per cent. Interestingly, when profitability is considered, highly concentrated markets seem to yield lower levels of profitability. Several factors may explain this pattern. High levels of concentration suggests oligopolistic competition where aggressive price competition cannibalizes profits. However, as the outline of the Spanish market suggests, implicit agreements among large banking institutions can serve to protect profit margins. Indeed, if this is the case it is less likely that institutions see the need to improve their efficiency through cost-cutting programmes. Alternatively, banks based in the less-concentrated markets, facing aggressive price competition, are compelled to cut costs and promote efficiency, which may prove to be a more effective way of preserving profit margins. A further explanation may

Table 12.5   Ownership of EC banks, 1987

Ownership	Number in top 100	Average assets $bn	Pretax profits $m	Staff numbers
Private	69	37.6	207	15 948
Public	67	31.1	159	7261
Cooperatives	14	41.4	243	12 124
Mutuals	12	10.4	78	4419

Source: *The Banker*

be derived from levels of differential competition – also a feature of the less-concentrated highly-competitive markets. Differentiation prompts a high degree of market segmentation. By adding value to products and services or capitalizing on local reputation and brand, banks can raise their profits. Equally, market segmentation supports the existence of regional banks and niche producers.

As a result of these disparities, there are, apparently, large opportunities for firms based in the less-concentrated, more-competitive markets to expand across Europe. How they achieve this expansion is less obvious. The importance of distribution networks and the cost of developing them cannot be overlooked. Achieving market penetration from scratch involves accepting lower profits by pricing products below competitors to attract customers, and takes a great deal of time to reach critical mass. Alternatively, banks may choose to acquire other European banks. However, as table 12.5 shows, 93 of the top 162 banks (in 1987) were either state-owned, mutual or cooperative, which means the likelihood of cross-border European takeovers involving the leading institutions is restricted, and will probably involve the smaller private/quoted banks, which are less politically sensitive.

Nevertheless, acquisition is proving to be an important strategy for expansion by EC firms as table 12.6 demonstrates. Although the figures are somewhat misleading as they involve acquisitions outside the EC and are not specific to the banking sector, they show those countries taking an aggressive stance in the lead up to 1992. The UK, which clearly dominates, is the most likely to yield misleading figures given the greater propensity for UK firms to expand internationally outside of Europe. Notwithstanding this fact, the level of activity shown by UK firms must been seen as indicative of a drive to expand internationally which, as Europe becomes one of the world's leading trading blocks, must incorporate the EC. Table 12.7 highlights the top European banks by assets.

Table 12.6 Cross-border acquisitions by EC companies, 1988*

Country of Acquiror	Number of Deals	(%)	Value of Deals £m	(%)
UK	884	67.8	44.5	69.5
France	143	11.0	11.2	17.5
Germany	99	7.6	2.8	4.4
Ireland	53	4.1	1.6	2.5
Netherlands	52	4.0	1.3	2.0
Italy	29	2.2	1.4	2.2
Others	46	3.5	1.2	1.9
Total	1305		64	

* Inc. Acquisitions of non-EC companies.
Source: SG. Waring Securities (KPMG)

Although not specifically focused at the retail sector, assets tend to reflect the extent of branch networks. It is interesting to note the dominance of French banks at the top of the rankings. However, rather than reflecting the competitiveness of these organizations, this may rather be indicative of the over-branched nature of the French market where rationalization at branch level was not, in the past, necessary in the heavily regulated and protected environment. Equally, branch restrictions prevalent in the Spanish market until recently, are reflected in the relatively low asset rankings for Spanish banks. This gives further credence to the high degree of interest being shown in the Spanish market as it suggests room for branch expansion. High ROE levels among the Spanish banks also signal a healthy environment for investment to foreign firms.

It should be noted, however, that it is not necessarily the largest banks, by assets, who are best placed to take advantage of European opportunities. It is more likely that it is those banks who have developed efficient systems, are effective innovators and have accessed, acquired or developed distribution networks who will be the winners in Europe. Thus, although size may be an important element, it is not sufficient to promote success.

12.6   Distribution

Distribution is a key element in the banking sector largely due to the nature of many of the products which are intangible and cannot be

Table 12.7 European banks ranked by assets, 1988

Bank	Assets $ bn	After Tax ROE	Ranking
Credit Agricole	214	5.6	1
Banque Nationale de Paris	183	12.9	2
Credit Lyonnais	168	13.2	3
Deutsche Bank	166	6.3	4
Nat West Bank	162	9.0	5
Barclays	158	4.8	6
Societe Generale	153	15.2	7
Dresdner Bank	129	6.9	8
Union Bank Switzerland	125	8.2	9
Parias	122	10.4	10
Swiss Bank Corp.	113	7.6	11
Commerzbank	101	9.2	12
West LB Girozentrale	94	2.5	13
Bayerische Vereins	93	6.6	14
Midland Bank	90	20.6	15
Algemeine B Nederland	85	9.4	16
Lloyds Bank	83	8.7	17
Credit Suisse	83	8.5	17
Amro Bank	81	9.9	19
Standard Chartered	55	29.5	20
S E Banken	40	21.1	21
Svenska Handels B	35	16.5	22
Banco Central	34	15.0	23
TSB Group	34	9.2	23
Royal Bank of Scotland	31	11.7	25
Banco Hispano-Amer	31	3.7	25
Banco de Bilbao	29	25.4	27
Union Bank Finland	29	14.0	28
Banco Espanol Credito	28	17.7	29
Banco de Vizcayo	27	29.8	30
Banco de Santander	26	18.9	31
Banco Popular	16	20.3	32

Source: IBCA/*Business Week*

stored and transported in the same way as goods. Because 'production' takes place in contact with the consumer it is necessary to develop systems to facilitate the interaction between suppliers and customers. Branch networks, characteristic of banks' domestic markets, created over a long period of historical development, are difficult to replicate on a European scale. This is partly the result of the cost of developing

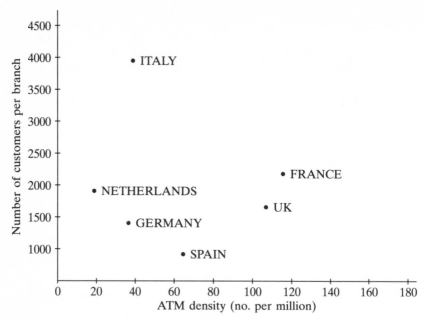

Figure 12.2   Branch structure and ATM density

distribution systems and partly due to the overbranched nature of many European markets, both of which factors militate against the greenfield development of networks.

This promotes acquisition and joint ventures as key strategies for accessing existing systems. The first option, whilst the most costly, allows banks to internalize the critical asset – the distribution network. Alternatively, joint ventures, whilst less costly generally involve the foreign partner to offer-up its product/service, which, unlike the distribution system, can be replicated very rapidly. Therefore joint ventures do not provide a long-term competitive option for the foreign investor, being more beneficial to the indigenous bank acquiring product/service knowledge, rather than the foreign investor, whose market share may only last as long as the joint venture. They may, however, prove to be part of a longer-term acquisition strategy where risk is minimized by testing the opportunity through a short-term joint venture.

Another important issue in distribution is the growing propensity of customers to use automatic teller machines (ATMs) for withdrawing money, which is more developed in some markets than others. Figure 12.2 highlights customers per branch and ATM density for a group of EC countries. The first measure serves to highlight the traditional branch coverage in each market, while the second demonstrates levels of technological development.

Italy is the least well-branched country although this rather reflects the banking restrictions in Italy as opposed to strategic directives. Spain with just over 1000 customers per branch may be regarded as overbranched. The other countries' banks lie in a band between 1500 to 2000 customers per branch, which tends to suggest relatively equally-developed traditional banking structures. Much wider differences, however, appear in the levels of technological development. France and the UK are clearly much more developed than Italy, Holland, Germany and Spain. Although this suggests room for expansion in the latter markets, it also raises a certain dichotomy. The technologically developed UK banks are now aware that the major proportion of banks withdrawals are done through their ATMs (Lloyds' banks estimates up to 80 per cent), which is turning bank branches into hollow vessels 'rarely visited by customers'. There is a growing concern, therefore, that siting of ATMs is possibly more critical than the existence of an extensive branch network. As they expand into European markets they cannot, however, make this assumption as the propensity of consumers to use ATMs is not as great and use of the traditional branch systems prevails. In the short-term, therefore, they must persevere with strategies for developing branch networks, while longer-term they foresee that these branches may become idle as customers turn to ATMs. What is apparent, however, is the need to access the shared ATM networks in Europe, which will prepare them for the long-term opportunities.

12.7 The Competitive Process

The measures of competitiveness highlighted in figure 12.3 are those cited by strategic managers from the banking sector. They serve to highlight the major forces driving competition in the industry.

As banks have traditionally been money managers, it is not surprising to find this reflected in their measures of performance. Strategic performance must equate with investment performance for it to be justifiable. To an extent, this constrains strategic investment, particularly expansion into Europe, and there are grounds for believing that, if the banks are to survive in the increasingly competitive European market, they must become more market focused than simply concerned with how well their money is working for them. This change to a market focus, whilst not universal, was evident with some banks who qualified their profitability measures in terms of 'profitability of customer relationships'. By realizing that their customer base is a critical asset that can be exploited to maximize profits, these banks are more clearly focused

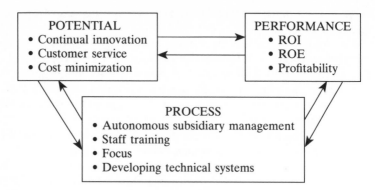

Figure 12.3 Measures of competitiveness in the banking sector

on generating new business, rather than trying to maximize returns from existing activities. This also reinforces the belief that there are profitable opportunities to be derived from a financial supermarket approach to the provision of retail financial services.

For some banks, the pursuit of profits was explicitly associated with cost minimization. By lowering costs banks can continue to preserve margins in the increasingly competitive environment. For all banks then, there is an implicit understanding that efficiency is a prerequisite for survival in the market place. This fact is further emphasized in the management process indicators wherein development of technical systems support the banks' activities specifically to promote efficiency, but also to open-up new opportunities in distribution. Banks view their major advantage to be in the area of product innovation. The highly-competitive deregulated UK market has resulted in high levels of product differentiation and the development of skills and systems for innovation and new product development. Many banks have drafted in marketing specialists from other retail fields to champion the new directives in an attempt to stay one step ahead of their competitors. Whilst most UK banks have reacted to this challenge by either developing the skills to innovate or becoming good 'follow-me' copiers of innovations, institutions in some of the less-developed European markets, particularly in the south, continue to sell less-sophisticated banking products and services. On the surface, then, the opportunities for UK institutions to consolidate their European activities or expand through the EC, appear extensive. Such an assumption, however, brings into question the nature of financial service products which, unlike many products, cannot be patent protected and rely only on administrative systems and relevant paper-work which can be replicated very quickly. Innovative products in themselves cannot provide UK banks with a sustainable competitive advantage. Many of the interviewed banks recognize this and believe that it is the continual introduction of new products based on good marketing skills which provides the advantage. Perhaps more importantly, the development of product innovation skills and systems to support the introduction of new products are the key factors offering UK banks potential over some of their European counterparts in less-developed markets. Although these skills and systems can be acquired and developed, the UK banks arguably have first-mover advantages in this respect.

Quality of service takes on a different perspective in the banking sector as compared to goods markets. Because many banking services are produced in conjunction with the customer, there is broad scope for banks' personnel to ensure that face-to-face interactions meet customer expectations and promote long-term relationships with the bank. Because there are few tangible differences between many of the leading UK banks – products and prices being broadly similar, most banks have refurbished their branches in response to a move towards greater customer orientation and branding being mostly absent – consumers judge the quality of service on intangible, experiential cues. In this respect, factors such as appearance, helpfulness, politeness of staff and tone of letters are likely to constitute the important indicators by which customers judge the quality of service provided. While attention to such factors does not help banks to win business, as potential consumers cannot judge the quality until they have experienced it, it avoids creating dissatisfied clients with a high propensity to move banks. It also serves to promote positive word-of-mouth promotion, an important factor in the service sector, where customers judge performance expectations through the experience of others. One of the banks interviewed also raised a further issue related to service quality in respect of costs and profits. There are additional costs associated with non-quality, due to lost sales, and therefore commitment to the provision of high-quality service can enhance the bottom line. As banks continue to exploit their customer bases through cross-selling, retention of customers through service-quality commitment may correspondingly become a key issue for all banks.

Banking staff, as has been noted, play an important role in the provision of quality customer service, which in turn emphasizes staff training. This is further compounded in the light of recent changes where 'backroom' staff, traditionally employed in administration and processing, have been released by computerization to perform 'front room' duties. In response to new opportunities identified in cross-selling products to the banks' customer bases, many banks have retrained staff to perform in-house sales functions. The effectiveness of this approach, has, however, raised questions, particularly in the light of the propensity of consumers to use ATMs and not enter the bank branch. Further difficulties arise as a result of the breadth of product range now offered by banks. As up to 250 products may be sold through each branch, it is by no means easy for the new front-room sales staff to have comprehensive knowledge of all products. Recent bank redundancies in the UK suggest efficiency from rationalization is preferable to the drive for additional sales.

The broad differences between European markets for banking products and different consumer preferences makes autonomous management by foreign subsidiaries an attractive strategy. Although the UK banks' opportunities depend for a large part on product innovation, there is an awareness amongst managers that products will not succeed simply because they are sophisticated. Products and services need to be matched to local needs and there is, in fact, a concern that some products are *too* 'sophisticated' for consumers in some of the less developed markets. Gradual introduction of innovative products, in-line with customer education, is required, the rate of introduction and the nature of innovations being most easily judged by local managers. Local managers are also best placed to understand the competitive environment and likely sources of future competitive threats.

A final point worthy of comment relates to the trend by some banks towards 'Allfinanz'. While large banking institutions with the resources to diversify may be able to take advantage of the economies of scope inherent in this strategy, it is potentially damaging for the smaller banks to try and be all things to all people as this would necessarily involve their spreading their resources too thinly. Specialism by smaller banks, and focusing on core strengths, therefore, is preferable – not least because it enables them to sustain shareholder performance and protect themselves from takeover. Focused strategies are not, however, restricted to the smaller banks. Larger organizations may also prefer this approach because of the simplified portfolio and coordination bringing with it lower costs. The overall outcome of specialization is an unbundling of activities among the banks. Such disaggregation, involving focused markets, limited segments and a narrow portfolio, involves a trade-off between economies of scale and higher-value added. Although there is little evidence that banks are actually following this route as the trend is towards banks mirroring goods retailers, it is possible that some banks will become retail specialists whilst others will concentrate on producing financial products and services. Cooperation between banks and other financial and non-financial firms is a way in which banks could concentrate on the things they do best.

12.8 Managing The Process

The nature of the European environment for banking services clearly defines the strategic options for achieving a competitive stance. Although ultimately 1992 may create opportunities to sell financial services across borders (exporting) such opportunities may not be realised in the short-term. Cross-border delivery is likely to become a reality when electronic means of delivery are accepted across Europe. In the meantime it is likely that, cross-border sales will be restricted to plastic cards – credit, debit and smart cards. As this area is well-developed in the UK market, a degree of cross-border activity in the short-term is probable.

Generally, however, financial products and services demands direct interaction between producer and customer and a broad distribution network to maximize the incidence of interactions. While this does not rule out greenfield branch establishment, as has been noted, the time to profitability, the overbranched nature of many EC markets and the difficulty of breaking down customer loyalty as a foreign bank all militate against banks taking this option. Hence banks focus attention on acquisitions and joint ventures.

Rationalization of branch networks by banks in certain EC markets opens up opportunities for acquiring divested branches with an established customer base. Not only does this provide firms with a strong market presence and distribution network but also allows them to avoid fragmentation of their capital base and preserve shareholder performance. There are, however, certain problems with this kind of approach not least the fact that branches which are divested are usually the least profitable in the poorer locations. There are also problems associated with establishing a strong image (while retaining customers) and thus acquiring branches in this manner may not allow banks to expand their pan-European image and identify. Alternatively, banks may opt for a strategy of acquiring an established bank and its in-place branch network thus overcoming the problems of only acquiring unprofitable outlets and being restricted in their image development. Currently, however, this strategy is proving less than favourable for many UK banks as 1992 has stimulated a frenzied period of European expansion, boosted demand for takeover opportunities, and pushed up the prices of potential take-over targets to quite ridiculous levels. Equally, those banks which are affordable are ailing casualties involving too high risks for the banks to contemplate. Whilst ultimately, therefore, bank takeovers may prove to be the most prolific expansionist strategy, UK banks seem prepared to play a waiting game, hedging their bets in the short-term to take advantage of good opportunities longer term when the market settles. Some observers of the UK banking industry argue that by waiting, UK banks are likely to miss the boat. However, Nat West and Barclays, as was noted earlier, have already established networks in those markets and niches they wish to be in and although there is evidence of intended consolidation and potentially small-scale expansion in new areas of business (such as high net-worth banking, unit trusts, life assurance and pensions) these will involve small-scale steps and major acquisitions are unlikely. The primary concern, in the short-term at least, is to ensure protection of the domestic market which is a very attractive investment base for foreign banks because of the sustained levels of profitability earned by UK based institutions. Where, however, European activities are developing is in the area of joint ventures and strategic alliances in an attempt to access new channels of distribution. Arguably, these strategies may also be regarded as 'trial periods' for testing the feasibility of bank takeover in the longer-term. Indeed, ultimate takeover may be essential as the foreign partner continues to control the distribution network – the critical asset. Whilst UK banks can offer innovative products in the short-term, their foreign partners can replicate these and the systems to produce them over time – negating the need for the partnerships and closing the UK banks out of the market. If the banks choose to reject the option of takeover, they are likely to find themselves without the essential distribution systems to operate in Europe.

What is apparent among the British banks is that there is little inclination for them to become pan-European in the sense of offering all their products and services in all European markets. They are more concerned with 'cherry picking' – opting to expand in the most profitable niches and markets with an aim to enhance profitability and not pursue European market share. While some observers would like to argue that their stance is more reactive than proactive in that their number one priority is to defend the UK market and number two to expand in Europe on a small scale – they are following the course of most European banks, few of whom see the potential to be truly pan-European. The possible exception here is Deutsche Bank which has made a public commitment to becoming pan-European, although here, too, there is a reluctance to jump on the acquisition bandwagon and risk large amounts of capital on less than convincing opportunities. They are also looking to foster joint ventures to test the waters with potential partners.

One further point of note is the fact that as banks expand into new product areas their strategies for European expansion may change accordingly. This is particularly the case as regards life assurance and pensions and here they may follow the strategies traditionally employed by the insurance companies to expand sales of their products and services. Employing agents and salesmen and becoming more adept at direct mail and direct marketing may be the key to success in these fields – and provide further opportunities for exploiting the new freedoms to sell cross-border.

12.9 The Future

Some suggestion has already been made about the potential for banks to disaggregate their business. This development may be given more momentum as banks seek to specialize in specific fields under threat from non-bank outsiders encroaching on traditional banking spheres in certain world markets. Retail stores and finance houses are increasing their stature in credit markets and banks are being used less by savers who are realising greater returns from high-interest money-market accounts. Retailers such as Marks and Spencers in the UK Sears Roebuck in the USA and Seiber Credit in Japan, are taking advantage of unrestricted bank regulations and are beginning to offer financial service products through their extensive distribution networks. As paper-processing which much money transfer business involves, is replaced by electronic systems the processing arm will become more accessible to non-banks and further erode the traditional banking spheres. Electronic Funds Transfer to Point of Sale (EFTPOS) and credit cards are allowing much business to by-pass the banks altogether. The question is how can the banks react to these growing challenges? Co-operation is likely to provide the best foundation for permitting banks to concentrate on their strengths, for example, joint arrangements between credit card firms and banks (viz Mastercard and Visa in the UK) whereby banks sell the cards through their branches and authorise payments and charge their customers. Other banks ensure retailers get paid. Banks therefore provide the link between the credit supplier and the retailers and customers. Specialization of this kind will enable banks to survive against new aggressive non-bank, less regulated institutions. It does not, however, mean that banks must become pawns in the non-bank retail financial service game. They have critical assets which they can exploit and enhance to sell profitable products. One feature, their distribution networks, cannot be overlooked. With branches in most high streets and with broad geographic coverage they apparently have a strong foundation for reaching a wide customer base. The major problem here is that few customers visit their branches preferring to use the ATM's. Banks may therefore be forced to review their distribution arrangements and move more towards practical location of ATM's (outside supermarkets, at petrol stations, outside major retail stores) and new distribution systems for the sale of products and services other than simple cash withdrawal.

The rate of development of new distribution systems will partly depend on consumer acceptance and changes in behaviour. Home banking systems, for example, whereby consumers could move money, buy shares and pay bills from home-based computer terminals did not prove popular with customers. Whatever developments occur, it is clear that banking will change quite considerably in the future, these developments depending on a change in ethos from competition to co-operation and technological developments based on effective marketing skills. The challenge facing banks, therefore, appears to be concerned with shrugging off their traditional mantle as pure money managers and accepting a new guise of specialists either in the production of products and services, processing and intermediation or marketing and distribution.

13

Industry Study 6: The European Housing Finance Market

13.1 Introduction

The European housing finance market is highly fragmented with broad differences in both supply and demand conditions between the twelve Member States. Lending institutions, funding systems and products all differ, which serves to insularize national competition. Mortgage lending is consequently the least Europeanized financial service sector. This fact is compounded by legislation, in markets such as the UK and Germany, which has restricted European expansion, protectionist attitudes, cultural differences and a general tendency for individuals to choose a local national producer to finance their largest single purchase. These factors have determined a market which is far from integrated but which, in the wake of 1992 legislation, offers up opportunities for foreign expansion where products developed for the home market have no equivalent in other Member States and are potentially attractive.

13.2 The European Environment

Table 13.1, which shows the growth in household formation to 1992, reveals a trend which exceeds the rate of EC population growth which is shown as table 13.2.

What is perhaps more interesting to the building societies is what constitutes this growth. Rather than demographic trends, social trends are influencing the growth. The younger end of the population are beginning to form households earlier and live for longer periods alone. Although the demographic trends suggest this is a declining sector of the population (see table 13.3), the propensity for household formation

Table 13.1 Household formation, 1988–92 (000s)

	1988	1989	1990	1991	1992
Total households	122 281	123 104	123 512	124 781	126 077
Growth in households	1.8%	0.6%	0.3%	1.0%	1.0%
Persons per households	2.65	2.64	2.63	2.62	2.60

Source: Euromonitor Database

Table 13.2 EC population by member state

Population (000s)	1995	(%)	2000	(%)	2010	(%)	2020	(%)
Belgium	9915	3.0	9880	2.9	9687	2.9	9387	2.9
Denmark	5169	1.5	5176	1.5	5075	1.5	4776	1.5
W. Germany	61 359	18.6	61 160	18.4	58 585	17.7	54 704	16.9
Greece	9975	3.0	10 115	3.0	10 300	3.1	11 149	3.4
Spain	40 094	12.2	40 746	12.3	41 193	12.4	40 699	12.5
France	57 060	17.3	57 880	17.4	58 763	17.8	58 664	18.1
Ireland	3500	1.1	3471	1.0	3412	1.0	3347	1.0
Italy	57 585	17.5	57 610	17.3	56 408	17.1	53 484	16.5
Luxembourg	374	0.1	375	0.1	375	0.1	369	0.1
Netherlands	15 329	4.7	15 716	4.7	16 101	4.9	16 160	5.0
Portugal	10 819	3.3	11 140	3.3	11 473	3.5	11 814	3.6
UK	58 144	17.6	58 858	17.7	59 391	17.9	59 838	18.4
EC TOTAL	329 321		332 127		330 761		324 318	

Source: European Commission

Table 13.3 Age structure of EC population

	1995		2000		2010	
0–14	58 964	17.9 %	59 011	17.8 %	54 170	16.3 %
15–44	142 878	43.3 %	139 971	42.1 %	129 288	39.1 %
45–64	77 089	23.4 %	80 092	24.1 %	89 686	27.1 %
65+	50 390	15.3 %	53 053	15.9 %	57 617	17.4 %
EC TOTAL	329 321		332 127		330 761	

Source: European Commission

Table 13.4   Key characteristics of the housing market

	Owner occupation (%)	Rental market (%)	Subsidised housing (%)	Construction as a % of GDP (1985)	No. of people per household	Extent of tax advantage
Italy	59	36	6	4.8	2.61	Medium
France	51	41	8	4.6	2.25	Medium
Germany	37	60	3	5.5	2.28	Medium
Spain	77	20	3	N/A	2.51	High
UK	62	10	28	3.6	2.54	High

Source: *International Housing Finance Fact Book BAH Analysis*

should compensate for the decline. Secondly, as divorce rates continue to rise, new household formation from broken homes will add to the trend. Finally, increased longevity in the population will add to the existing housing stock.

Table 13.4 highlights some key housing-market characteristics for a group of European countries.

These key characteristics are important for their contribution to individual country demand conditions. Comparing back to table 13.2, some of the largest markets in the EC in terms of population, notably France and Germany, reveal relatively low levels of owner-occupancy (51 per cent and 37 per cent respectively). Nevertheless, the size of these markets puts them among the leading countries in terms of new advances with France equivalent to £30 billion, the UK £29 billion and West Germany £22 billion (the figures relating to 1987). It should be pointed out, however, that the figures for Germany are somewhat misleading for although only 37 per cent of the population are owner-occupiers, as there is little motivating tax incentive, around 60 per cent own property as there are advantages of owning property for investment. Alternatively, Italian advances were between £7 and £8 billion and Spanish £3 billion, small amounts given their population and owner-occupancy levels. These low levels can be explained by cultural quirks of the two markets. Spanish customers traditionally believed that credit for house-purchase was an indication of poverty and not something wealthier people did. Alternatively, Italians tended to finance their housing purchases from savings and inherited wealth. However, times are changing in both countries with consumers becoming less credit averse and market conditions – notably tax relief in Spain and growing property values – encouraging customers to consider mortgage-credit.

Levels of owner occupancy can clearly be seen as a reflection of the sophistication of the rented property market. In Germany, for example, the rented market for all income levels is well-developed, which is clearly not the case in the UK where the rented market is heavily biased towards low income groups. In the UK, therefore, this tends to engender a high degree of upward mobility as there is a certain stigma attached to renting property on a permanent basis. However, this is not solely the result of supply-side conditions, the old axiom 'an Englishman's home is his castle' holds true in shaping UK cultural attitudes towards home-ownership. Across all countries, however, owner-occupation levels are rising and mortgage markets correspondingly growing, reinforcing opportunities for cross-border expansion, and as legislation harmonizes across Europe, traditionally 'closed' and protected markets will be opened up to new competition.

13.3   Mortgage Funding

1992 will permit housing finance lenders to provide mortgage credit and fund their loans in other Member States in the same way they do at home. Therefore, the differences between funding systems may determine relative positions of competitive strength. There are three traditional techniques – the open system, the closed system and the mortgage bond – each relating to specific types of institution, the building society, the Bausparkasse and the mortgage-bond institution. The 'open' system of the British building societies involves no contractual obligation to save with the institution prior to the granting of the mortgage loan. Savers and borrowers are not necessarily the same, and savers' deposits comprise shares on which interest is paid, and which can be withdrawn on sight or with a fixed period of notice. Thus, long-term loans are financed by short-term deposits, both subject to variable interest rates which can be adjusted to suit changing market conditions. Conversely, the 'closed' system of the Bausparkasse in Germany and Austria involves contractual savings before the granting of mortgage credit. Individuals are required to deposit money with the savings institutions and loans are subsequently granted to the same individuals for house purchases after a particular period of time. The contract, whilst binding the investor to the savings bank, also gives him legal claim to a loan at a favourable fixed rate of interest. Low rates of interest can be charged as loans are made out of savings on which there is a correspondingly low interest rate.

In the German Bausparkasse system, the time when the loan is granted is not established in advance as it depends upon the ratio between the amount saved and the property value and the length of the saving period. Alternatively, in the closed French system, 'e'pargne logement', the time for the granting of the loan must be outlined beforehand and any shortfall between the guaranteed loans and savings contracts made up by external funding.

The third system, the mortgage-bond scheme is the most popular across Europe, and involves institutions procuring capital for long-term mortgage loans at fixed rates through the sale of securities at equal fixed interest rates. The contracts are written by institutions authorized by law including mortgage banks in West Germany, France, the Netherlands, Denmark, and Spain and the independent departments of credit institutions in Italy. Loans and interest are paid to issuing institutions from the pledged property. The financial circle is closed by credit institutions paying interest on this money to the bondholders and redeeming the bonds at nominal value on maturity. The key factor is that the value of bonds must be equally matched by the value of the mortgages, and the loans granted from the funds obtained must not exceed a certain proportion of property value.

13.4   European Market Analysis

Although EC markets show a high degree of similarity in the limited penetration from mortgage institutions based in other Member States, the differences in the nature of individual countries' mortgage markets are extensive.

13.4.1   The German market

The German market is peculiar in that it is usual for customers to obtain mortgage credit from a variety of sources. Although this appears complicated, the 'package' is usually put together by the organization first contacted by the customer. Loans of up to 60 per cent are usually made by the 37 mortgage banks which are subsidiaries of other financial institutions, notably the big three banks, Deutsche, Dresdner and Commerzbank. These loans are funded by mortgage bonds. Top-up loans of up to 80 per cent of the loan to valuation ratio may then be made by the Bausparkassen, restricted to lending within their own state, and funded through contractual savings arrangements. The final 20 per cent of the property value is normally made up from savings. These may be deposited with the savings banks, 591 publically owned firms (in 1984) with 17 131 offices. Despite the relatively low levels of owner-occupation in Germany, the market is one of the largest in the EC, with £150 billion loans outstanding at the end of 1985.

13.4.2 The French market

The French market with £130 billion loans outstanding is equally complex. Approximately half the market is made up of the banks – specifically, Credit Agricole, Societe Generale, Banque Nationale de Paris and Credit Lyonnais. Credit Foncier, a private institution run by government appointed managers, accounts for a further 20 per cent of the market. It lends on both state-aided and commercial terms and plays a key role in government housing policy. Loans are usually fixed rate (with mortgage-bond funding) although variable rate products do exist. The loan to valuation ratio is limited to 80 per cent (50 per cent in the case of Credit Foncier). Compagnie Bancaire, a general retail bank, has recently made known its ambitions to be a European mortgage financier and has established a subsidiary in the UK, UCB Home Loans, to launch its attack on the highly developed UK market.

13.4.3 The Italian market

The Italian housing finance market, like the banking market is highly fragmented, comprising both banks and specialized credit institutions. The market is very small and not well developed. Relatively few individuals have mortgages, with a large proportion of the market, as much as two thirds, being funded directly from personal savings. The loan-to-valuation ratio is usually 50 per cent, with loans at fixed rates and funding through mortgage bonds.

13.4.4 The Spanish market

Although larger than the Italian market, the Spanish market is relatively small with loans outstanding at the end of March 1986 valuing £14 billion. More than half the market is comprised of the 81 savings banks which are highly regionalized. A further third is made up by The Mortgage Bank of Spain which is a public institution, funded to a considerable extent by the government. In 1982, the government allowed the development of a further sector, based on the issue of mortgage bonds and certificates, which is dominated by the savings banks. Loans are usually variable rate, although, if funded by bonds or certificates, this rate can only vary every two to three years. There is a statutory ceiling of 80 per cent on the loan-to-valuation ratio.

13.4.5 The UK market

The UK mortgage market is the largest and most sophisticated in Europe with £187 billion of loans outstanding at the end of 1987. Traditionally dominated by the building societies, funded by the issue of securities backed by mortgage loans, the market is now open to competition from a wide variety of sources. In 1987, the building societies accounted for 52 per cent of the market for new loans, domestic banks 34 per cent. Although more recently there has been a swing back to the building societies, the banks still pose a major threat. Mortgage loans are usually restricted to 85 per cent of the loan-to-valuation ratio, but are frequently topped up to 100 per cent by life assurance companies. This has served to attract a large number of first-time buyers in their early twenties along with low-start mortgages in an attempt to extend the size of the market. The popularity of endowment mortgages has also forged close links between insurance companies and mortgage institutions, be they banks or building societies. There is also evidence that the UK market is becoming more fragmented with different institutions, some of them non-financial, specializing in different aspects of mortgage provision, generating funding and administering. Two building societies, Abbey National and the Woolwich have recently established joint ventures with European institutions in Spain and Italy in an attempt to exploit the advantages derived from their relatively sophisticated products and services.

13.4.6 European overview

The differences between countries clearly suggest opportunities for cross-border expansion. For example, the relatively underdeveloped Italian market offers great potential for firms offering more than 50 per cent loan-to-valuation ratio. Equally, there is potential in the German market to offer mortgage credit to first-time buyers without the need for them to save over a long period of time. However, this will depend on the scope for foreign institutions to import their local laws and regimes. It is unlikely, for example, that British firms will be allowed to offer 100 per cent mortgages in Italy (effectively doubling the size of the market) as such practices may be blocked by the Italian government, being against the 'public good'. Consequently, the extent of some opportunities may be diluted by local authorities being granted the freedom to legislate on certain issues. Nevertheless, broad differences, particularly in terms of funding systems and the resultant nature of products, remain.

13.5 Mortgage Lenders' Products

By dictating whether interest on mortgage loans is fixed or variable, funding systems help to shape the nature of products offered in the different Member States. As a result of the mortgage-bond system being dominant across Europe, fixed interest products prevail. These involve the mortgage institution adjusting for fluctuations in market conditions rather than the consumer, as in the case of variable-rate mortgages. It is probable, if inflation rises, that fixed interest rates will prove preferable. This should open up opportunities for Bausparkasse and mortgage-bond institutions to sell fixed-rate products in the UK, which is currently dominated by variable-rate products. Alternatively, there are potential opportunities for mortgage-bond institutions and building societies to offer immediate mortgage credit in Germany, France and Austria.

Other differences between types of product offered can be attributed to a wide range of factors, not least tax incentives on mortgage loans which determine relative product attractiveness. Tax relief on life assurance premiums in the UK prompted the popularity of endowment mortgages, interest only mortgages where the capital sum is paid off at the end of the mortgage-term, by a life assurance policy. Likewise, Personal Equity Plans (PEPs) mortgages have been, and may continue to be, encouraged by tax incentives. Similarly, recent increases in fixed-rate repayment mortgages in Spain (where both capital and interest are paid back over the loan-term) may be partly contributed to growing tax-relief. However, based on the experiences of the UK market, some EC authorities may be reluctant to raise tax relief on mortgage related products. Mortgage tax incentives in the UK served to raise the demand for house-purchase, which, combined with low interest rates in the mid-1980s led to a dramatic increase in the price of houses. Owner-occupiers took advantage of this boom raising their mortgage debt, withdrawing equity from their appreciating property assets and going on a spending spree resulting in high inflation. The fear now is that, linked to the ERM and correspondingly lower interest rates, a further round of excessive property inflation will ensue.

Levels of state intervention are also likely to have an impact on products. In Greece, Portugal, Spain, France and Germany, the state subsidises housing finance. This has tended to dampen competitive pressures reducing the range of products, and limiting competition on services, interest rates and types of supplier. It has also complicated mortgage lending which characteristically involves the customer dealing with more than one institution.

Taking a wider view of the products offered by mortgage institutions, it is essential to consider the changing nature of the players and their portfolios. Specialist mortgage institutions prevail in most markets – Italy, France, Spain, the UK, Germany, Ireland and Greece. Equally, the savings banks play an important role across many EC markets. Increasingly, however, commercial banks have begun to make inroads into housing finance markets in an attempt to maximize returns from their existing customers through cross-selling. This has been brought about by financial deregulation which is continuing apace across Europe and redefining the boundaries between traditionally specialized financial service institutions. In the UK, for example, deregulation for building societies was manipulated via the 1986 Building Societies Act which permitted the societies, for the first time, the freedom to offer ancillary financial services to their customers. This has resulted in their offering current accounts, cheque cards, credit cards and automatic teller machine (ATM) services, traditionally the sphere of UK banks. Alternatively, in Germany, many of the Bausparkasse have signed deals with German commercial banks to access their extensive geographic networks. Actions of this kind have served to stir up competition.

British banks were encouraged to pay interest on current accounts to compete with building societies for investments and develop their own mortgage products to counteract the competitive challenge from the societies. In Germany, certain banks without deals with the Bausparkasse have begun to sell their own mortgages. Traditional lines of demarcation between institutions are disappearing with important implications for the nature of competition and the extent of individual institution's coverage. Much rests on the different regulatory environments and the freedom of mortgage providers to diversify, but where they are permitted to redefine their business as deregulation takes effect, the main question they face is whether to specialize or whether to diversify and become retail financial-service providers. In this sense, mortgage providers are facing up to the same competitive challenge now confronting the banks – specialization or 'Allfinanz'. There are strong arguments supporting both options. By focusing on core strengths, institutions can concentrate their resources on the most profitable areas of their business rather than spreading their funding across a range of products and services some of which may yield low profits and be a drain on resources. Equally, there are economies in simplifying the product portfolio and having a single processing system for all their business. Arguably, however, there are scope economies to be earned from diversifying into a range of financial-service products through cross-selling to the existing customer base. Furthermore, there is also the option of diversifying out of the mature housing finance market into new growth areas, in life assurance and unit trusts and in so-doing extending the business into longer-term savings offering the possibility of capital appreciation.

Supporting this argument is the changing demography of the population. The decline in the 0–14 and 15–44 age ranges, typically associated
with net borrowing and asset accumulation, and a substantial growth in
the over-65 group concerned with net savings and asset management
(see table 13.3) suggests a changing emphasis in retail financial services
in the future. However, experience of diverisification by UK building
societies into the estate-agency sector suggests a degree of caution. While
there are apparent benefits from integrating backwards and accessing
customers at an early stage in the house-buying process, the expense of
building up chains and the necessary capital depletion has placed a high
degree of financial strain on the building societies, many of which have
suffered substantial losses. Although much can be attributed to the
unforeseen downturn in the housing market, many societies overlooked
the problems of management and integration in their attempts to secure
new mortgages and protect their core business. Principally, the fact that
the business cultures of building societies and estate agencies differ
markedly was obscured by the apparent advantage of business generation. Many customers, rather than viewing the organization of their
mortgage through the estate agent as a simple process, were wary of the
scheme as a result of their traditional perception of estate agents as
unethical aggressive sales and profit centres. Despite the efforts of some
societies to associate their estate agencies with the umbrella corporate
image, the venture has proved an expensive diversion for many organizations. Given such unfavourable experiences, specialization, with its
greater productivity, cost efficiency and profitability, may, after all, prove
favourable.

Some institutions will have little choice as a result of their size, which
will prevent them from contemplating diversification in the provision of
products and services, and specialization, particularly in profitable niche
sectors and regions, is likely to be the only safe strategy for securing
long-term survival. Nevertheless, these small firms, and those that opt
for specialization, need not be precluded from the trend towards
Allfinanz – indeed, they may perpetuate it. The move towards establishing financial surpermarkets does not necessarily involve the 'production' of all products and services by the retailer. Strategic links
between insurance companies and banks or mortgage companies (in the
UK, Commercial Union with Midland Bank and Standard Life with
Halifax Building Society, in France, GAN with CIC Bank and in
Germany, AHB and Bfg Bank and alliances between Dresdner Bank
and several regional Bausparkasse) demonstrate how banks and mortgage financiers can sell a broad range of products through their branches
whilst remaining specialist producers. What this suggests is a splitting
up of functions – production and retailing no longer necessarily being
conducted by the same institution.

Table 13.5 Relative cost/price positions* for banking products

	Belgium	*Spain*	*France*	*W. Germany*	*Ireland*	*Netherlands*	*UK*
Consumer Credit	−41	39	105	136	N/A	31	121
Credit Cards	74	26	−30	60	89	43	15
Mortgages	31	118	78	57	−4	−6	−20

* per cent discrepancies from price of average of lowest four producers.
Source: Price Waterhouse

At this point in time, it is not clear how the retail financial-service market will ultimately develop. What is clear, however, is that the mortgage market is becoming more competitive, and this is likely to continue into the foreseeable future. House purchase constitutes the most significant single transaction an individual will undertake and thus mortgage provision is arguably the pivotal financial relationship between a financial retailer and his customer. With this being the case, the encroachment by commercial banks into this sector is not surprising as they aim to maximize returns from their customer base. Equally, it may be necessary for mortgage providers to extend their product range or offer their products in conjunction with those of other financial service firms to satisfy the broad needs of their customers and raise the profitability of existing customer relationships.

Cost/price differences across Europe differ widely which reinforces the argument that there are opportunities for cross-border expansion. For example, the annual cost of a mortgage in Spain (measured by the excess of mortgage rates over money-market rates) is more than twice that in the UK. Table 13.5 highlights the percentage discrepancies from the average price of the four lowest producers for a range of EC countries. In the areas of mortgage finance, UK, Irish and Dutch firms look well-placed to take advantage of the market imperfections between the different EC countries. Spain and France appear as potential target markets where the cost advantages are greatest. So, as well as deciding to specialize or diversify, societies are faced with the equally perplexing question of whether to Europeanize or protect their domestic market from increased competition. Firms which decide to specialize are arguably the best placed to contemplate expansion as they can concentrate their resources on geographic rather than product diversification. More importantly, however, it is profitability which gives firms the scope to invest abroad, which provides equal opportunities for profitably diversified organizations. In addition, disaggregation of separate business functions in the mortgage field provides scope for cross-border expansion through cooperation. The Skipton Building Society in the UK recently signed a deal with Societé Generale of France, wherein the funding is provided by Societé Generale, the administration and retail functions by the Skipton. More deals of this nature are likely, particularly where the retail coverage of a mortgage financier is able to generate more business than the institution can fund itself.

13.6 Distribution

Traditionally, most mortgage business has been conducted through the branch networks of the specialist housing financiers and the banks. As in the banking sector, distribution is a critical element in formulating strategies for European expansion. The intangibility of mortgages (and their often complicated nature) dictates direct interaction between the seller and the customer, necessitating establishing, acquiring or accessing branch outlets. Greenfield establishment, whilst potentially attractive for tapping niche sectors (such as provision of finance for the purchase of holiday homes to nationals from the domestic market), is costly and fails to overcome the barrier of 'foreignness' which is high in the mortgage market due to individuals preference for investing their money with national institutions afforded higher levels of trust. Acquisition, which allows local branding, also involves acquiring institutions with very different funding systems and products, raising problems of cultural difference and integration. Nevertheless, as acquisition permits the internalization of the distribution network, which provides a key competitive asset, this strategy cannot be ruled out. In the UK, the banks were able to penetrate rapidly the mortgage market, quickly establishing themselves as the second largest group of lenders with 25–30 per cent of the market, not because they had any specific skills in mortgage provision but because they had an extensive customer base and branch coverage. In the short-term, however, as mortgage institutions' attention is focused on Europe as a result of '1992', they may prefer to enter into joint ventures as a way of 'getting a toe in the water' without exposing themselves to potential risk by fragmenting their capital base at a time when defending their domestic market may take precedence over expansion.

   The disaggregation of functions, as noted above, may provide scope for the establishment of joint ventures, particularly in the light of cost differentials and the widely differing financial instruments for funding mortgages which has produced large market imperfections and potential

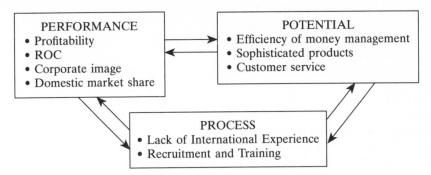

Figure 13.1   Measures of competitiveness for mortgage providers

opportunities across the EC. Notwithstanding these factors, however, as in the banking sector, the ownership of distribution systems is the key to long-term sustainable competitive advantage as products and services can be replicated, whereas physical distribution systems cannot. In addition, while banks may take advantage of developing technologies for the provision of their core products – savings and credit – mortgage delivery appears to be remaining a more personalized service. Innovative distribution systems, independent financial advisers, direct marketing and non-financial outlets such as estate agents and solicitors, are largely untapped outside the UK and France and even here the channels are only directed at niche markets, or, as we have noted in the case of backward integration by UK building societies into estate agencies, have proved relatively unsuccessful.

13.7   The Competitive Process

Figure 13.1 highlights the measures cited by managers from the mortgage institutions interviewed reflecting key factors determining the nature of competition.

Mortgage providers are in a state of change with a wide range of factors influencing the development of a new competitive focus. Traditionally, money managers provide long-term loans out of short-term deposits. There is still evidence of an investment performance mentality. Focus on return on capital and how hard assets are working for the company in measuring performance and efficiency in money management are all indicative of the traditional mortgage-credit institution. Recent deregulation and increased competition are, however, serving to alter this traditional focus as institutions move more towards a marketing orientation. The pursuit of profitability and domestic market share and concern with the development of sophisticated (differentiated) products shows a shift in focus from managing money to strategic management of the business. This refocusing of effort is following a similar path to that in the banking sector – unsurprising given the blurring of traditional boundaries between the two sectors. The factors affecting concentration on profitability, product innovation, customer services and staff recruitment and training, all mirror those discussed earlier for the retail banking sector.

Where the mortgage sector differs from the retail banking sector is principally in its early stage of European expansion. Wide differences in mortgage markets, particularly in terms of legislation, and protectionist and anti-expansionary attitudes on the part of EC governments have almost totally restricted foreign expansion by mortgage-credit institutions. However, the move towards a Single European Market is refocusing attention on potential expansionary strategies. There is a growing recognition that with freedom of establishment in other EC Member States and growing harmonization of legislation, the differences in mortgage markets emerge as opportunities rather than barriers to cross-border business. In the case of UK building societies, the impact of deregulation has resulted in greater efficiency and skills in product innovation and development, providing advantages for UK-based organizations over those based in the comparatively regulated markets of Southern Europe. Nevertheless, there are major hurdles to be faced before these potential opportunities can be realized – not least the fact that mortgage-credit institutions have no retail networks across Europe. This problem is compounded by the fact that mortgage institutions generally lack staff with any European experience.

Although these hurdles are not insurmountable, they serve to perpetuate the argument that mortgage markets are, and will continue to be nationally focused. This argument is given further weight as 1992 directives become apparent, indicating that governments will continue to be allowed the freedom to legislate against certain products and services on the basis of protecting the 'public good'. As housing finance is an integral part of each national economy and each country's housing and social policy, total freedom of product and service provision is obviously not feasible. It is likely then that real opportunities will be restricted to niche sectors – the likelihood of pan-European mortgage providers being remote. The small incidence of foreign expansion by British institutions can be explained, therefore, by the difficulties of expanding abroad in this sector and is not indicative of a reluctance to take risks and establish operations in other EC Member States. There are feasibly greater opportunities in product rather than geographic diversification. For example, why should a UK building society prefer to sell unsecured loans in the highly-competitive British market as opposed to mortgage credit in the chaotic and under-developed Italian market? Although they have no experience in personal loans, and are experts in providing housing finance, in the first instance they are selling products to existing customers in a market where they have high credibility, a well-developed distribution system and other tried and tested credit products.

Alternatively, expansion into the Italian market requires the development of a distribution system, brand awareness and an understanding of the market. Expansion by British firms to-date has been relatively small scale – joint ventures being established with institutions in Spain and Italy to tap specific areas of potential – while minimizing the risks by going in with a local partner. Firms based in other EC markets show equally limited rates of expansion, preferring to concentrate on their own national markets and exploit the profit potential from existing customer bases or those of the local banks where cooperative arrangements are established.

To some extent, it is more likely that mortgage credit will Europeanize through the banks who have already developed distribution networks and who are thus better placed to realize the potential opportunities. This raises further incentives for cooperative arrangements between mortgage funders and banks. In the UK, however, the fact that the banks have developed their own mortgage products closes the door on such opportunities for the building societies. Nevertheless, there is potential for their establishing cooperative links with foreign banks, seeking to diversify their product ranges. Equally, the disaggregation of various functions in the provision of mortgage credit opens up opportunities for cross-border cooperation.

13.8   Managing the Process

The lack of distribution networks has already been highlighted as a major barrier to expansion by European mortgage institutions. What is less clear, however, is why so much emphasis is being placed on joint ventures as a way of tapping niche opportunities. Cross-border delivery of mortgages is not likely to be a reality in the short-term as customers traditionally buy their mortgages through branch outlets. Furthermore, given that a mortgage is the largest individual loan taken out by customers and quite a complicated contract, explanation of the contract and reassurance are often regarded as key services in mortgage delivery. Easily achieved through face-to-face interaction, these services are not so simple to provide across borders. Although market-based sales representatives could provide these services, and in the longer-term firms may be tempted to experiment with this approach, this would necessitate a change in consumer behaviour which would take time to achieve. Alternatively, greenfield development of branch outlets is both costly and high risk. Faced with unknown and highly diverse European markets in terms of both legislation and competition and lacking the personnel to champion EC expansion, mortgage financiers are understandably reluctant to develop their own activities from scratch. While acquisition would allow institutions to buy in these skills, without any experience in Europe this is considered equally high risk, not only in terms of up-front costs, but also as regards the difficulty of integrating an organization whose funding systems, products and services are so far-removed from the acquirer's.

Unlike the banking sector there are no scale-economy advantages to be derived from expanding the organization through acquisition. Due to the diverse nature of funding and systems for product administration there is little scope for real integration following acquisition. Although acquisition may enhance profitability by extending an organization's distribution coverage it will also raise the costs of administration, which may potentially offset the advantages. Acquisition may consequently present diseconomies – further reinforcing the argument for product rather than geographic expansion.

Joint ventures, therefore, appear to be the only feasible option for cost-effective, low-risk expansion and also provide mortgage institutions with important learning experiences and a forum for testing market opportunities without their committing themselves to wholly-owned ventures. Coupled with this, as the profile of cooperative arrangements has risen, as many retail financial service firms have become part of the trend towards Allfinanz, new opportunities for cross-border cooperation have opened up between financial-service providers operating in different product sectors. Equally, the breaking down of mortgage-finance provision into its constituent elements of generation, funding and administration adds further scope for cross-border liaisons and joint ventures.

13.9   The Future

Like the banks, there is some evidence to suggest that disaggregation of mortgage business and specialization by firms in specific areas is likely. Although the diversion into estate agencies has been less successful than imagined, it is likely that mortgages will increasingly be sold through intermediaries further down the channel with the potential of capturing customers at an earlier stage in the buying process. Estate agents and solicitors are likely, then, to play an increasingly important role in the retailing of mortgages – although acquisition of estate agents, which was the approach followed by many UK building societies, may be supplanted by greenfield agents or cooperative agreements. In addition, many mortgage institutions have recognized the natural synergies between mortgages, life assurance and building contents insurance. Consequently the incidence of cooperative arrangements and tied relationships between mortgage providers and insurance companies is likely to increase.

Unlike the banking sector, technological developments are not expected to have a major impact on the distribution of mortgages. Although many UK building societies have developed or accessed ATM networks, these support the delivery of their current account money provision and, to some extent, deposits but merely serve to advertise the building societies' core products – their mortgages. Nevertheless, computerization has served to simplify the processing of mortgage applications and administration of accounts which has helped to promote increased efficiency – and development of this kind is likely to continue. Whether there is scope for exploring technology-based systems for the provision of mortgages is debatable. Although computers are becoming more user-friendly, their ability to provide detailed explanations and reassure customers regarding such a major transaction is limited. Thus mortgage provision, whilst changing quite considerably in the face of deregulation and intensified competition is likely to remain a personalized service.

14

Industry Study 7: The European Insurance Industry

14.1 Introduction

The European insurance industry has traditionally been characterized by a high degree of national compartmentalism and fragmentation. The high political and social profile of insurance opens nations up to government legislation which shapes national markets independently. In the past, this has restricted the amount of foreign competition, as has the high cost of establishing the extensive distribution networks necessary to sell insurance. Mergers and acquisitions are an obvious way of overcoming these hurdles, and with many domestic markets reaching capacity, European firms' growing interest in cross-border expansion is following this route. This spate of merger activity is also reducing levels of market concentration and as insurance companies link up with banks, housing finance organizations and other financial firms, the face of European insurance is clearly changing.

14.2 Sectoral Analysis

Insurance can be divided into three categories: (1) Life (2) Non Life/General, and (3) Reinsurance.

Life Insurance incorporates life-cover and pensions and unlike other types of insurance payments are made at the end of a fixed period against a certain event such as retirement or death. The business is, therefore, not susceptible to fluctuations in earnings and centres on investment of accumulated premiums. The long-term liability involved reduces the capital base required by firms. Policies have traditionally

Table 14.1   Age structure of EC population, 1995, 2000, 2010

	1995 (000s)	(%)	2000 (000s)	(%)	2010 (000s)	(%)
0–14	58 964	17.9	59 011	17.8	54 170	16.3
15–44	142 878	43.3	139 971	42.1	129 288	39.1
45–64	77 089	23.4	80 092	24.1	89 686	27.1
65+	50 390	15.3	53 053	15.9	57 617	17.4

Source: European Commission

been sold through salesmen, which has tended to restrict activity to local regions or national markets.

Whereas Japanese consumers, on average, have life premiums valued at \$1560 and Americans \$725, European premiums are estimated at \$390 which suggests great scope for future growth. Growth rates in the life sector of 'under-insured' markets of Europe – France, Italy, Spain, Portugal and Greece – are expected to exceed 20 per cent. In the more developed markets such as Germany and the UK, although more modest, growth is still expected to be between 5 and 10 per cent. Demographic trends also support this growth in insurance. Life expectancy across Europe is increasing, and the overall age structure of the population is changing. As consumers' demands for financial products change over their life-time, the changing age structure has an important bearing on the demand for specific products. Table 14.1 shows the changing pattern up to the year 2010.

The population is clearly ageing, and, given the growing tendency for people to make adequate provision for their retirement, the beneficial impact on the life insurance sector is quite apparent. However, the real value for the industry will depend upon the propensity to save (which in turn is related to local economic conditions – interest rates and taxation) and the level of state pension provision. Thus, for example, although the British show a low propensity to save, they spend by far the most in the EC on life assurance as a result of the low state-pension provision. Thus, these two factors may have a counterbalancing effect.

General Insurance includes both 'personal lines'/'mass risk', which are the policies taken out by individuals to cover damage to, for example, their property or their car, and 'large risks' which are those taken out by commercial customers to protect against large-scale disasters or product/professional liability. Claims are unpredictable and thus the capital base of firms must be high. Demand generally follows the pattern of national economic performance, in particular rates of growth and the resulting impact on disposable income. The sector is also susceptible to trends in competition and capacity as reflected in its underwriting results. Europe, however, shows far less fluctuation in its underwriting cycle than North America as a result of national-market insulation wherein the lack of cross-border activity reduces the amount of mobile capital entering markets. This may well change in the wake of Single-European-Market initiatives designed to promote cross-border trade in the non-life sector.

Reinsurance occurs when the 'direct' insurer passes on part of the risk on a policy to one or more 're-insurers'. This sector of the market grew in stature in the 1970s following the oil crisis, which depressed global economic performance, affecting demand for corporate, personal line and life insurance, but promoting insurance against industrial failure. The advantages of reinsurance are quite clear: it allows firms to spread risk and it permits small firms to extend their direct business beyond the level that their capitalization would otherwise allow. The resultant boom in this sector led to over-capacity and expansion into the long-tail sector (where there is a significant time lag between the inflow of revenues and the paying of claims). This led to many firms getting their fingers burned as US courts continually found in favour of consumers in major product liability cases. Nevertheless, the future of this sector looks favourable given the limited amount of regulation and the fact that European firms reinsure a higher proportion of risks than their Japanese and American counterparts. It is estimated that approximately one tenth of all global premiums are reinsured. As reinsurance does not involve direct sale to consumers it cannot be considered a part of the retail financial service sector.

14.3   Overview – Europe in Perspective

Table 14.2 shows the level of gross premium payments across various markets. These data serve to highlight the difference in *scale* between the United States (in particular) and Japan, and individual European countries, which show lower levels of insurance business as a per cent of GNP. The UK is exempted from this latter categorization, being a relatively heavily-insured market. Scale, it can be argued, is an important factor in the insurance industry as underwriting large volumes of insurance allows firms to spread risk. Consequently, the establishment of a single European market and resultant expansion cross border by European firms should raise the profile of European insurers in the world market as large-scale players with a global outlook. Progress to that position is hampered, however, by the fragmented nature of the

Table 14.2 Gross premium payments in 1985 in US dollars

	Life	(%)	Non-Life	(%)	Total	% of GNP
United States	156.2	52	145.6	48	301.8	7.6
Japan	65.6	74	23.0	26	88.6	6.7
United Kingdom	19.5	46	23.3	54	42.8	9.4
Germany	14.0	38	22.9	62	36.9	5.9
France	8.6	31	18.8	69	27.4	5.4
Canada	8.2	40	12.5	60	20.7	6.2

Source: OECD

European market. The 325 million people in Europe will be served by more than 4000 insurance companies as opposed to the 54 firms serving 122 million customers in Japan. A degree of industry rationalization is inevitable, and necessary, if European firms are to take opportunities of the advantages offered by a single Europe.

14.4   Leading Markets

The twelve member states of the EC reveal very different markets for both life and non-life insurance. UBS Philips & Drew European Insurance Review (1989) defines the basic characteristics of the major markets. Table 14.3 presents a summary of these factors.

14.4.1   France

The major issue currently confronting the French market is growing awareness by consumers of the value of supplementing state pensions with personal provisions. It is estimated that the life-assurance market will grow at 20 per cent a year, although profits will be less attractive due to the costs associated with generating and supporting such high levels of new business. In the non-life sector, aggressive competition yields low returns as continual price cutting, coupled with high numbers of claims in all sectors continue to depress the market.

There are three main sectors of insurance companies in France:

1 Private Stock Companies
2 Nationalized Companies. There are four groups of nationalized companies – AGF, UAP, GNP and GAN. In 1987, they accounted for approximately 42 per cent of premium income in the life sector and 22 per cent in non-life.

Table 14.3 Life and non-Life geographical breakdown, 1988

	Population (millions)	Life Insurance	(%)	General Insurance	(%)	Growth Life 1988 (%)	Growth General 1988 (%)
France	54.9	F87 476m	37	F153 742m	63	15.0	6.0
Italy	57.3	L4 994bn	22	L18 084bn	78	25.0	10.5
The Netherlands	14.7	Dfl13 345m	45	Dfl16 380m	55	20.0	8.0
Spain	38.9	Pts424 511m	36	Pts727 620m	64	35.0	30.0
W. Germany	61.0	Dm51 100m	42	Dm70 830m	58	7.5	6.0
UK	56.6	£21 455m	68	£10 084m	32	11.0	10.0

Source: UBS Phillips & Drew Global Research Group *European Insurance Review*, January 1989

3 Mutual Sector. This is particularly strong in France for private line insurance, especially in the motor sector. They generally offer cheaper rates as they have no agents and thus no costly intermediate fees.

14.4.2 Italy

As with France, life insurance in Italy shows great potential for growth. Between 1984 and 1989, premiums for life and endowment policies rose by nearly 270 per cent, and although growth has slowed, it is likely to continue favourably. Italian customers are growing more aware of the benefits of insurance and, given their propensity to save and their demand for savings instruments managed by professional specialists, there is great scope for sophisticated quality products from the insurance sector. As the life sector in 1989 accounted for only 24.5 per cent of the insurance market, exploiting growth potential in this sector should allow a better balance to be achieved with other risks. Growth is also being stimulated by the authorities who, fearing the burden that the ageing Italian population will have on the country's social security system, are actively encouraging people to make provision for their futures.

The Italian market is also geographically unbalanced with per capita expenditure in Northern Italy outweighing the South by approximately three times. This partly reflects lower economic development in the South as well as cultural differences with awareness of the value of insurance running much lower in the mezzogiorno than in the North.

14.4.3 Spain

Spain's insurance market offers enormous opportunities with a young, upwardly mobile population in possession of growing disposable incomes. However, culturally, there is a tendency to spend not save and thus maximizing apparent potential depends on a period of education, wherein firms must persuade customers that there are benefits from long-term investment in their futures rather than short-term profit tax-dodge schemes. Investment in single premium life policies allowed consumers to pour black-market money into bonds on which the interest was non-taxable and for which the policyholder did not have to disclose his name. This, whilst now prevented by law, perpetuated a market in search of a 'quick fix'. Before the laws were passed, the rapid increase in investment in single policies distorted the growth rate of the market. Nevertheless, as consumers become increasingly aware of the importance of life insurance and pension policies, the underlying growth rate is expected to be around 35 per cent. Alternatively, non-life opportunities are far fewer, despite the expected growth rate of 30 per cent. Competition is extremely intense in all areas and profit margins low. Although the motor sector accounts for over 47 per cent of the market, notoriously bad driving by Spanish motorists and rising claims costs and frequencies make the sector far from attractive. The health sector, whilst relatively developed in Spain given that the public health service is not available to all, is likely to remain at a break-even level due to spiralling claims costs.

14.4.4 Germany

Population ageing is a particularly acute problem in the German market accentuating the fears of the state about their ability to provide for the population and awareness by individuals that self-provision is essential. Growth rates are expected to continue around 7.5 per cent despite recent changes to taxation of life policies. Although a 10 per cent tax is levied on interest over the guaranteed 3.5 per cent, life policies remain the most tax-efficient form of saving. However, such taxation policies clearly make equity-linked products unattractive to high-income consumers. Buoyant economic conditions help to sustain a strong and healthy non-life sector with modest rates of growth.

14.4.5 The UK

The UK life assurance industry is still adjusting following the 1986 Financial Services Act. The introduction of the polarization requirement wherein market intermediaries for life assurance are required to be completely independent and deal with the whole market *or* be the representative of only one firm, has had an important impact on the industry. In particular, smaller companies, heavily reliant on referrals from independent intermediaries, have therefore had to strengthen their own distribution networks. Awareness of the importance of life assurance by British consumers is already high, but growth is expected to continue in a market whose culture determines that insurance is regarded highly. The UK general insurance market is highly profitable with most firms earning a pre-tax profit on equity in excess of 20 per cent – likely to attract foreign firms to the market, increase competition and reduce returns. This has resulted from lower levels of fragmentation in the UK market which is dominated by a limited number of quoted companies. Two thirds of the business written in the UK is controlled by ten firms which gives them a powerful position, but does not prevent stiff competition.

Table 14.4 Relative cost/price positions* insurance products

	Belgium	Spain	France	W. Germany	Ireland	Netherlands	UK
Life Insurance	78	37	33	5	83	−9	−30
Home Insurance	−16	−4	39	3	81	17	90
Motor Insurance	30	100	9	15	148	−7	−17

* per cent discrepancies from price of average of lowest four producers
Source: Price Waterhouse

14.5 Products

As insurance companies are becoming the main mediums for savings in the EC, government intervention is inevitable. This includes policy wording/prior approval, price controls, definition/restriction of profits, mortality tables and interest rates, applied to different degrees in different markets. All countries also control insurance reserves and areas of investment. The focus of these controls is the consumer, but the specific objective varies from emphasizing consumer choice to stressing consumer protection. Such controls and restrictions impact on the nature of products offered in the twelve Member States, and the degree to which markets are regulated influences the extent of product development and innovation. In the heavily regulated markets of Germany, Italy, Greece and Portugal, product controls have restricted the degree to which products are adapted and differentiated. Competition centres on price, which can result in cut-throat competition and low profit margins. The least regulated markets – the Netherlands and the UK – through aggressive product innovation have been able to preserve profits and re-invest in systems for lowering production costs and sustaining profitability long-term. Table 14.4 shows the relative cost/price positions for a range of countries. Britain and Holland's efficiency, in life and motor insurance particularly, is quite clear. Adding to this efficiency is the market size in each country, which allows firms to attain a critical mass, particularly in processing, and benefit from economies of scale.

Thus, regulations shape the types of product offered and the way they are sold. What further adds to the disparity between countries is customer preference. For example the Germans spend up to $25 per head a year on legal insurance compared to less than $2 per head for the British; 'all-risk' insurance is popular in the UK but less so in continental Europe where individuals prefer to itemize specific risks. In the past, these factors have added to national insularity.

14.6 Distribution

Distribution is probably the key to successful insurance business and it is here where competition is most intense and most innovative. The old axiom 'insurance isn't bought it's sold' underlies the reasoning behind personal selling which has dominated the insurance sector for so long. Motor insurance, which in many markets is a legal necessity for all car owners and which is thus actively sought by customers, provides an exception, and is rather determined by availability and price giving rise to an important broker sector in some markets, notably the UK. Alternatively, insurance has historically been sold through branch network outlets. However, channels of distribution and sales methods are changing as firms seek to reduce their costs in increasingly competitive markets wherein the heavy burden of sales commission paid to company or independent agents, and the high costs of establishing extensive branch networks, simply cannot be justified. Such change has been particularly acute in Britain where legislation introduced in 1988 has changed the relationship between the insurance companies and independent intermediaries. The tied status which many former independent agents have opted for has raised their bargaining power *vis-à-vis* the insurance companies raising commissions by up to an estimated 30 per cent. The impetus has turned insurance company focus away from establishing and managing their own distribution arrangement to a round of co-operative agreement and joint ventures with banks and building societies who have extensive branch-networks far beyond the scope of insurance firms. For example, Commercial Union has established a distribution arrangement with Midland Bank, Standard Life with the Halifax. Standard Life has further ensured access to a wide customer base by acquiring 35 per cent of the Bank of Scotland.

Similar, if not so extreme, patterns can be seen across Europe. As tied and semi-tied agents dominate insurance in many European markets (see table 14.5) the stimulus to move to less costly cooperative options is quite apparent. In France, GAN, the state-owned insurance company, has linked with CIC bank and in Germany AHB has combined forces with Bank für Germeinwirtschaft (BfG). These links are also being fostered by the banks themselves who are keen to benefit from the economies of scope offered by extending their product portfolio to include insurance as their objectives change from traditional banking activities to an 'Allfinanz' financial supermarket approach. For some

Table 14.5 Insurance selling methods

	W. Germany Total	Holland Total	Italy Life	Italy Non-Life	France Life	France Non-Life	Britain Life	Britain Non-life
	Market Share (%) 1986							
Firms without intermediaries	3	25	–	–	10	27	3	N/A
Banks	2	13	–	–	32	–	3	N/A
Brokers	16	20	20	10	26	21	44	70
Agents & salesmen	79	42	80	90	32	52	50	N/A

Source: *L'Argus*

banks, this move is involving their developing their own insurance lines in-house , and, although some may argue that this will raise administrative costs unnecessarily above those of banks who have opted for cooperative arrangements, the returns accrue solely to the bank and the control over activities is total. Indeed, while the trend towards banks offering their own insurance provides a competitive challenge to insurance companies to become more efficient in terms of cost cutting by finding more effective means of distribution, it provides some cause for concern about the competitive vulnerability of insurance companies in the wider market for financial services, which includes banks and housing-finance providers. Whereas insurance products and administrative systems are easy to replicate by other financial institutions, branch networks remain a costly barrier to insurance companies attaining similar market potential. Insurance companies in an attempt to reduce costs and gain access to established customer bases in the short-term may be vulnerable in the longer-term if banks and other institutions decide to do their own thing.

Other forms of distribution are being explored by firms, particularly those who are not willing to become beholden to powerful banks. Direct Response Advertising and Direct Mail techniques are being used aggressively in many markets which provide an assured way of cutting costs. What is less sure, however, is the effectiveness of these techniques. Some industry specialists continue to assert that direct personal selling will continue to be the most effective mode of sale. Because products are often complicated and require a considerable amount of explanation, and because after-sales service and 'hand-holding' are important product-related offerings, they argue that sales agents will continue to dominate the industry. There are also some who question the ability of bank staff to conduct the traditional selling role of company sales agents, reacting passively to enquiries made in the bank branches, which are now visited infrequently as a result of automatic teller machines (ATM's) which negate the need for entering bank premises. However, with bank overheads running (in many instances) at less than 5 per cent of premiums compared to 10–25 per cent with a direct sales force, training bank staff to affect an aggressive approach towards in-house insurance sales may ultimately be the optimum approach. Whichever way the market develops, it is undoubtedly true that it is changing, as are the rules of the competitive game. In terms of international expansion, cooperative arrangements with foreign organizations, particularly banks, are providing a key point of access for insurance companies wishing to enter European Markets. Commercial Union's distribution arrangement with Credit Italiano provides a good example of a Southern European bank seeing the advantage of liaising with a UK insurance firm to provide sophisticated life assurance products for a rapidly developing market. Equally, it reveals how the relative sophistication of products provided by firms based in the most developed European markets such as Britain acts as an incentive for banks and other indigenous firms to give them access to their distribution networks. Similarly Allianz and Banco Popular Espanol have agreed to form two joint ventures in Spain – a life insurance firm and a management company for pension funds, each party aware of the potential synergies from the pooling of skills and resources.

14.7 The Competitive Process

The measures of competitiveness in figure 14.1 are those most frequently cited by managers interviewed in the study.

The measures cited reflect the key forces determining the competitive process in the insurance industry for British firms.

Underlying the whole insurance industry is the fact that it is an investment business wherein performance is not only linked to sales and the volume of business generated, but also depends upon the skill and acumen of company investors. It is not surprising therefore, to find that investment-income fund performance and profitability are the focus of performance measures. The volume of business generated (and indeed the size of the organization) dictate the amount of money with which the firm can generate profits. Although profitability is not only a British phenomenon, aggressive competition in the UK market has possibly raised the focus of profitability in recent years as firms have recognized that to survive they need to invest in technologies and systems

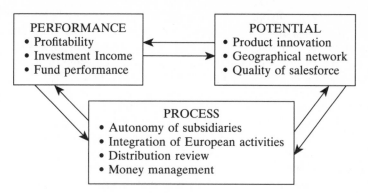

Figure 14.1   Measures of competitiveness in the insurance industry

whereby they can reduce their production costs and preserve profit margins long-term.

The technologies and systems in which profits are being invested are highlighted in the potential measures. In order to avoid cut-throat pricing, particularly following a period when deregulation has added to the competitive pressures facing many financial-service firms, organizations have opted for product innovation and competition based on differentiation rather than price. This has led to a point now where many British firms boast of their product 'superiority' *vis-à-vis* European competitors, particularly those of Southern Europe, and see this as providing them with competitive advantages over their rivals. Whilst such firm-specific advantages are short lived, as insurance products are easy to replicate, product innovation may be the lynch-pin in establishing cooperative arrangements with indigenous firms with well-established distribution networks. As distribution is such a key element in the selling of insurance, the importance of establishing or gaining access to a wide geographical network is an inevitable inclusion in the measures of potential. For some firms this involves the developing of ties with other financial institutions at home and abroad. For others, attaining a geographic spread and an extensive customer base relies on their attracting and training a quality salesforce. This latter factor reflects the importance still attributed to the direct sales function by some organizations who believe that, despite the cost, the direct salesforce still provides the best selling medium. These firms, however, stressed the importance of technology in making the salesman more efficient and effective. Computerization is allowing certain administrative roles to pass to the sales representative – particularly gathering and computer logging of customer data at the point of sale. Although this represents a degree of cost saving the high costs traditionally associated with this mode of selling, along with others, make constantly reviewing distribution methods and searching for new options a central task of the insurance marketing function. As competition intensifies and strategic alliances abound, exploring potential innovations in distribution and the newer, low-cost strategies, such as Direct Response Advertising and Direct Mail, takes on a new significance as a key management function.

There is, however, a certain dichotomy in the investment decisions for European expansion by insurance firms. Because the insurance business is investment orientated, it is necessary that the growth option pursued by firms yields the same (if not better) returns than could be made on the money markets. This is arguably a problem affecting only British firms, who, unlike their European counterparts are not prepared to witness a dilution of their earnings per share in the event of favourable expansionist options.

Whichever way distribution systems develop, it is unlikely that they will develop in the same way in all European markets. Although the Single European Market Act is actively concerned with establishing directives to eliminate legislative disparities between the twelve Member States, they can do little to change the different buying behaviours of customers, which have been shaped by the historical development of such legislation and the individual country cultures. Adaptation to local needs will remain a critical issue, and for some firms this determines a high degree of autonomy being afforded to their subsidiaries with freedom to plan strategies and develop products as individual markets demand. Other firms, whilst not overlooking the need for local adaptation, rather view the management of the European firm as involving as much centralization of activities as possible – particularly in areas such as administration where there are economies of scale to be earned.

14.8   Leading European Players

Table 14.6 shows the relative standing of European insurers according to premium. Northern European insurers are all well represented, particularly the UK which boasts seven of the top 18 players compared to three for Germany and France, and two for Switzerland and Holland. Nevertheless, despite this apparent large-firm dominance, UK insurers have not developed a particularly strong European coverage, as table 14.7 shows. This has sometimes been attributed to their early expansion into the Commonwealth and America which means many of their interests lie outside the EC. However, given the amount of American and other international business performed by the other leading European firms this argument is less than convincing. It would rather appear that

Table 14.6 Insurance company premiums

	Premiums				Nationality
	Total (£m)	*Life (%)*	*General (%)*	*Reinsurance (%)*	
Allianz	5913	40	53	7	German
Zurich	5086	25	64	11	Swiss
UAP	4962	43	48	9	French
SWISS Ro	4348	7	37	56	Swiss
Royal Insurance	4033	20	77	3	British
Prudential	3882	69	16	15	British
Nat. Nedelanden	3542	53	38	9	Dutch
Munich Re	3494	–	–	100	German
Commercial Union	2845	29	69	2	British
Sun Alliance	2755	28	72	–	British
AGF	2676	46	54	–	French
General Accident	2383	9	91	–	British
Axa	2226	23	70	7	French
GRE	2141	32	68	–	British
Aegon	1658	55	45	–	Dutch
Legal & General	1536	75	15	10	British
AMB	1335	31	69	–	German

Source: UBS Philips & Drew, *European Insurance Review*, 1989

until very recently the British failed to realize the potential a wider European market could offer. This is changing to some extent as firms are attempting to develop strong European networks, although there is a degree of caution. The Prudential's activities reveal more of a series of small dabblings than a concentrated effort to develop a strong pan-European network. Reluctant to jump on the bandwagon of expensive acquisitions and rapidly-formed partnerships they appear to be playing a waiting game. Mr Mick Newmarch, Prudential's chief executive is reported as having said, 'The question is how urgent do we feel we have to be. The answer is not very. Most of these big expensive deals have my blessing since it is my competitors who are doing them'. The drive for expansion across Europe by British firms lacks the aggression evident with some of their German, French and Italian counterparts. The Italians are included here as a result of Generali's recent expansionist efforts. In 1988, Generali ranked fifth in Europe behind Allianz, Zurich, UAP and the Prudential and above Royal Insurance. More impressive in many ways, however, is the fact that around 65 per cent of its business is generated outside its home market, 60 per cent in other European

Table 14.7 Geographical distribution of premium income, 1988

(£m)	Belgium	Denmark	Eire	France	Germany	Italy	Netherlands	Spain	Switzerland	UK	Rest of Europe	US	Other
Allianz –													
General	–	–	–	146	2653	536	19	108	68	345	509	385	51
Life	–	–	–	–	2400	398	–	–	–	58	–	–	–
Zurich –													
General	49	–	–	121	558	216	83	118	698	213	72	922	745
Life	21	–	–	23	251	49	67	15	592	45	14	43	217
UAP –													
General	106	–	119	1552	53	66	161	–	15	–	–	425	129
Life	–	–	–	1775	–	–	–	–	–	–	–	–	–
Royal –													
General	–	–	–	–	–	–	117	27	–	1060	88	1363	555
Life	–	–	–	–	–	–	–	–	–	823	–	–	–
Prudential –													
General	55	3	5	–	1	–	5	–	–	430	37	–	326
Life	11	–	83	–	–	–	–	–	–	1813	12	756	348
Commercial Union –													
General	52	–	–	27	–	17	240	23	–	838	38	590	189
Life	–	–	–	–	–	–	306	–	–	353	103	68	1
Sun Alliance –													
General	15	95	50	15	50	15	40	15	–	1179	–	216	301
Life	–	55	–	–	100	–	–	–	–	554	–	–	55

Source: UBS Phillips and Drew European Insurance Review, 1989

markets. In a relatively short space of time it has become one of the most Europeanized firms in the community, with a network in German speaking Europe (a throwback to its Austro–Hungarian roots), a minority shareholding in Compagne du Midi in France (which itself has recently merged with Axa to Generali's annoyance) and small operations in Belgium, Holland and the UK.

Allianz, however, is probably the best-placed insurer in Europe. Acquisitions in the UK (Cornhill) and Italy (RAS), the latter of which had a strong European network of its own, have given it a strong position in the rapidly-growing markets of Spain and Italy, the highly fragmented, buoyant UK market and the French market, which is growing increasingly difficult to penetrate. Added to this, its unassailable position in its domestic market, where it is more than twice as big as its nearest rival, give it an enviable position in the new wider Europe.

UAP, the state-owned French market leader is also making rapid strides to extend its coverage. It has strengthened its position domestically by taking a 34 per cent stake in Groupe Victoire, it has acquired operations in Ireland, Italy (Allsecures, a subsidiary of the Fiat-group Toro Insurance), Belgium (Royale, Belge) and Spain, and bought stakes in firms in the UK (Sun Life) and Greece.

Mutual societies, prevalent in France and the UK deserve some comment. Mutual companies, owned by their policyholders, are restricted in their capital formation to what can be generated internally from their own resources. Many have done this with great success and achieved a strong position in their domestic markets, and through boom-market periods have accumulated very large free reserves. However, growing competitive pressures have tempted some firms to maintain market share by paying higher commissions out of their reserves, and the inability for firms to seek outside funding in a period of intense competition and recession clearly puts mutuals at a disadvantage. Ultimately, they face three options. Firstly, they could choose to demutualize. Experience among American mutual insurance companies who have opted for this route, however, shows a poor track record for survival. Most firms, with few exceptions, have been acquired by outside financial institutions immediately following demutualization. Secondly, the small mutual firms could choose to focus their efforts in the niche sectors where their limited funds can be concentrated on specific sectors rather than diluted across a broad product range. This appears to be the direction most preferred amongst both French and British mutuals. Finally, they could group together through merger to form larger, more robust institutions whose combined reserves would permit greater earning power. This latter option, which theoretically looks beneficial, has not been considered, or has been rejected by firms seeking to retain their independence. Whatever path they take, the future may well prove to be rocky.

14.9 Managing the Process

The foreign market servicing strategies employed by firms are critical in attaining a competitive position in ever-changing European markets. The brief outline of the leading players in Europe has shown a high propensity for takeover and merger. Because it allows firms to 'hit the ground running', returns are rapid and the outlay can more easily be justified as potentially it can produce similar returns to fund investments. The principal advantage of takeovers, however, relates to the established distribution network and customer base which is inherently acquired. Developing greenfield businesses are long-term ventures, and penetration is not assured, given the high degree of entrenchment by indigenous producers in most markets. This would apparently suggest the option being ruled out, but surprisingly there are a number of firms, particularly British insurers, who have opted for this approach. In the field of general insurance, firms can expect to gain business from independent brokers where they exist. For large firms with an assured reputation, the likelihood of winning business this way is greater, as brokers tend to recommend firms with a high profile and proven track record. This is particularly true for UK insurers in Southern European markets where the relative small size of indigenous firms and the attractiveness of sophisticated UK firms gives British general insurers a potentially strong foothold to earn a high proportion of recommendations. In markets such as Spain, however, where there is no indigenous broker network, following this option will depend upon the rate of Europeanization of the brokers.

Greenfield investment for life assurance appears less attractive still with the prospect of hiring and training an indigenous salesforce to persuade customers away from long-established local firms. But some firms are following this route and with some success. National Nederland started a greenfield life company in Greece and has gained 12 per cent of the market and its Spanish operation is one of the best new companies in the country. Here, the major advantage is the control over the organization which this option naturally affords; control over the types of products, distribution arrangements and nature of customers is complete and permits companies to grow organically without diluting their share performance. Furthermore, the cultural affinity between subsidiary and parent company makes the new venture easy to integrate into the company, which is often a problem with takeovers and mergers and can consequently lead to poor results in the early years. Although the lead to scale of business is obviously small in the short-term, the rate of penetration slow and the opportunities for spreading risk limited, it provides an option for Europeanization for small niche firms wishing to expand beyond their domestic markets.

Alternatively, firms are looking to establish partnership or cooperative arrangement with foreign firms, primarily for the access to distribution networks this provides. Some of these are with local banks who, in many ways, are better than the local insurance firms who have limited branch networks. In the same way that there are synergistic benefits in domestic markets for insurance companies to establish links with local banks, there are clear advantages of tying activities to those of foreign banks in search of insurance products to extend their portfolios. That is not to say that there aren't benefits to be derived from establishing joint ventures with foreign insurance companies. Insurers often offer very different products and therefore a complementary portfolio can be established through a joint venture. Of equal interest to some firms is the potential to establish joint ventures with non-financial retailers. As the differences between goods retailers and financial-service retailers narrow (viz. the Allfinanz approach being adopted by some and the growing importance of issues such as store ambience), there is apparent potential to exploit the vast network of outlets owned by non-financial firms. Although this is not currently a fully explored area or one which has yielded any degree of success (Benetton has recently pulled out of its joint venture with the Prudential in Italy), it is a strategy which cannot be ruled out in the future.

Whatever form joint ventures and cooperations may take, it is probably the firms who *control* the distribution channels who are best placed to exploit opportunities in the wider European market over time. It is quite clear that distribution channels are a critical asset, their ownership providing firms with firm-specific advantages which cannot be replicated and which cannot easily be established from scratch (if at all). Firms who are beholden to other firms for their distribution are in a very precarious position as their long-term potential is in no way assured. Certain joint-ventures may, therefore, simply be the first steps by some firms to acquire total control of the foreign firm and its distribution network. This is obviously making some firms reluctant to enter into joint arrangements with firms they see as stronger than themselves for fear of later takeover. Finding a potential joint-venture partner, particularly for relatively large UK insurers in the less developed South-European markets, may not therefore be possible.

14.10   The Future

Some observers believe it likely that, ultimately, Europe will be dominated by around ten heavily capitalized companies with pan-European coverage. As the dominant firms grow ever-larger through acquisition and benefit from scale advantages in investment and greater capital to invest in new technology for handling, administration and distribution, they will gain a leading edge over smaller rivals. Furthermore, as consumer behaviour becomes more standardized in the wake of the Single European Market, large pan-European firms will be well-placed to exploit scale economies in centralizing functions – notably adminis-tration. As firms see this as the future direction of the industry and the threat of takeover is very real, rationalization is likely to continue apace as those firms wishing to be one of the major league large-scale players continue to grow by acquisition. In so doing, these firms will come to control major distribution networks in the twelve member states, rais-ing barriers to entry and perpetuating the trend towards large-firm dominance.

This does not, however, preclude small firms from the industry, specifically niche specialists who may gain a strong European coverage by concentrating on specific skills not available to all. Those firms likely to be casualties in the rationalization process are the medium-size firms who fall between the two stools of scale and specialism. It is also likely that American and Japanese firms will show a growing interest in the Single European Market, intensifying competition still further.

The future of the industry is also likely to witness continuing innova-tion in the distribution of insurance, this development going hand-in-hand with new technological developments such as home-computerized shopping. With changing demographics – particularly the increasing number of women in the workforce – it is inevitable that shopping habits will change in the future. Exploring potential new routes of delivery may consequently be a key element in future competitiveness.

15

Conclusion

15.1 Context

The aim of this piece of research was to establish the impact of foreign market servicing strategies on the international competitiveness of UK firms.

The context of this investigation was given in the introduction. The choice of industries and individual firms was governed by a number of principles. These included: a mix of foreign market servicing techniques in use and available to the firms, a range of firm size in the industry, identifiable foreign competitors, easily defined industry boundaries and some coherence in competitive strategies.

The industries chosen covered both manufacturing and services. In manufacturing, pharmaceuticals, scientific instruments, consumer paint and glass and industrial gases (the latter two grouped together as national champions) gave a mix of size and scope of firms, industrial and consumer orientation and international experience. The key market focus to narrow the scope of the investigation led us to concentrate on Japan/ USA, and France/Germany as highly competitive markets, together with Sweden to represent a sophisticated non-EC European market, and Australia as a means of capturing a developed but non-central market. This industry/country mix meant that great diversity is present in the consideration of market servicing 'switches', which presents analytical problems of attributing the impact on competitiveness to the switch rather than to other factors. However, it does enable the complexity of company policy to be appreciated and it illustrates the difficulties of management in formulating a strategic direction.

The service firms are all in retail financial services. They include banks, housing finance (building societies in the UK context) and insurance firms. The orientation here is firmly pan-European and our major concern was to trace the European expansion of UK firms and their Continental European competitors.

Because competitiveness is a relative concept it is important to use comparators and one of the most important of these is foreign competitor firms. Differences and similarities in attitudes to competitiveness and in foreign market servicing policy are therefore a crucial aspect of the research. Similarly, a key issue facing all firms competing in the world economy is the creation and consolidation of trade blocs or common markets and this project provided an ideal opportunity to examine the importance of the Single European Market Act to both British and foreign competitor firms.

15.2   Competitiveness

Investigation of the concept of international competitiveness, both in the literature and by direct investigation of managerial attitudes, yielded a view of competitiveness as dynamic, relative and many faceted. Competitiveness cannot be considered at a point in time, as a static, single measure. Many performance measures are of this kind and because they ignore sustainability, they are fatally flawed. Similarly, it is essential to bench-mark any notion of competitiveness against an alternative state. This measure may be relative to a different point of time (including therefore the notion of a *loss* of competitiveness), against a different part of economic space (for example, cross national comparisons at macro level, comparing one firm with another of different nationality) or taking a counter-factual position (what would have happened if some crucial event had not taken place). Finally, single measures cannot capture all the necessary elements of competitiveness. Our investigations led us to three interrelated elements of competitiveness: performance, potential and managerial process.

At the level of the firm, it is virtually universal across industries and countries that the key measures are profitability and market share. Clearly there is room for variation in the way in which these are combined or prioritized. There is also often an implicit tradeoff between the two, which varies according to circumstances. Generally though, performance measures are uncontroversial.

Measures of competitive potential vary largely according to industry group. This is unsurprising. What is important in sustaining competitiveness over time does vary greatly according to industry circumstances. In the pharmaceutical industry, research and development is central to future competitive success, in financial services it is more dependent on human resources and therefore on skills and training.

Finally the management process provides a vital underpinning to the competitiveness of firms. It is management which is the active ingredient or prime mover in the competitiveness process. Management has perforce to balance the investment needs of competitive potential with the consumption needs of competitive performance. Too great a performance with little investment in potential will lead to rapid burn-out through non-sustainability and too weak a performance with excessive investment in potential will lead to take-over or bankruptcy. The use of managerial skills and their correct focusing is central to competitive success.

This model provides a useful, clear and theoretically grounded model of competitiveness. It is possible to examine the impact on this process of an external change. The change investigated in detail is a switch in market servicing policy in one particular market.

15.3 Foreign Market Servicing Strategies

The text of this book has illustrated that far from being a simple choice of mode of doing foreign business (export, license, direct foreign investment), foreign market servicing decisions are complex, dynamic and inter-related.

In any single market, the choice of market servicing mode must be built on company objectives, past achievements, logistical possibilities and constrained by product and market realities. The whole of the channel of distribution must be considered and due attention must be paid at all stages to optimum location and mode of control (internal versus external).

However, markets do not exist in isolation one from another. An overview must be taken of the whole system, the total network of the company. Selling in particular markets must be coordinated and rationalized where necessary. Forecasting must be used so as to coordinate foreign market servicing activities through time. As we have seen, many problems become focused through the foreign market servicing network. Good decisions on foreign market servicing will not however compensate for bad ones elsewhere – a bad product will not sell through even the most ideal network.

It is in this context that a foreign market servicing network should be considered. In no sense does the firm have a free choice of market servicing techniques. It will be constrained by the nature of the product, the market, the past history of involvement in the country and, not least, by the action of competitors. Timing too is crucial. A correct decision is entirely dependent on its coincidence with favourable factors. Perforce, many market servicing decisions are incremental, involving perhaps a minor adjustment in strategy, perhaps not involving a change of mode. Indeed, several of the most successful switches were within-mode changes (for example, a change in export arrangements).

Again it is important to take a comparative stance. Foreign competitors which are doing things differently are a source of evidence that other methods of doing business are feasible. This is true of market servicing where British managers could experience the impact of their competitors decisions but sometimes were constrained in their desire to emulate their most successful foreign rivals.

15.4 The Impact of Foreign Market Servicing Strategies on Competitiveness

Our results show that switches in foreign market servicing arrangements in particular markets can, and often do, have a profound effect on competitiveness in that market. This impact may be felt directly on performance and potential, and on management process separately or collectively. However, the interaction between the three elements of competitiveness may bring about a second-order effect.

Mistakes in switching modes of doing business abroad will have an adverse effect on the ability of the firm to compete effectively and may well adversely affect competitiveness in a wider area than just the market where the poor switch was made. Incorrect foreign market servicing decisions can impair performance, reduce competitive potential (perhaps by diverting resources away from essential investment sites) and damage management process by diverting management attention to repair the damage, destroying morale or derailing the strategic direction of the firm.

A number of interesting considerations arise from the firms sampled. Some firms found exporting through agents/distributors to be 'unsatisfactory' and switched to alternative modes of market servicing. However, it should be emphasized that many firms have forged highly successful relationships with their agents/distributors. A key factor in this respect is the selection of the 'right' intermediary (one which has the resources and incentives to promote the firm's products to the maximum effect), and the establishment of a good *two-way* dialogue and commitment between the two (or more) parties. The firms sampled generally avoided licensing because of its potential for undermining competitive advantages, although, again, it can be usefully employed by financially constrained firms or used to secure entry into 'difficult' markets. There was a consensus of opinion that some form of market presence is required to service effectively overseas markets. For firms who choose not to manufacture abroad, the nature of the ideal presence is a sales/marketing subsidiary. The major benefit offered by pursuing this strategy is 'closeness to customers' which is perceived by most managers as a way of overcoming problems of cultural and business naivety when selling abroad, allowing firms a better understanding of consumers and competitors in targeted markets.

15.5 1992

It is impossible to ignore the impact of 1992 either when examining the markets, firms and countries within its borders, or those outside them. For outsiders, particularly the Japanese, 1992 may be presented as a confidence trick, causing Japanese exporters to Europe to switch to direct investment so as to avoid the ill effect of 'Fortress Europe'. For insiders, an intensification of competition by removal of artificial barriers by governments and an influx of new competitors with a presence in the Single Market is likely to result. For our sample of UK firms, the results are industry specific. Within this, there seems to be little overt difference between British firms and their continental European rivals within the same industry. The exception to this rule is that Continental European firms are far more likely to envisage pan-European rationalization of facilities than are UK firms.

15.6 Summary of Major Themes

The comparison of manufacturing and service industries demonstrates the importance of industry-specific factors on the choice of foreign market servicing strategies, partly arising from the different competitive advantages necessary for success. Several common themes however arise across *all* our sample (1) Firms whose aim is short-term profitability are constrained in their choice of foreign market servicing strategies. This prevents many firms from following an optimum approach to their foreign activities, as this strategy restricts the available resources for foreign investment and increasing commitment to overseas markets. (2) Without exception, management of the process is a critical element of the firm's perception of competitiveness. (Many managers were highly critical of their own management styles and structures as barriers to improving competitiveness.) The opinion of several managers was that myopia within their organizations prevents firms from attaining a truly global perspective. Many of the larger firms are actively promoting a more international outlook and style in their organization. (3) Many firms behave in an opportunistic manner and the development of international activities stems from decisions based on highly imperfect information, which then need to be followed by an extensive period of adjustment. This adds further weight to the importance of the management process as it suggests that strategic planning is partly dependent on idiosyncratic decision making and that decisions, once made, require creative management in order to correct previously suboptimal strategies.

15.7   Lessons of the Research

It is appropriate to draw up a list of lessons for management which arise from this research:

1 Foreign market servicing strategy is an important component of international competitive success.
2 Foreign market servicing strategy in any one particular market must be constantly monitored with regard to its success relative to well-understood targets and with regard to the stance (and likely future stance) of competitors. Benchmarking against rivals is here, as well as elsewhere, a useful process.
3 Changes in foreign market servicing strategy need not be dramatic to be effective. Minor adjustments in arrangements can often achieve great results.
4 The correct foreign market servicing stance is not a substitute for other elements of successful business policy and operation. 'It ain't what you do, it's the way that you do it' might be a useful adage in that the management of the particular mode chosen is crucial.
5 It is not possible to make a success of foreign market servicing unless the inter-relations between markets are understood. It is essential to consider knock-on effects, inter-relationships and complementarities between markets.
6 The whole channel has to be considered in foreign market servicing. In particular, two sets of decisions are paramount. One is control of the particular stage of the channel. The other is its location. These two sets of decisions are interdependent.
7 The overview of foreign market servicing strategy – the whole network of the international firm – must be a paramount concern of top management, if international competitiveness is to be maintained or improved upon.

Above all, even where firms have a well defined approach to foreign market servicing the need for a *long-termist* and *flexible* outlook is considered to be particularly important. The former underpins learning-curve effects (understanding local cultures and customer needs, establishing harmonious and mutually beneficial supplier and distributor relations) and encourages the firm to seek long-term rather than short-term profit returns; the latter emphasizes (given the different nuances and characteristics of different markets) the need to approach each market separately – looking to the optimum mode of servicing individual markets, rather than attempting an holistic, global strategy.

Bibliography

Abernathy, W. J. and Wayne, K. (1974), 'Limits of the learning curve', *Harvard Business Review*, September–October 1974, pp.109–19.

Aliber, R. Z. (1970), 'A theory of foreign direct investment' in *The International Firm* (ed. by C. P. Kindleberger), Cambridge, Mass: MIT Press.

Anderson, E. and Coughlan, A. T. (1987), 'International market entry and expansion via independent or integrated channels of distribution', *Journal of Marketing*, Vol.51, pp.71–82.

Artto, E. W. (1987), 'Relative total costs: an approach to competitiveness measures of industries', *Management International Review*, Vol.27, No.2, pp.47–58.

Balassa, B. (1965), 'Trade liberalisation and "revealed" comparative advantage', *The Manchester School*, Vol.XXXIII, No.2, pp.99–123.

Balassa, B. (1977),' "Revealed" comparative advantage revisited: an analysis of relative export shares of the industrialised countries 1953–1971', *The Manchester School*, Vol.XLV, No.4, pp.327–44.

Baumol, W. J., Blackman, S. A. B. and Wolff, E. N. (1989), *Productivity and American Leadership: The Long View*, Cambridge, Mass: MIT Press.

Berg, T. L. (1971), 'Designing the distribution system' in *The Social Responsibility of Marketing* (ed. by W. D. Stevens), Chicago: American Marketing Association.

Boddewyn, J. J., Halbrich, M. B. and Perry, A. C. (1986), 'Service multinationals: conceptualization, measurement and theory', *Journal of International Business Studies*, Vol.16, No.3, pp.41–57.

Bowen, H. P. (1983), 'On the theoretical interpretation of indices of trade intensity and revealed comparative advantage', *Weltwirtschaftliches Archiv*, Vol.119, No.4, pp.464–72.

Brown, W. (1984), 'Firm-like behaviour in markets: the administered channel', *International Journal of Industrial Organisation*, Vol.2, pp.263–76.

Buckley, Peter J. (1983a), 'New theories of international business: some unresolved issues' in Mark Casson (ed) *The Growth of International Business*, London: George Allen & Unwin.

Buckley, Peter J. (1983b), 'New forms of international co-operation: a survey of the literature', *Aussenwirtschaft*, Vol.38, No.2, pp.195–222. Reprinted in Buckley and Casson (1985), op. cit.

Buckley, Peter J. (1987), 'An economic transactions analysis of tourism', *Tourism Management*, Vol.8, No.3, pp.190–4.

Buckley, Peter J. (1988), 'The limits of explanation: testing the internalisation theory of the multinational enterprises', *Journal of International Business Studies*, Vol.XIX, No.2, pp.181–93.

Buckley, Peter J. and Artisien, P. F. R. (1987), *North–South Direct Investment in the European Communities*, London: Macmillan.

Buckley, Peter J. and Casson, Mark (1976), *The Future of the Multinational Enterprise*, London: Macmillan.

Buckley, Peter J. and Casson, Mark (1979), 'A theory of international operations' in J. Leontiades and M. Ghertman (eds) *European Research in International Business*, Amsterdam: North Holland.

Buckley, Peter J. and Casson, Mark (1981), 'The optimal timing of a foreign direct investment', *Economic Journal*, Vol.92, No.361, pp.75–81. Reprinted in Buckley and Casson (1985), op. cit.

Buckley, Peter J. and Casson, Mark (1985), *The Economic Theory of the Multinational Enterprise: Selected Readings*, London: Macmillan.

Buckley, Peter J. and Davies, H. (1981), 'Foreign licensing in overseas operations: theory and evidence from the UK' in R. G. Hawkins and A. J. Prasad (eds) *Technology Transfer and Economic Development*, Greenwich, Conn: JAI Press.

Buckley, Peter J. and Ghauri, P. N. (1991), *The Internationalisation of the Firm*, Oslo: Norwegian University Press, and Oxford: Oxford University Press.

Buckley, Peter J. and Mirza, H. (1985), 'The wit and wisdom of Japanese management: an iconoclastic analysis', *Management International Review*, Vol.25, No.3, pp.16–32

Buckley, Peter J., Mirza, H. and Sparkes, J. R. (1984), *European Affiliates in Japan*, Report to the Japan Foundation.

Buckley, Peter J., Mirza, H. and Sparkes, J. R. (1987a), 'Direct foreign investment in Japan as a means of market entry', *Journal of Marketing Management*, Vol.2, No.3, pp.241–58.

Buckley, Peter J., Mirza, H. and Sparkes, J. R. (1987b), 'Planning operations in Japan: the practices of British companies on entry and operation in the Japanese market', *University of Wales Business and Economics Review*, No.2, Winter 1987, pp.33–40.

Buckley, Peter J., Newbould, G. D. and Thurwell, J. (1988), *Foreign Direct Investment by Smaller UK Firms* London: Macmillan. (First edition, 1978), *Going International – The Experience of Smaller Companies Overseas*, London: Associated Business Press.)

Buckley, Peter J., Pearce, R. D. (1979), 'Overseas production and exporting by the world's largest enterprise – a study in sourcing policy', *Journal of International Business Studies*, Vol.10, No.1, pp.9–20.

Buckley, Peter J. and Pearce, R. D. (1981), 'Market servicing by multinational manufacturing firms: exporting versus foreign production', *Managerial and Decision Economics*, Vol.2, No.4, pp.229–46.

Buckley, Peter J. and Pearce, R. D. (1984), 'Exports in the strategy of multinational enterprises', *Journal of Business Research*, Vol.12, No.2, pp.209–26.

Buckley, Peter J. and Prescott, K. (1989), 'The structure of British industry's sales in foreign markets', *Managerial and Decision Economics*, Vol.10, No.3, pp.189–208.

Cable, V. (1983), *Protectionism and Industrial Decline*, London: Hodder and Stoughton.

Cantwell, J. (1987), 'Historical trends in international patterns of technological innovation', University of Reading Discussion Paper in Economics, series A, No.191.

Casson, Mark (1985), 'Multinationals and intermediate product trade' in Buckley and Casson, op. cit.

Casson, Mark (1987), *The Firm and the Market: Studies in Multinational Enterprise and the Scope of the Firm*, London: George Allen & Unwin.

Casson, Mark (1988) 'Controversies in the economic theory of the multinational enterprise: some methodological considerations', University of Reading Mimeo.

Christopher, M. (1972), 'The marketing channel' in *Marketing Logistics and Distribution Planning*, Christopher, M. and Wills, G. (eds), London: George Allen & Unwin.

Davidson, W. H. and McFetridge, D. G. (1985), 'Key characteristics in the choice of international technology transfer mode', *Journal of International Business Studies*, Vol.11, pp.5–21.

Davies, H. (1977), 'Technology transfer through commercial transactions', *Journal of Industrial Economics*, Vol.26, No.4, pp.161–75.

Dertouzos, M. L., Lester, R. K. and Solow, R. M. (1989), *Made in America: Regaining the Productive Edge*, (The MIT Commission on Industrial Productivity), Cambridge, Mass: MIT Press.

Diamantopoulos, A. (1987), 'Vertical quasi-integration Revisited: the role of power', *Managerial and Decision Economics*, Vol.8, pp.185–94.

Dunning, John H. (1972), 'The location of international firms in an enlarged EEC: an exploratory paper', Manchester Statistical Society.

Dunning, John H. (1981), *International Production and the Multinational Enterprise*, London: George Allen & Unwin.

Dunning, John H. (1985), 'The eclectic paradigm of international production: an up-date and reply to its critics', University of Reading Discussion Papers in International Investment and Business Studies, No.91.

Dunning, John H. (1989), 'Multinational enterprises and the growth of services: some conceptual and theoretical issues', *Service Industries Journal*, Vol.9, No.1, pp.5–39.

Dunning, John H. and Buckley, Peter J. (1977), 'International production and alternative models of trade', *The Manchester School*, Vol.LXV, No.4, pp.392–403.

Economist (1990), 'A survey of international banking', March 25, 1990.

Edvinsson, L. (1981), 'Some aspects on export of services', University of Stockholm, Working Paper.

Enderwick, P. (1989), 'Some economics of service-sector multinational enterprises' in *Multinational Service Firms*, Peter Enderwick (ed.), London: Routledge.

European Management Forum (1984), *Report on Industrial Competitiveness*, Switzerland: EMF.

Fagerberg, J. (1988), 'International competitiveness', *Economic Journal*, Vol.98, pp.355–74.

Feenstra, R. C. (ed.) (1989), *Trade Policies for International Competitiveness*, Chicago: University of Chicago Press.

Francis, A. (1986), 'The concept of competitiveness', ESRC Working Paper.

Giddy, I. H. and Rugman, A. M. (1979), 'A model of trade, foreign direct investment and licensing', New York: Columbia University Mimeo.

Graham, M. G. (1972), 'The through transport concept' in Christopher, M. and Wills, G. (eds) *Marketing Logistics and Distribution Planning*, London: George Allen & Unwin Ltd.

Greenaway, D. and Milner, C. (1986), *The Economics of Intra-Industry Trade*, Oxford: Blackwell.

Hannay, N. B. and Steele, L. W. (1986), 'A study of US competitiveness in seven industries', *Research Management*, Vol.29, No.1, pp.14–22.

Hennart, J. F. (1986), 'What is internalization?', *Weltwirtschaftliches Archiv*, Vol.122, No.4, pp.791–804.

Hirsch, S. (1976), 'An international trade and investment theory of the firm', *Oxford Economic Papers*, Vol.28, pp.258–70.

Hirsch, S. (1986), 'International Transactions in services and in service intensive goods', Tel Aviv University Working Paper.

Hood, N. and Young, S. (1979), *The Economics of Multinational Enterprise*, London: Longman.

Horst, T. O. (1971), 'The theory of the multinational firm – optimal behaviour under different tariff and tax rates', *Journal of Political Economy*, Vol.79, pp.1059–72.

Horst, T. O. (1972), 'Firm and industry determinants of the decision to investment abroad: an empirical study', *Review of Economics and Statistics*, Vol.54, pp.258–66.

Horst, T. O. (1974), 'The theory of the firm' in *Economic Analysis and the Multinational Enterprise*, John Dunning (ed.), London: George Allen & Unwin.

House of Lords Select Committee (1985), *Report from the Select Committee of the House of Lords on Overseas Trade* (The 'Aldington Report'), London: HMSO.

Jensen, M. C. and Meckling, W. H. (1976), 'The theory of the firm: managerial behaviour, agency costs and ownership structure', *Journal of Financial Economics*, Vol.3, pp.305–60.

Kaldor, N. (1978), 'The effect of devaluations on trade in manufacturers' in *Further Essays in Applied Economics*, London: Duckworth.

Kirpalani, V. H. and Balcome, D. (1987), 'International marketing success: on conducting more relevant research' in Philip J. Rosson and Stanley D. Reid (eds), *Managing Export Entry and Expansion*, New York: Praeger.

Kotler, P. (1984), *Marketing Management: Analysis Planning and Control*, fifth edition, London: Prentice Hall.

Krugman, P. R. and Hatsopoulus, G. N. (1987), 'The problem of US Competitiveness in manufacturing', *New England Economic Review* (Federal Reserve Bank of Boston), Jan./Feb. 1987, pp.18–29.

Leamer, E. E. (1987), *Sources of International Competitive Advantage: Theory and Evidence* (Cambridge, Mass: MIT Press.

Lipsey, R. E. and Kravis, I. B. (1987), 'The competitiveness and comparative advantage of US multinationals 1957–84', *Banca Nationale Del Lavoro Quarterly Review*, Vol.161, pp.147–65.

Luostarinen, R. (1978), 'Internationalization process of the firm', Working Papers in International Business 1978, Helsinki: Helsinki School of Economics.

Luostarinen, R. (1980), *Internationalization of the Firm*, Helsinki: Helsinki School of Economics.

Munro, H. J. and Beamish, P. W. (1987), 'Distribution methods and export performance' in Philip J. Rosson and Stanley D. Reid (eds), *Managing Export Entry and Expansion*, New York: Praeger.

Nicholas, S. J. (1983) 'Agency contracts, institutional modes and the transition to foreign direct investment by British manufacturing multinationals before 1939', *Journal of Economic History*, Vol.43, pp.675–86.

Nicholas, S. J. (1986), 'Multinationals, transaction costs and choice of institutional form', University of Reading Discussion Papers in International Investment and Business Studies, No.97.

Ohmae, K. (1985), *Triad Power: The Coming Shape of Global Competition*, New York: The Free Press.

Oral, M. and Reisman, A. (1988), 'Measuring Industrial Competitiveness', *Industrial Marketing Management*, Vol.17, pp.263–72.

Owen, N. (1983), *Economies of Scale, Competitiveness and Trade Patterns within the European Communities*, Oxford: Clarendon Press.

Pascale, T. R. and Athos, A. G. (1982), *The Art of Japanese Management*, Harmondsworth: Penguin.

Patel, P. and Pavitt, K. (1987), 'The Elements of British Technological Competitiveness', *National Institute Economic Review*, November 1987, pp.72–83.

Pavitt, K. (1984), 'Sectoral Patterns of technical change: towards taxonomy and a theory', *Research Policy*, Vol.13.

Piore, M. J. and Sabel, C. F. (1984), *The Second Industrial Divide*, New York: Basic Books.

Porter, M. E. (1980), *Competitive Strategy: Techniques for Analyzing Industries and Competitors*, New York: Free Press.

Porter, M. E. (1985), *Competitive Advantage: Creating and Sustaining Superior Performance*, New York: Free Press.

Porter, M. E. (ed.) (1986), *Competition in Global Industries*, Boston: Harvard University Press.

Porter, M. E. (1990), *Competitive Advantage of Nations*, London: Macmillan.

Pratten, C. F. (1976a), *A Comparison of the Performance of Swedish and UK Companies*, Cambridge: Cambridge University Press.

Pratten, C. F. (1976b), *Labour Productivity Differentials within International Companies*, Cambridge: Cambridge University Press.

Root, F. R. (1989), *Entry Strategies for International Markets*, Lexington Books.

Rugman, A. (1987), 'Strategies for National Competitiveness', *Long Range Planning*, Vol.20, No.3, pp.92–7.

Scherer, F. M. et al (1975), *The Economics of Multi-Plant Operation*, Cambridge Mass: Harvard University Press.

Sciberras, E. (1986), 'Indicators of technical intensity and international competitiveness: a case for supplementing quantitative data with qualitative studies in research', *Research and Development Management*, Vol.16, No.1, pp.3–19.

Scott, B. R. (1985), 'National strategies: key to international competition', in Bruce R. Scott and George C. Lodge (eds) *US Competitiveness in the World Economy*, Boston, Mass: Harvard Business School Press.

Scott, B. R. and Lodge, G. C. (eds) (1985), *US Competitiveness in the World Economy*, Boston, Mass: Harvard Business School Press.

Shepherd, D., Silberston, A. and Strange, R. (1987), *British Manufacturing Investment Overseas*, London: Methuen.

Shostack, G. L. (1977), 'Breaking free from product marketing', *Journal of Marketing*, Vol.41, pp.73–80.

Slater, J. R. (1988), 'Product quality and UK trade performance', *International Journal of Quality and Reliability Management*, Vol.5, No.3, pp.7–14.

Smith, A. D., Hitchens, D. W. M. N. and Davies, S. W. (1983), *International Labour Productivity: A Comparison of Britain, America and Germany*, Cambridge: Cambridge University Press.

Teece, D. J. (ed.) (1987), *The Competitive Challenge*, Cambridge, Mass: Ballinger Publishing Co.

Terpstra, V. (1983), *International Marketing*, 3rd Edition, Chicago: Dryden Press.

Thirlwall, A. P. (1979), 'The balance of payments constraint as an explanation of international growth rate differences', *Banca Nazionale del Lavoro Quarterly Review*, Vol.32, No.128, pp.45–53.

Thompson, S. (1988), 'Agency costs of internal organisation' in Steve Thompson and Mike Wright (eds) *Internal Organisation, Efficiency and Profit*, Oxford: Philip Allan.

United Nations Industrial Development Organization (1986), *International Comparative Advantage in Manufacturing – Changing Profiles of Resources and Trades*, UNIDO Publication.

United States Department of Commerce, International Trade Administration (1987), *Improving US Competitiveness*, Washington DC.

Vandermerwe, S. and Chadwick, M. (1989), 'The internationalisation of services', *Service Industries Journal*, Vol.9, No.1, pp.79–93.

Vernon, R. (1966), 'International investment and international trade in the product cycle', *Quarterly Journal of Economics*, Vol.80, pp.190–207.

Watanabe, S. (1971), 'Subcontracting, industrialisation and employment creation', *International Labour Review*, Vol.104, pp. 51–76.

Watanabe, S. (1972), 'International subcontracting: employment and skill promotion', *International Labour Review*, Vol.106, pp.425–49.

Webster, A. (1988), 'Measuring revealed comparative advantage Ex Ante: an application to UK industry', University of Reading Discussion Paper in Economics, Series A, No.199.

Whittaker, D. H. (1990), *Managing Innovation: A Study of British and Japanese Factories*, Cambridge: Cambridge University Press.

Young, S. (1987), 'Business strategy and the internationalization of business: recent approaches', *Managerial and Decision Economics*, Vol.8, No.1, pp.31–40.

Index